Asiatic So[...]

VOL. XVII.

LALLĀ-VĀKYĀNI,

OR

THE WISE SAYINGS OF LAL DĔD,

A MYSTIC POETESS OF ANCIENT KASHMĪR.

EDITED WITH TRANSLATION, NOTES AND A VOCABULARY

BY

SIR GEORGE GRIERSON, K.C.I.E.,
PH.D., D.LITT., M.R.A.S.,

AND

LIONEL D. BARNETT, LITT.D., M.R.A.S.

LONDON:
PUBLISHED BY THE ROYAL ASIATIC SOCIETY,
74, GROSVENOR STREET, W.1
1920

PRINTED AT OXFORD, ENGLAND
BY FREDERICK HALL
PRINTER TO THE UNIVERSITY

CONTENTS

PREFACE

THE collection of songs edited in the present volume possesses a twofold interest. Composed so long ago as the fourteenth century A. D., it claims the attention not only of the philologist as the oldest known specimen of the Kāshmīrī language, but also, and still more, that of the student of religions.

In ancient times, the religious system based on Śaiva Yōga was the object of much study amongst the learned men of Kashmīr. From that remote corner of North-Western India their teaching influenced the whole peninsula,—so much so that we even read that Rāmânuja, the leader of a rival Vaiṣṇava belief, felt compelled to travel from distant Madras to Kashmīr, with the special object of combating the hostile creed at its fountain head. There is an imposing mass of Kashmīr Śaiva literature still extant. Much of it has been published in the original Sanskrit, and more than one English work has been devoted to it.

Lallā, or Lal Dĕd, the authoress of the following verses, was a wandering ascetic, and a devoted follower of this cult. The importance of her songs consists in the fact that they are not a systematic exposé of Śaivism on the lines laid down by the theologians who preceded her, but illustrate the religion on its popular side. What we have here is not a mere book-religion as evolved in the minds of great thinkers and idealists, but a picture of the actual hopes and fears of the common folk that nominally followed the teaching of these wise men whom they had accepted as their guides. The book, in short, gives an account, often in vivid and picturesque language, of the actual working out in practice of a religion previously worked out in theory. As such, it is a unique contribution to the body of evidence that must necessarily form the basis of a future history of one of the most important religious systems of India.

A word may be added as to the respective shares of those responsible for the preparation of this edition. While each has considered and has discussed what the other has written, it may be roughly assumed that, while the account of the Yōga system and the many notes referring to it are directly, or indirectly, from the pen of Dr. Barnett, the preparation of the text, its translation, the various appendixes, and the vocabulary are the work of Sir George Grierson.

WORKS QUOTED IN THE FOLLOWING PAGES

WALTER, H.—The *Haṭha-yōga-pradīpikā* of Svâtmârāma, translated into German. Munich, 1893.

DEUSSEN, PAUL.—*Allgemeine Geschichte der Philosophie.* Leipzig, 1899, 1906.

SHRINIVAS IYENGAR, P. T.—The *Śiva-sūtra-vimarśinī* of Kṣēmarāja, translated into English. Reprinted from 'Indian Thought'. Allahabad, 1912.

SRIS CHANDRA VASU.—*The Yōga Śāstra, Śiva-saṁhitā.* In 'Sacred Books of the Hindus', vol. xv, Part I. Allahabad, 1913.

An Introduction to Yōga Philosophy: Sanskrit Text, with English Translation of (1) the Śiva-saṁhitā, and of (2) The Ghēraṇḍa-saṁhitā. Ibid., Parts II and IV. Allahabad, 1914-15.

CHATTERJI, J. C.—*Kashmir Shaivism*, vol. ii, Fasciculus I. The Research Department, Kashmir State, Srinagar, 1914.

PANCHAM SINH.—The *Haṭha-yōga-pradīpikā* of Svâtmârāma, Sanskrit Text and English Translation. In 'Sacred Books of the Hindus', vol. xv, Part III. Allahabad, 1915.

PŪRṆÂNANDA.—*Ṣaṭ-cakra-nirūpaṇa.* Text often printed in India.

BARNETT, L. D.—Translation of the *Bhagavad-Gītā.* In the Temple Classics. London, 1905.

SYSTEM OF TRANSLITERATION USED

The system of transliteration is the same as that employed by Sir George Grierson in his *Kāshmīrī Dictionary*.

The *Mātrā*-vowels are represented as follows:

क्क $k^{a}ka$, क्कि $k^{\dot{a}}k^{i}$, क्कु $k^{o}k^{\dot{u}}$, क्कू $k^{\ddot{u}}k^{\ddot{u}}$; कि k^{i}, कु k^{u}, कू $k^{\ddot{u}}$.
क्य $k^{\breve{e}}$, क्व $k^{\breve{o}}$.

The ordinary vowels are represented as follows:

क *ka*, का *kā*, कि *ki*, की *kī*, कु *ku*. कू *kū*, क्य *kĕ*, के *kē*, कै *kai*, क्व *kŏ*, को *kō*, कौ *kau*, कंकि $k\dot{a}k^{i}$, कंकु kok^{u}, कंकू $k\ddot{u}k^{\ddot{u}}$, कांकू $k\ddot{o}k^{\ddot{u}}$, कोकु $k\hat{o}k^{u}$, क्वंकु $k\d{o}k^{u}$, क्वांकू $k\breve{\ddot{o}}k^{\ddot{u}}$.

ऋ is no longer a vowel, and is represented by *ru*. ॠ is similarly represented by *rĕ*. Anunāsika is represented by ˜. Thus कँ *kã*

The Kāshmīrī consonants are:

क *ka*, ख *kha*, ग *ga*, (घ) *gha*, (ङ) *ṅa*.
च *cĕ*, छ *chĕ*, ज *jĕ*, (झ) *jhĕ*, ञ *ñĕ*.
च़ *tsa*, छ़ *tsha*, ज़ *za*.
ट *ṭa*, ठ *ṭha*, ड *ḍa*, (ढ) *ḍha*, (ण) *ṇa*.
त *ta* थ *tha*, द *da*, (ध) *dha*, न *na*.
प *pa*, फ *pha*, ब *ba*, (भ) *bha*, म *ma*.
य *yĕ*, र *ra*, ल *la*, व *va*.
श *shĕ*, (ष) *shĕ*, स *sa*, ह *ha*.

Letters enclosed in brackets are found only in borrowed words, and do not belong to the language.

For further particulars Sir George Grierson's *Kāshmīrī Dictionary*, in course of publication by the Asiatic Society of Bengal, and his *Manual of the Kāshmīrī Language*, published by the Clarendon Press, may be consulted.

For Sanskrit, the ordinary system of the Royal Asiatic Society is followed.

INTRODUCTION

The verses in the following collection are attributed to a woman of Kashmīr, named, in Sanskrit, Lallā Yōgīśwarī. There are few countries in which so many wise saws and proverbial sayings are current as in Kashmīr,[1] and none of these have greater repute than those attributed by universal consent to Lal Dĕd, or 'Granny Lal', as she is called nowadays. There is not a Kāshmīrī, Hindū or Musalmān, who has not some of these ready on the tip of his tongue, and who does not reverence her memory.

Little is known about her. All traditions agree that she was a contemporary of Sayyid 'Alī Hamadānī, the famous saint who exercised a great influence in converting Kashmīr to Islām. He arrived in Kashmīr in A.D. 1380, and remained there six years, the reigning sovereign being Quṭbu'd-Dīn (A.D. 1377–93).[2] As we shall see from her songs, Lallā was a Yōginī, i.e. a follower of the Kashmīr branch of the Śaiva religion, but she was no bigot, and, to her, all religions were at one in their essential elements.[3] There is hence no inherent difficulty in accepting the tradition of her association with Sayyid 'Alī. Hindūs, in their admiration for their coreligionist, go, it is true, too far when they assert that he received his inspiration from her, but the Musalmāns of the Valley, who naturally deny this, and who consider him to be the great local apostle of their faith, nevertheless look upon her with the utmost respect.[4]

Numerous stories are current about Lallā in the Valley, but none of them is deserving of literal credence. She is said

[1] See, for instance, the *Dictionary of Kāshmīrī Proverbs and Sayings*, compiled by Mr. J. Hinton Knowles (Bombay and London, 1885).
[2] *Panjab Notes and Queries*, ii. 432.
[3] Compare verse 8 in the following collection.
[4] Cf. Lawrence, *Valley of Kashmir*, p. 292.

to have been originally a married woman of respectable family. She was cruelly treated by her mother-in-law, who nearly starved her.[1] The wicked woman tried to persuade Lallā's husband that she was unfaithful to him, but when he followed her to what he believed was an assignation, he found her at prayer. The mother-in-law tried other devices, which were all conquered by Lallā's virtue and patience, but at length she succeeded in getting her turned out of the house.[2] Lallā wandered forth in rags and adopted a famous Kāshmīrī Śaiva saint named Sĕd Bôy^{u} as her *Guru* or spiritual preceptor. The result of his teaching was that she herself took the status of a mendicant devotee, and wandered about the country singing and dancing in a half-nude condition. When remonstrated with for such disregard for decency, she is said to have replied that they only were men who feared God, and that there were very few of such about.[3] During this time Sayyid 'Alī Hamadānī arrived in Kashmīr, and one day she saw him in the distance. Crying out 'I have seen a man', she turned and fled. Seeing a baker's shop close by, she leaped into the blazing oven and disappeared, being apparently consumed to ashes. The saint followed her and inquired if any woman had come that way, but the baker's wife, out of fear, denied that she had seen any one. Sayyid 'Alī continued

[1] Compare the Kāshmīrī saying:—

honḍ^{u} marān kina kaṭh,
Lali nalwūṭ^{ü} ṭsali na zāh.

'Whether they killed a big sheep or a small one, it was all the same; Lal had always a stone for her dinner.' For, when she dined in the presence of other people, the mother-in-law used to put a lumpy stone on her platter and thinly cover it with rice, so that it looked like quite a big heap. Still she never murmured. Cf. K. Pr., p. 82, and *Panjab Notes and Queries*, ii. 743.

[2] For these, and other stories, see *Panjab Notes and Queries*, l.c.

[3] See K. Pr. 20, quoted in full on p. 122, below. PNQ. makes another saint, a contemporary of Sayyid 'Alī named Nūru'd-dīn, the hero of the story; but every version that we have seen or heard elsewhere gives it as above. PNQ. adds that Nūru'd-dīn, 'not to be outdone in miracles, then disappeared on the spot, and after much searching she found him between two platters in the form of a diamond'. A story very similar to that given above will be found in Mērutuṅga's *Prabandhacintāmaṇi*, where the hero is a Kṣatriya named Jagaddēva, and the unclothed lady a dancing-girl: Bombay edition (1888), p. 296, and Tawney's translation, p. 186.

his search, and suddenly Lallā reappeared from the oven clad in the green garments of Paradise.

The above stories will give some idea of the legends that cluster round the name of Lallā. All that we can affirm with some assurance is that she certainly existed, and that she probably lived in the fourteenth century of our era, being a contemporary of Sayyid ʻAlī Hamadānī at the time of his visit to Kashmīr. We know from her own verses[1] that she was in the habit of wandering about in a semi-nude state, dancing and singing in ecstatic frenzy as did the Hebrew *nābī's* of old and the more modern Dervishes.

No authentic manuscript of her compositions has come down to us. Collections made by private individuals have occasionally been put together,[2] but none is complete, and no two agree in contents or text. While there is thus a complete dearth of ordinary manuscripts, there are, on the other hand, sources from which an approximately correct text can be secured.

The ancient Indian system by which literature is recorded not on paper but on the memory, and carried down from generation to generation of teachers and pupils, is still in complete survival in Kashmīr. Such fleshy tables of the heart are often more trustworthy than birch-bark or paper manuscripts. The reciters, even when learned Paṇḍits, take every care to deliver the messages word for word as they have received them, whether they understand them or not. In such cases we not infrequently come across words of which the meaning given is purely traditional or is even lost. A typical instance of this has occurred in the experience of Sir George Grierson. In the summer of 1896 Sir Aurel Stein took down in writing from the mouth of a professional story-teller a collection of folk-tales, which he subsequently made over to Sir George for editing and translation. In the course of dictation, the narrator, according to custom, conscientiously reproduced words of which he did not know the sense. They

[1] Nos. 77 and 94.

[2] See, for instance, p. li of the late Professor Bühler's *Detailed Report of a Tour in Search of Sanskrit MSS. made in Kaśmīr, &c.* (Bombay, 1877), where two of these collections are mentioned.

were 'old words', the signification of which had been lost, and which had been passed down to him through generations of *ustāds*, or teachers. That they were not inventions of the moment, or corruptions of the speaker, is shown by the facts that not only were they recorded simultaneously by a well-known Kāshmīrī Paṇḍit, who was equally ignorant of their meanings, and who accepted them without hesitation on the authority of the reciter, but that, long afterwards, at Sir George's request, Sir Aurel Stein got the maṇ to repeat the passages in which the words occurred. They were repeated by him *verbatim, literatim, et punctatim*, as they had been recited by him to Sir Aurel fifteen years before.

The present collection of verses was recorded under very similar conditions. In the year 1914 Sir George Grierson asked his friend and former assistant, Mahāmahôpâdhyāya Paṇḍit Mukunda Rāma Śāstrī, to obtain for him a good copy of the *Lallā-vākyāni*, as these verses of Lallā's are commonly called by Paṇḍits. After much search he was unable to find a satisfactory manuscript. But finally he came into touch with a very old Brāhmaṇ named Dharma-dāsa Darwēsh of the village of Gush.[1] Just as the professional story-teller mentioned above recited folk-tales, so he made it his business, for the benefit of the piously disposed, to recite Lallā's songs as he had received them by family tradition (*kula-paramparâcāra-krama*). The Mahāmahôpâdhyāya recorded the text from his dictation, and added a commentary, partly in Hindī and partly in Sanskrit, all of which he forwarded to Sir George Grierson. These materials formed the basis of the present edition. It cannot claim to be founded on a collation of various manuscripts, but we can at least say that it is an accurate reproduction of one recension of the songs, as they are current at the present day. As in the case of Sir Aurel Stein's folk-tales, this text contains words and passages which the reciter did not profess to understand. He had every inducement to make the verses intelligible, and any conjectural

[1] The Goosh of the maps. It is about thirty miles from Bāramūla, and is not far from the famous shrine of Śāradā. See Stein's Translation of the *Rājataraṅgiṇī*, ii. 280 and 288.

emendation would at once have been accepted on his authority; but, following the traditions of his calling, he had the honesty to refrain from this, and said simply that this was what he had received, and that he did not know its meaning. Such a record is in some respects more valuable than any written manuscript.

Besides this collection, we have also consulted two manuscripts belonging to the Stein Collection housed in the Oxford Indian Institute.[1] Both were written in the Śāradā character. Of these, one (No. cccxlvi of the catalogue, and referred to as 'Stein A' in the following pages) is but a fragment, the first two leaves and all those after the seventeenth being missing. It is nevertheless of considerable value; for, besides giving the text of the original, it also gives a translation into Sanskrit verse, by a Paṇḍit named Rājānaka Bhāskara, of songs Nos. 7–49. The Kāshmīrī text, if we allow for the customary eccentricities of spelling, presents no variant readings of importance and is in places corrupt. We have, therefore, not taken account of it; but, so far as it is available, we reproduce the Sanskrit translation under each verse of our edition.[2]

The other manuscript (No. cccxlv—referred to herein as 'Stein B') demands more particular consideration. It contains the Kāshmīrī text of forty-nine of the songs in the present collection. The spelling is in the usual inconsequent style of all Kāshmīrī manuscripts written before Īśvara-kaula gave a fixed orthography to the language in the concluding decades of the nineteenth century,[3] and there are also, as usual, a good many mistakes of the copyist. It is, however, valuable as giving a number of variant readings, and because the scribe has marked the metrical accentuation of most of the verses, by putting the mark ॥ after each accented word.[4] For this reason, and also because it gives a good example of the

[1] See JRAS., 1912, pp. 587 ff.

[2] Since the above was written, a complete edition of Rājānaka Bhāskara's translation has been printed in Kashmīr. It covers altogether sixty of Lallā's verses. From this edition, the verses missing in Stein A have been supplied.

[3] Iśvara-kaula's spelling is that followed in our printed text.

[4] Regarding the accentual nature of Lallā's metre, see Appendix III.

spelling of Kāshmīrī before Īśvara-kaula's time, under each verse of our text we reproduce, in the Nāgarī character the corresponding verse, if available, of this manuscript. Except that we have divided the words—a matter which rarely gives rise to any doubt—we print these exactly as they stand in the manuscript with all their mistakes and inconsistencies of spelling.

The order of verses in this manuscript is different from that of Dharma-dāsa's text, and we have therefore, in Appendix IV, given a Concordance, showing the correspondence between the two.

Although there is not much consistency in old Kāshmīrī spelling, the following general remarks may facilitate the reading of the text of Stein B. No attempt is made in it to indicate the existence of *mātrā*-vowels or the consequent epenthetic changes of vowels caused by them.[1] For instance, the word *tot*^{u} (तंतु॒) is spelt ततो, and the termination -*wŏn*^{u} (वोनु॒) is spelt वानो. As a rule, long vowels are written in the place of these *mātrā*-vowels, the spelling of the old Prakrit from which Kāshmīrī is derived being thus perpetuated. Thus, we have just seen that *u*-*mātrā* is represented by *ō*. Similarly, *i*-*mātrā* is represented by *ī*. For instance, *tàm*^{i} (तंमि॒) is spelt तमी, and *töp*^{i}*tan* (तांपि॒तन्) is spelt तापीतन्. Again, *ü*-*mātrā* is represented by *ū*, as in *tröv*^{ü} (त्रांवू॒), written त्रावू.

Kāshmīrī possesses a series of affricatives च़ *ća*, छ़ *ćha*, and ज़ *za*. In Īśvara-kaula's system these are indicated, as shown here, by dots put under the corresponding palatal letters. In Stein B, on the contrary, they are indicated by the palatals without any distinguishing mark—thus च, छ, ज. The true palatals are then distinguished by adding to each the letter *ya*. Thus—च्य *ca*, छ्य *cha*, and ज्य *ja*.

It is a universal rule in Kāshmīrī that every final surd consonant is aspirated. Thus, *rāt*, night, is pronounced *rāth*,

[1] In our printed text in the Roman character, these are indicated by small letters above the line. Īśvara-kaula indicates them with the help of the sign for *virāma*. Thus, ु॒, ि॒, ू॒.

and in Īśvara-kaula's spelling is written राथ्. Before his time it was not customary to indicate this aspiration in writing, and accordingly Stein B spells this word as रात्, and so on in other cases.

Lallā's songs were composed in an old form of the Kāshmīrī language,[1] but it is not probable that we have them in the exact form in which she uttered them. The fact that they have been transmitted by word of mouth prohibits such a supposition. As the language changed insensibly from generation to generation, so must the outward form of the verses have changed in recitation. But, nevertheless, respect for the authoress and the metrical form of the songs have preserved a great many archaic forms of expression.[2]

As already said, Lallā was a devout follower of the Kashmīr school of Yōga Śaivism. Very little is yet known in Europe concerning the tenets of this form of Hinduism, and we have therefore done our best to explain the many allusions by notes appended to each verse. In addition to these, the following general account of the tenets of this religion has been prepared by Dr. Barnett, which will, we hope, throw light on what is a somewhat obscure subject.

[1] Kāshmīrī, as a distinct language, is much older than Lallā's time. A still more ancient form is preserved by Kalhaṇa (twelfth century A.D.) in *Rājataraṅgiṇī*, v. 398. See Stein's note to his translation of the passage.

[2] This matter of Lallā's language is considered at length in Appendix II.

PRELIMINARY NOTE ON YŌGA

I.

1. The object of the discipline called Yōga is to emancipate the individual soul (*puruṣa*) from its bondage to the material universe (*prakṛti*). In the term *prakṛti* is included the mental organism, commonly styled in the Yōga-sūtra *citta*. The emancipation is effected by a mental and bodily discipline culminating in a spiritual transformation, in which there comes into existence a permanent intuition revealing the essential distinction (*vivēka*) between *puruṣa* and *prakṛti*. This is the state of *kaivalya*, isolation, which is salvation.

2. The *citta* has five intellectual functions, *vṛttis*. They are: (1) *pramāṇa*, right judgement of real things; (2) *viparyaya*, false judgement of real things; (3) *vikalpa*, imagination without corresponding reality, based on mere words; (4) *nidrā*, 'sleep', i.e. the negative action that occurs in sleep, based on no conception of reality; (5) *smṛti*, memory, continuance of connexion with an object that has been perceived. *Citta* has also five moral functions, the *klēśas*, or 'afflictions', viz. (1) *avidyā*, primal ignorance, by which *puruṣa* imagines itself to be identical with the material *citta*; (2) *asmitā*, the conception of an 'I am', egoism identifying the powers of *puruṣa* and matter; (3) *rāga*, material desire; (4) *dvēṣa*, hate; (5) *abhinivēśa*, clinging to embodied life. The *klēśas* move the subject of thought constantly to works, *karma*, from which arise *saṁskāras* and *vāsanās*, mental predispositions moving him to corresponding future works; and so the vicious cycle goes on in birth after birth for ever, until salvation can be found. To gain salvation the Yōgī attempts to paralyse the five *vṛttis* of *citta* and wear down the *klēśas* by the various ascetic exercises included under the term *aṣṭâṅga*, 'eight members'. These are: (1) *yama*, moral discipline in

relation to others; (2) *niyama*, moral discipline in relation to oneself; (3) *āsana*, suitable modes of sitting during meditation; (4) *prāṇāyāma*, regulation of breathing; (5) *pratyāhāra*, retracting the sense-organs from objects of sense; (6) *dhāraṇā*, negative fixation of *citta* by pinning it to an object; (7) *dhyāna*, meditation, positive fixation of *citta*; (8) *samādhi*, perfect stillness of thought, in which all sense of individuality is extinguished. In the course of these the Yōgī is supposed to win various miraculous powers (*vibhūti*), in addition to the 'light of intuition', *prajñālōka*. The last three *aṅgas* collectively make the stage of training called *saṁyama*, and culminate in the condition styled *sabīja samādhi*, 'the stillness of spirit with the seed', namely, the seed of future activity of *citta* and consequent *karma*; or what is nearly the same thing, *samprajñāta samādhi*, stillness of spirit in which, however, the *vṛttis* of *citta* are not yet paralysed. To attain the final stage, this kind of *samādhi* has to be converted into *nirbīja*, 'seedless', or *asamprajñāta* 'unconscious', *samādhi*. This takes place in three phases, called *nirōdha-pariṇāma*, *samādhi-pariṇāma*, and *ēkāgratā-pariṇāma*. In the first of these the activity of the waking state of *citta* is arrested, and its *vṛttis* are temporarily paralysed; in the second, the power of *citta* to relate itself to manifold objects is destroyed, and its cognitions are restricted to a single object of inward or outward perception; in the third, the two previous conditions are combined in equal proportion. These are permanent transformations, as a result of which all sense of objectivity disappears from the matter of thought, leaving only the intuition of the distinction between *puruṣa* and *prakṛti*, wherein the *puruṣa* shines for ever in its perfectly pure still radiance.

II.

3. From the first the method of gnosis which we have outlined presupposed certain mystic conceptions of the natural and spiritual world. These in course of time have become more and more important in the Yōgic systems, and have tended to obscure the philosophical and ethical elements in

the primitive Yōga. They may be classified broadly under two heads: (1) the theory of Nature and of salvation by means thereof; (2) the practice of physical means supposed to be efficacious in attaining the latter object. We shall now endeavour to give a general outline of the Yōgic theory of nature in its developed form, noting in advance that it represents only one of the various aspects which have been assumed by Yōga, though perhaps the most important aspect. Our exposition is based upon the following works: *Śiva-saṁhitā*, an anonymous work of some antiquity (quoted as SS.); *Ṣaṭ-cakra-nirūpaṇa*, by Pūrṇânanda (quoted as SCN.); and *Haṭha-yōga-pradīpikā*, by Svâtmârāma (quoted as HYP., in the German translation by H. Walter, Munich, 1893). The references to SS. are according to the text as published in *Sacred Books of the Hindus*, Allahabad, 1914.

4. In Yōgic theory the human body is conceived as a miniature copy or replica of the world without it; the forces by which this microcosm is controlled at the same time operate upon the macrocosm outside, and thus by certain physical and mental processes the Yōgī can win for himself not only supernatural powers over his own body and mind but also a miraculous control over the universe, culminating in the complete translation of his soul into the highest phase of Being, the Absolute (usually conceived as Supreme Śiva) for ever and ever.

5. In the human body the vertebral column is conceived as Mount Mēru, the central mountain of Hindū cosmology. As the macrocosmic sun and moon are imagined to turn round Mēru, so we have a microcosmic sun and moon in the human body: the moon at the top of the vertebral column and the sun at its base (SS. II. 6–12). Among the numerous *nāḍīs* (veins or arteries: see HYP. p. iv) there are three of supreme importance, *Suṣumnā*, *Iḍā*, and *Piṅgalā*, which descend from the brain into the pit of the abdomen; and HYP. (p. iii, and text III. 113) says that between the pudendum and navel is a 'bulb' (*kanda*), into which the *nāḍīs* debouch. Suṣumnā is identified with Agni, fire. At the upper end of Iḍā is the moon, and they are identified; at the lower end of Piṅgalā is

the sun, and they too are identified (SS. II. 13–20). These three *nāḍīs* are in immediate conjunction, Iḍā being on the left hand of Suṣumnā, and Piṅgalā on the right. Suṣumnā rises vertically from the pelvic region along the vertebral column as far as the Brahma-randhra (on which see below); there it bends round to the right of the Ājñā circle (see below, § 18) and passes up into the left nostril. In the centre of Suṣumnā is a *nāḍī* called *Citrā*, which is said to be of five colours, and to be the *upâdhi* of the body, and to have the Brahma-randhra at its upper end (SS. II. 18–19, V. 124). The Brahma-randhra is the upper extremity of Suṣumnā, and of the inner *nāḍī* enclosed in Suṣumnā.

6. SCN. refines somewhat upon this theory by asserting that inside Suṣumnā there is a bright *nāḍī* called Vajrā, and that inside Vajrā is another *nāḍī* called Citriṇī, which passes through all the six circles attached to the spine, to which we shall come presently (§§ 9 ff.). In the centre of Citriṇī is the Brahma-nāḍī, a subtile duct representing pure knowledge and bliss. At the lower mouth of Suṣumnā is the *Brahma-dvāra*, or 'Door of Brahma', where are the 'knots' (*granthi*: see HYP. p. xvii [1]). Cf. also HYP. pp. v, vii.

7. Sometimes, to continue the analogy of microcosm to macrocosm, Iḍā is identified with the Ganges, Piṅgalā with the Jamnā, and Suṣumnā with the Saraswatī, and the point where they meet, at the mouth of the Brahma-randhra, is called *Trivēṇī* (Tribeni, the meeting place of the Huglī or Ganges, Jamnā, and Saraswatī, in Hooghly District); by daily spiritual contemplation of this union, corresponding to the physical act of bathing at the real Tribeni, the Yōgī may win salvation for his ancestors and himself (SS. V. 103 ff., 130 ff.). Sometimes the sacred city of Benares (*Vārāṇasī*) is localized in the microcosm by styling Iḍā *Vāraṇā* and Piṅgalā *Asi*, so that their place of union at the Brahma-randhra is Vārāṇasī, the residence of Viśvanātha, the Lord of the Universe (SS. V. 100–1).

[1] Some writers speak of three knots: the *Brahma-granthi* in the Anāhata-circle, the *Viṣṇu-granthi* in the Viśuddha, and the *Rudra-granthi* in the Ājñā.

8. The microcosmic moon at the top of the vertebral column, which is said to consist of eight and sometimes of sixteen digits, is always exuding nectar, which flows downwards. Half of this nectar passes through Iḍā, on the left side, and there becomes water for the nourishment of the body. The other half goes through Suṣumnā into the vertebral column, and thence down to the base of the latter, where it meets the microcosmic sun. This sun, which has twelve digits, casts its rays upwards through Piṅgalā along the right side of the body, and thence through the system (SS. II, 6–12, V. 145).

9. In the abdomen, in the middle of the sphere of the sun, is the Vaiśvānara fire, which effects the process of digestion in the body (SS. II. 32–34). In the same region is situated the first of the *cakras* or circles, which are conceived as being of the form of lotuses, attached at intervals to Suṣumnā (cf. HYP. p. xiv). The first circle is the *Mūlādhāra*, or simply *Ādhāra*, and is imagined to be a lotus of four digits in width, situated two digits above the anus and two digits below the penis. In the pericarp of this lotus is a triangular space representing the *yōni* or female organ. On this space dwells the *Kula-Kuṇḍalinī* (or simply *Kuṇḍalinī*), who is the *Śakti* or *Cic-chakti*, the power of spirit, the creative force of the phenomenal universe (cf. HYP. p. xiii). She is golden of hue, like a streak of lightning; when at rest, she sleeps rolled up in three and a half coils, like a serpent, with her tail in her mouth, inside the lower orifice of Suṣumnā. On her left is Iḍā, which coils round Suṣumnā and finally enters the right nostril; on her right is Piṅgalā, proceeding in the reverse way upwards and debouching into the left nostril (SS. II. 21–31, V. 56 ff., 124). SCN. 5 ff. adds to these details the information that Mūlādhāra represents earth, and is the seat of Brahma, and it locates the *yōni* (which is called Traipura; cf. below, § 21) at the mouth of Vajrā (§ 6).

10. Kuṇḍalinī is sometimes termed *Vāg-dēvī* or Goddess of Speech, the *Śakti* of Viṣṇu, the mother of the three *Guṇas*, the Seed of Being (*bīja*). Over her sleeping form broods the *Kāma-bīja* or 'seed of Love', a bright spiritual radiance endowed with the powers of knowledge and action, which

circulates through the body. This Kāma-bīja is also styled *Svayambhū-liṅga*, the phallic symbol of the Self-created Being Śiva (SS. V. 57–62).

11. SCN. 9–12 has a very similar account: it adds that around the *yōni* there blows a red wind called Kandarpa (the same as Kāma, Love); in the *yōni* is the Svayambhū-liṅga, having the hue of molten gold, and facing downwards; above this is Kuṇḍalinī, who is like a lotus-fibre and lightning, and covers with her face the orifice of Suṣumnā. It also states that in the midst of Kuṇḍalinī is *Paramā Kalā* or *Paramēśvarī*, or *Mahāprakṛti*, the super-subtile principle of Bliss which is like lightning, and illuminates the universe (SCN. 13).

12. The *yōni* and the *liṅga* upon it are known as the *Kula* or Home, the site of the Power of Phenomenal Being: we shall return to this anon (§ 19).

13. A little distance above Mūlâdhāra, at the base of the penis, is the second circle, *Svâdhiṣṭhāna*, conceived as a red lotus with six petals (SS. V. 75 ff.). It represents Varuṇa, and is the seat of Viṣṇu (SCN. 15 ff.).

14. The third circle is *Maṇipūra*, a golden lotus of ten petals by the navel (SS. V. 79 ff.). SCN. holds that it is blue, and that it represents Agni, and that Rudra dwells on the inverted triangle (*yōni*) at its centre (SCN. 20 ff.).

15. The fourth circle is *Anāhata*, a red lotus of twelve petals situate in the heart; in it is a flame styled *Bāṇa-liṅga* (SS. V. 83 ff.). It represents Vāyu or Wind; in the double triangle within it dwells Īśāna; in the middle of this double triangle is a *yōni* or triangle known as *Trikōṇā Śakti*, within which is the golden Bāṇa-liṅga, on the head of which is a lotus of eight petals, the seat of Lakṣmī (SCN. 23 ff.).

16. In this lotus dwells the *Prâṇa* or breath of life,[1] together with the *vāsanās* or influences of former works upon the soul, the *karma* thereof, and its *ahaṁkāra* or principle of egoity (SS. III. 1–8).

[1] Besides *Prâṇa* or outward breath Yōga recognizes also *Apâna*, breath going downwards in the anus; *Samāna*, in the navel; *Udāna* in the throat; *Vyāna*, circulating through the body, besides some others: SS. III. 1–8, *Ghēraṇḍa-saṁhitā*, V. 60 ff. &c.

17. Above Anāhata, and situate in the throat, is the circle *Viśuddha*, a golden lotus of sixteen petals (SS. V. 90 ff.). SCN. adds that it represents Ākāśa or ether, and is the residence of Sadāśiva, and ascribes to it the colour of smoke (SCN. 29 ff.).

18. The sixth circle is *Ājñā*, a lotus of two petals between the eyebrows, which contains the mystic force called *akṣara-bīja* (SS. V. 96 ff., 145 ff.). It is of the colour of the moon. In its pericarp is the seat of Śiva called *Itara*, in the form of a *liṅga*, like a series of lightnings; it is *parama-kula-pada*, the highest stage of the Kula, in which Śiva and his consort Śakti are half and half, *ardhāṅgī*, in mutual fusion. In it is envisaged Paramâtman, the Supreme Self, as creator of origin, maintenance, and dissolution of the cosmos, like a halo of the light of fire, sun, and moon. After death the Yōgī who has fixed his breaths on this seat of Viṣṇu enters here into Paraṁ Brahma (SCN. 34–40).

19. Above all these circles is the highest of all, *Sahasrâra*, conceived as a lotus with a thousand petals, situated at the base of the palate. On its pericarp is a reversed triangular space or *yōni*, in the centre of which is the Brahma-randhra or upper extremity of Suṣumnā. On this *yōni* (or below it, according to SS. V. 145) is the Moon, whose nectar flows downwards through the system (SS. V. 103 ff., 122 ff.); its place is within the sinus of the forehead (SS. V. 148). Sahasrâra is conceived as Mount Kailāsa, the home of Śiva; and as representing the sphere of the Absolute or Transcendental Being, Parama-Śiva or Paramêśvara, as opposed to the sphere of cosmic action or Kula, it is styled *A-kula* or *Na-kula*. It is thus the physical as well as the spiritual antithesis of the Kula at the lower end of Suṣumnā (SS. V. 151 ff.).

20. As usual, SCN. refines on this. It describes Sahasrâra as having a thousand red petals facing downwards, and containing fifty letters of the alphabet from *a* to *kṣa*. It contains the full moon without the hare (our 'man in the moon'), and in its central *yōni* the Yōgī should contemplate the Void (SCN. 42 ff.). In the void of this *yōni* is the sixteenth digit of the Moon; it is called *Amā* or *Anā*; it is like lightning,

and is thin as one-hundredth part of a lotus-fibre ; it conveys the nectar flowing from Sahasrâra. Inside Amā is the digit *Nirvāṇa*, which is fine as a thousandth part of a hair, curved like the new moon, bright as twelve suns, the tutelary deity (*adhidaivata*) of living creatures. In the middle of Nirvāṇa is *Apūrva-nirvāṇa-śakti*, which is thin as the ten-millionth part of a hair and bright as ten million suns, the creator of the threefold world and dispenser of the knowledge of Brahma, the life of all creatures. Inside this Apūrva-nirvāṇa is the *Śiva-pada* or seat of Siva, or Paraṁ Brahma, also called *Haṁsa-sthāna*, the Swan's Home, the revelation of salvation and state of eternal bliss (SCN. 48–51).

21. As the object of metaphysical contemplation is to merge the individual soul into the absolute All-Spirit, so the object of Yōgic contemplation is to absorb the Kuṇḍalinī in the microcosm, representing the macrocosmic Energy, into Sahasrâra, typifying the Absolute, whereby the Cosmos is merged into the infinite bliss of Paramêśvara. In order to effect this transit of Kuṇḍalinī through Suṣumnā and the Brahma-randhra into Sahasrâra, the *nāḍīs* must, by the exercise of *prâṇâyāma*, be blocked up with air introduced into them by inspiration (*pūraka*) and retained in them (*kumbhaka*) ;[1] the normal circulation of the air through the system, which causes the continuance of the soul's imprisonment in the body, is arrested by this stoppage of the air. Then Kuṇḍalinī, when she has been aroused to sufficient energy by mystic exercises, passes up through Suṣumnā, bursting the eight knots (§ 6) that bind the *nāḍīs*, and enters through the Brahma-randhra into Sahasrâra, the realm of the Absolute (SS. V. 127 ff.). But long training is needed before Kuṇḍalinī can be stimulated to this supreme effort. An earlier stage of the training is passed in Mūlâdhāra. The Yōgī after taking a deep inspiration fixes his thought upon the lotus of Mūlâdhāra and compresses the *yōni* in it, meditating upon Kāma, the Spirit of Love, who dwells in the *yōni*, and conceiving in the flame above it a union as Śiva and Śakti. Then Kuṇḍalinī, styled Tripurā

[1] The final expiration of this retained air is called *rēcaka*.

as comprising the three principles fire, sun, and moon, begins to rise in Suṣumnā, and after drinking the nectar streaming down it returns to the Kula (SS. IV. 1–5, V. 61 ff.). *Mudrās*, or various postures of the body, are practised in order to increase mechanically the activity of Kuṇḍalinī. These methods, with further contemplation of the higher circles up to Ājñā, stimulate Kuṇḍalinī to such a degree that in the last stage the Yōgī is able to bring her up into Sahasrâra. By long practice his *citta-vṛttis* (activities of the material organ of thought) become absorbed in the Akula, the Absolute; his *samādhi* becomes one of perfect stillness. Drinking the lunar nectar of Sahasrâra, he overcomes Death (cosmic, conditioned being) and the Kula (SS. V. 151 ff.).

22. SCN. 52 instructs the Yōgī, after due practice of the *yamas* and *niyamas* (above, § 2) and spiritual purification, to stimulate Kuṇḍalinī to burst the Svayambhū-liṅga, and to bring her with the sound of the mystic syllable *huṁ* to the Brahma-dvāra (§ 6), in the centre of Mūlâdhāra. She then bursts the *liṅgas* in Anāhata and Ājñā, and at the Brahmarandhra unites with Parama-Siva, shining like a bright thread of lightning. The Yōgī should bring her together with his soul (*jīvātman*) into Sahasrâra, and there contemplate her as supreme and as Caitanya, spirit. When she has there drunk the red nectar from Śiva, she returns to Mūlâdhāra by the way whereby she came. Then he should make a libation of this nectar to the deities of the cosmos, whereby he obtains immunity from future birth and assurance of absorption into the Infinite.

23. Yōgic writers often dwell upon the phenomena of the Nāda. Of the cosmological significance of this term we shall speak below (§ 24); here we need only notice its physical aspect, in which it signifies the mystic sound, or *anāhata-dhvani*, heard by the Yōgī in the Suṣumnā in the interior of his body. Several varieties of this Nāda are mentioned in HYP. IV. 69 ff. The first of them is the sound caused in the ether of the heart when the exercise of *prâṇāyāma* (§ 2) has loosened the *brahma-granthi* or knot of Brahma in the Anāhata circle. Sometimes the sound is identified with the mystic syllable *Ōṁ*.

Probably the idea was suggested by the noise heard on closing the ears with the hands, to which HYP. IV. 82 refers.

24. Yōgic works, in common with the Tantras, often refer to a theory of cosmogony of which the leading idea is as follows. The Puruṣa, Absolute Spirit, Para Siva, or Brahma, and the Prakṛti, identified with the Supreme Śakti, are eternally coexistent. Like Puruṣa, Prakṛti is to be conceived as both unqualified and qualified; through Her universal presence as the principle of cosmic Bliss, Puruṣa reveals Himself in all finite being. Essentially they are two in one and one in two. Creation begins when from Him as affected by Her, i.e. as *niṣkala*, there issues the primal Bindu or 'drop' (the dot representing the final nasal sound at the end of the mystic syllable Ōṁ). The same idea is sometimes expressed more fully by the statement that Prakṛti by contact with Puruṣa becomes spiritualized (*cin-mātrā*), and in an effort towards creation She becomes solidified and changes into the primal Bindu. In the latter Śiva and Śakti exist together in an as yet undissolved union, shrouded in the bonds of Māyā, bearing the potentialities of cosmic creation, continuance, and dissolution. It is imagined as existing in the form of a grain of gram or pulse in the Sahasrâra of the microcosm (see above, § 19), where it composes the Void (§ 20) or Brahmapada there. This primal Bindu—under the influence of Time, according to some—divides itself into three, a gross or seminal Bindu, the germ of the material universe, a subtle Bindu which contains the *guṇas* or modes of matter (the well-known Sattwa, Rajas, and Tamas), which is termed Nāda, and a supreme Bindu. Nāda literally means 'sound', and denotes or is denoted by the semicircle under the *bindu* or dot on the syllable Ōṁ (ओँ). From the Bindu as it thus divides itself arises an inarticulate sound styled Śabda-Brahman, 'Śpeech-Brahman', from which emerge, according to some, the three cosmic Powers of Knowledge, Will, and Action: others derive from it the genesis of the material principle of the finite universe, Mahat or Buddhi, and its evolutes. The theories of cosmic evolution that are connected with all this are extremely complicated and obscure, and

hardly repay study. But it may be well to call attention to the similar theory of the Śaiva Siddhânta, one school of which teaches that from Pure Māyā emanates Nāda (Vāk), the elemental sound or Logos, and from Nāda the Bindu or cosmic germ, from which are successively evolved the principles of the finite universe; in this theory Śiva includes the Trinity consisting of *Pati*, *Paśu*, and *Pāśa*, or 'Lord', 'Herd', and 'Bond', i.e. Supreme Being, souls bound in the fetters of finitude, and the three forces binding them, which are *Māyā*, *Āṇava* or *Avidyā*, the power of darkness obscuring the native light of the soul, and *Karma*, the mechanical influence of former works upon present experience. Pure Māyā is almost the same conception as that of Śakti as explained above.

25. So far we have dealt with Nāda and Bindu in their general macrocosmical aspects, but they also play a prominent rôle in the microcosm of the individual. The following account is taken from the *Śiva-sūtra-vimarśinī*[1] of Kṣēmarāja. We have seen (§ 9) that Kuṇḍalinī, or Śakti, resides within the Mūlâdhāra, ordinarily sleeping rolled up in coils like a serpent. This serpent-like Kuṇḍalinī surrounds the microcosmic Supreme, who is in the shape of a minute dot of light. The first stage towards enlightenment occurs when a man obtains glimpses of this dot of light. By this the dot is set in motion, and rouses the Kuṇḍalinī, or Śakti, from her sleep. She wakes with a great sound (*nāda*) and becomes conscious. The soul is thus illuminated by a flash of the supreme light of consciousness. The Śakti, being merely the immanent aspect of the Supreme, is identical with Him. It is this flash of light, or *bindu*, and this sound of Sakti, or *nāda*, that are mystically represented by the *nāda-bindu* of the syllable *ōṁ*, written ओँ, with *anunāsika* (ँ), of which the dot represents the *bindu*, and the semicircle the *nāda*. By a further extension of the metaphor, this *nāda-bindu* is thus considered to be a representation of the Ultimate Supreme.

26. Inasmuch as the divine Śakti reveals herself in sound,

[1] A translation of this work by P. T. Shrinivas Iyengar has been published in the *Indian Thought* Series, Allahabad, 1912.

Word or Logos, the elements of speech, namely the syllables and their combinations, have a profound mystic significance in Śaiva doctrine. Hence there has arisen a copious literature on the mysteries of the letters of the alphabet and their groupings in spells (*mantras*), of which some idea may be gathered from the paper 'On the Sāradā Alphabet' in *Journ. Royal Asiatic Society*, October, 1916.

27. Appendix. In the preface to the translation of SS. in the *Sacred Books of the Hindus* it is suggested that the *cakras* and other terms of Yōgic anatomy correspond more or less to real parts of the human body, and the following identifications are proposed:—

Citrā: the grey matter of the spinal cord.

Brahma-randhra: the central canal of the spinal cord (but by modern Hindus identified with the anterior fontanelle).

Mūlādhāra: the sacral plexus.

Maṇipūra: the epigastric plexus.

Anāhata: the cardiac plexus.

Viśuddha: the laryngeal or pharyngeal plexus.

Ājñā: the cavernous plexus.

Sahasrāra: the medulla oblongata.

Suṣumnā: the spinal cord.

Iḍā: the left sympathetic cord.

Piṅgalā: the right sympathetic cord.

INDEX TO THE NOTE ON YŌGA

[*References are to paragraphs. If a word occurs more than once, the more important references (if any) are in italics, and precede the others.*]

ERRATUM.

Page 131, l. 3 from bottom, *after* cerebrals *add* and dentals.

Lallā Vākyāni

LALLĀ-VĀKYĀNI

1.

abhyös^{i} savikās layĕ wŏthū
gaganas sagun myūl^{u} sami tsaṭā
shūñ gol^{u} ta anāmay mŏtū
yuhuy wŏpadēsh chuy, baṭā!

2.

wākh mānas kŏl-akŏl nā atē
tshŏpi mudri ati nā pravēsh
rōzan shiwa-shĕk^{a}th nā atē
mŏt^{u}yĕy kūh ta suy wŏpadēsh

[Rājānaka Bhāskara's Sanskrit translation of 1 and 2.

abhyāsēna layaṁ nītē dṛśyē śūnyatvam āgatē
sākṣirūpaṁ śiṣyatē tac chāntē śūnyē 'py anāmayam
vāṅ mānasaṁ ca tanmudrē śivaśaktī kulākulē
yatra sarvam idaṁ līnam upadēśaṁ paraṁ tu tat

(From the printed edition.)

The following is the text of 1 and 2 in Stein B:—

अभ्यासो सविकास् ॥ लय् उत्थो [v. l. चन्द्र्]
गगनस् ॥ गगुन् [sic] मिलो संभ्रट्टा ॥
शून्य् गलो ता अनामय् ॥ मुतो
एक्रुय् ॥ उपदेश ॥ छोयी भट्टा ॥ १५ ॥

वाक् मानुस् ॥ कुलकौल् ॥ ना यत्ति ॥
छुपिय् मुद्रा नाति नाति प्रवेश् ॥
रजन् दिवस ॥ शिवशत्त ना यत्ति ॥
मुतो को ॥ ता सोयी उपदेश् ॥ १४ ॥]

1. When by repeated practice (of *yōga*) the whole expanse (of the visible universe) hath ascended to absorption;

When the qualified (universe) hath become merged within the Ether;

When the ethereal Void itself hath become dissolved, then naught but the Weal hath remained.

The true doctrine, O Brāhmaṇa, is but this alone.

2. There is there no word or (thought of) mind. There is there no non-transcendent or transcendent.

Not by vow of silence, not by mystic attitudes, is there entry there.

Not there dwell Śiva and his Śakti.

If there remaineth somewhat, that is what the doctrine teacheth.

1. The universe is here called 'that which has wide expanse', i.e. the wide expanse of creation. In the consciousness of the devotee who has attained to enlightenment it is recognized as being really an illusive emanation from the Supreme, and this recognition causes, to the consciousness of the devotee, its reabsorption in Him. Before the absorption of the universe, it has qualities.

Gagan, the sky, means the wide expanse of empty space, and, hence, the principle of *ākāśa*, ethereality, or of vacuity, with which it is identified in the third line. *Ṭraṭh* is the splash of water upon water, and, just as water falling with a splash into water is utterly united with that into which it falls, so the perception of the visible world is, as it were, at one splash, lost in and becomes one with the Void. This Void is not the ultimate Supreme, but is the first stage in His apparent evolution, in which he associates Himself with *Māyā*, or cosmic illusion, and thereby becomes subjected to limited individual experience. For further particulars, see the Note on Yōga, § 24 and Vocabulary, s. v. *shūñ*.

Transcending this stage, the soul loses all consciousness of limited individuality, and becomes absorbed in the

Supreme as unlimited pure consciousness and nothing else. This it is that is the aim of the devotee.

2. 'There', i.e. in the Supreme. The *kŏl*, or family (Sanskrit *kula*), is the group consisting of the *jīva* (individual soul), *prakṛti* (primal matter), space, time, ether, earth, water, fire, and air. The *akŏl* is that which transcends these. Hence, *kŏl-akŏl* means the totality of all creation, or the visible creation and that which transcends it. For the transcendental meaning of these words, see Note on Yōga, §§ 12, 19.

Vows of silence and the like do not lead directly to Him. The utmost they can do is to lead the mind to that knowledge of the Supreme which brings it into union with Him.

The 'somewhat', i.e. the ineffable Supreme, is not even Śiva and his Śakti, or energic power, for these have form and name, while the Supreme has neither.

3.

Lal bŏh drāyĕs lōla rē
ṭshāḍān lūstum dĕn kyōh rāth
wuchum panḍith panani garē
suy mĕ roṭᵘmas nĕchatur ta sāth

4.

damāh dam korᵘmas daman-hālē
prazalyōm dīph ta nanyēyĕm zāth
ạndᵃryumᵘ prakāsh nĕbar ṭshoṭum
gaṭi roṭum ta kürᵘmas thaph

[Rājānaka Bhāskara's Sanskrit translation of 3 and 4.

lallâhaṁ nirgatā dūram anvēṣṭuṁ śaṁkaraṁ vibhum
bhrāntvā labdhō mayā svasmin dēhē dēvō gṛhē sthitaḥ
tataḥ prâṇâdirōdhēna prajvālya jñānadīpikām
sphuṭaṁ dṛṣṭō mayā tatra citsvarūpō nirāmayaḥ

(From the printed edition.)]

3. With passionate longing did I, Lallā, go forth. Seeking and searching did I pass the day and night.

Then, lo, saw I in mine own house a learned man,

And that was my lucky star and my lucky moment when I laid hold of him.

4. Slowly, slowly, did I stop my breath in the bellows-pipe (of my throat).

Thereby did the lamp (of knowledge) blaze up within me, and then was my true nature revealed unto me.

I winnowed forth abroad my inner light,

So that, in the darkness itself, I could seize (the truth) and hold it tight.

In these two verses Lallā relates her own spiritual experiences.

3. She had wandered fruitlessly far and wide in search of the truth. In other words, she had made pilgrimages to holy places, and sought for salvation through formal rites, but all in vain. Then suddenly she found it in her own home, i.e. in her own soul. There she found her own Self, which became to her the equivalent of a *guru*, or spiritual preceptor, and she learned that it and the Supreme Self were one.

4. Suppression of breath is one of the most necessary *yōga* exercises. See Note on Yōga, § 21, and Vocabulary s. vv. *nāḍi* and *prān*, 2. Lallā compares the air-passages to the pipe of a bellows, by gently compressing which the feeble light of a lamp is allowed to blaze up. Otherwise it would be blown out.

It was the light, not the lamp, which she winnowed forth abroad. That is to say, the light which had at first burnt dimly in the inmost recesses of her soul, now suffused her whole being.

5.

par töy pān yĕm[i] *som*[u] *mŏn*[u]
yĕm[i] *hyuv*[u] *mŏn*[u] *dĕn kyōh rūth*
yĕmisạy aduy[u] *man sȭpon*[u]
tȧmiy ḍyūṭhuy sura-guru-nāth

[Rājānaka Bhāskara's Sanskrit translation.

ātmā parō dinaṁ rātrir yasya sarvam idaṁ samam
bhūtam advaitamanasas tēna dṛṣṭō 'marēśvaraḥ

(From the printed edition.)

The following is the text of Stein B:—

पर् ता पान् ॥ यमी समोय् मानो
हिहोय् मानोन् दिन् त रात् ॥
यमी अद्वय् मन् सम्पन्नो
तमी दिट्ठो सुरगुरुनाथ् ॥ २९ ॥

The MS. numbers this 20 by error.]

He who hath deemed another and himself as the same,
He who hath deemed the day (of joy) and the night (of sorrow) to be alike,
He whose mind hath become free from duality,
He, and he alone, hath seen the Lord of the Chiefest of gods.

Duality is the considering God and nature to be distinct. The true believer, who 'sees God', is one who recognizes that God is all in all, and that all creation, and all experiences, are but modes of Him. For the curious expression *sura-guru-nāth* for 'the Supreme', see Vocab. s. v. *guru*.

6.

ṭsidānandas jñāna-prakāshĕs
yimav ṭsyūn[u] tim zīwānt[i] mọkh[ụ]t[i]
vishĕmis samsāranis pāshĕs
abŏd[i] gaṇḍāh shĕth-shĕt[i] dit[i]

[Rājānaka Bhāskara's Sanskrit translation.

cidānandō jñānarūpaḥ prakāśākhyō nirāmayaḥ
yair labdhō dēhavantō 'pi muktās tē 'nyē 'nyathā sthitāḥ

(From the printed edition.)

The following is the text of Stein B:—

चिदानन्दस् ॥ त ज्ञानप्रकाशस् ॥
यमु चिनो तीम् ॥ जूवन्तीय् ॥ मुक्ती ॥
विषमीस् संसारनीस् ॥ पाशस् ॥
अबुधि गण्डा शत् ॥ शत् दिती ॥ ३१ ॥]

They who have gained experience of the Knowledge-light,—of that Self which is compact of pure spirit and of bliss,

They, while yet alive, have gained release (from earthly births).

But, to the tangled net of continual rebirth,

Have ignorant fools added knot by knot in hundreds.

Parama Śiva, the Supreme Self, has two aspects, as the *Śiva-tattwa* and the *Śakti-tattwa*. The former is pure Spirit, the pure light of Intelligence, without anything to shine upon. The latter is perfect Bliss, the supremest Self-satisfaction, absolute Rest. The ideas of pure Spirit and Bliss therefore comprise the whole idea of the Supreme Deity. The object of the devotee is to gain a perfect knowledge of Him, and to recognize that He is the Absolute Self of all things. The 'ignorant fools' are those who have not acquired this knowledge, and who are therefore born and reborn again. See *Kashmir Shaivism*, pp. 62, 64.

7.

*nātha! nā pān nā par zônum**
sadöy^{i} bôdum yih kŏdēh †
ts^{a}h bŏh bŏh ts^{a}h myul^{u} nā zônum
ts^{a}h kus bŏh kŏssa chuh sandēh •

* V. l. *nā parzônum*

† V. l. *sadöy^{i} gôrum yēkuy dēh*

[Rājānaka Bhāskara's Sanskrit translation in Stein A.[1]

[1] See p. 5.

nātha na tvaṁ na cátmápi jñātō dēhábhimānataḥ
svasyâikyaṁ ca tvayā tēna ka āvāṁ iti saṁśayaḥ
(MS. has *svasyâikaṁ.*)

The following is the text of Stein B :—

नाथा पाना ना पर्जाना
साधित् बाधिम् एह् कुदेह् ॥
चि भु चू मि मिलो ना जाना
चू कु भु कु क्यों सन्देह् ॥५॥]

7. Lord, I have not known myself or other than myself.

Continually have I mortified this vile body.

That Thou art I, that I am Thou, that these are joined in one I knew not.

It is doubt to say, 'Who am I?' and 'Who art Thou?'

Or, if we adopt the alternative readings :—

Lord, I have not recognized myself (as one with Thee).

Continually have I shown affection for this single body.

That Thou art I, &c., as above.

An impassioned declaration of the oneness of the Self with the Supreme Self. Lallā declares that in her ignorance she has not known the true relation of herself to others. In other words, she has clung to the conception of her personal identity, and been ignorant of the real nature of her Self, as only one manifestation of the Supreme. She has worn her body out by attempting to gain salvation by good works, not recognizing that these lead only to further transmigrations and are all in vain. The only hope of salvation is the recognition of the identity of her Self with the Supreme. To wonder who I am, and who He is, i.e. to doubt this identity, is indeed the fatal doubt of doubts.

In the alternative text, the meaning is much the same, though couched in somewhat different language.

8.

Shiv wā Kēshĕv wā Zin wā
Kamalaza-nāth nām dörin yuh
mĕ abali kösᶦtan bhawa-ruz
suh wā suh wā suh wā suh

[Rājānaka Bhāskara's Sanskrit translation in Stein A.

śivō vā kēśavō vā́pi jinō vā druhiṇō 'pi vā
saṁsārarōgēṇā́krāntām abalāṁ māṁ cikitsatu

The following is the text of Stein B:—

शिव् वा केशव् जिन् वा कमलुज् ॥
नाथा नाव् धारिनिय् यी यो ॥
सो मि अबलि कासीतन् भवरुज्
सो वा सो वा सो वा सो ॥ २ ॥]

Let Him bear the name of Śiva, or of Kēśava, or of the Jina, or of the Lotus-born Lord,—whatever name he bear,—

May he take from me, sick woman that I am, the disease of the world,

Whether He be he, or he, or he, or he.

By whatever name the worshipper may call the Supreme, He is still the Supreme, and He alone can give release. Kēśava means Viṣṇu; by the name of 'Jina' is indicated both a 'Jina', the Saviour of the Jains, and also the Buddha. I suspect that here it is confused with the Arabic *Jinn*, the 'genius' of the Arabian nights. The Lotus-born Lord is Brahmā.

9.

bān golᵘ töy prakāsh āv zūnē
ċandᵃr golᵘ töy mŏtuy ċĕth
ċĕth golᵘ töy kĕh-ti nā kunē
*gay bhūr bhuwaḥ swar vĕsarzith-kĕth**

* V. l. *swar mīlith ta kotᵘ*

[Rājānaka Bhāskara's Sanskrit translation from Stein A.

bhānau naṣṭē kāśatē candrabimbaṁ
tasmin naṣṭē kāśatē cittam ēva
cittē naṣṭē dṛśyajātaṁ kṣaṇēna
pṛthvyādīdaṁ gacchati kvāpi sarvam

The following is the text of Stein B :—

भान् गलो सुप्रकाश्॒ा जोनि
चन्द्र् गलो ता मुतो चित्त् ॥
चित्त् ॥ गलो ता किंह् ना कोनि
गय् भवा विसर्जन् कित् ॥ २१ ॥]

When the sun disappeared, then came the moonlight;

When the moon disappeared then only mind remained;

When (absorbed in the Infinite) mind disappeared, then naught anywhere was left;

Earth, ether, and sky all took their departure.

Or, if we take the variant reading, the last line would run:—

Then whither did earth, ether, and sky go off (absorbed) together (in vacuity)?

Regarding this verse, see Vocab. s.v. *sōm.* The moon and the sun represent, respectively, the uppermost and lowest seats of action, or *cakras.* When, by intense mental absorption, or *yōga*, these disappear, or cease to be present to consciousness, the devotee is conscious of the existence of nothing except his thinking faculty or mind. When this is finally absorbed in the Supreme, all sense of difference between the individual spirit and the Universal Being is sunk in the all-consuming consciousness of All-Being, All-Light. See Note on Yōga, §§ 5, 21.

10.

wŏth rainyā! arʦun sakhar
athē al-pal wakhur hĕth
yod[u]*wanay zānakh parama-pad akhĕr*
hishiy khŏsh[i]*-khŏr kĕtha khĕth*

[Rājānaka Bhāskara's Sanskrit translation from Stein A.
uttiṣṭha śāktikastri tvaṁ pūjayēśaṁ surádibhiḥ
yadi jñātam akṣaraṁ tat tvayā tēnápi kā kṣatiḥ
(MS. has *jñānam*, corrected to *jñātam*.)

The following is the text of Stein B :—

उत्थ् रैन्या अर्चने सखर् ॥
अथि अल् ॥ पल् ॥ ता अखुर् ॥ हित् ॥
यिद् जानक् परमो पद् ॥ अक्षुर् ॥
खशि खर् ह्रंशि खुम्प् कित् ॥ १६ ॥

The last line has been corrected in the MS., and this is what seems to be intended. But the reading is unintelligible, and very doubtful. A better reading will be found in verse 77.]

Arise, O Lady, set out to make thine offering,
Bearing in thy hand wine, flesh, and cates.
If thou know the syllable that is itself the Supreme Place,
Thou (wilt also know that) if thou violate the custom it is all the same. What loss is there therein?

The lady is a diligent worshipper of Śiva, with all the necessary rites, and is apparently a follower of the left-handed sect, that consumes wine and flesh, and performs less reputable acts as a part of worship, which are not consonant with regular Hindū *ācāra*, or custom.

Lallā points out that the violation of her Hindū custom, by the performance of these Kaula sacraments, is unobjectionable, or, indeed, praiseworthy, provided she knows the mystic syllable *ōṁ*, regarding which, see verse 15. The 'lady' is probably the Śakti abiding in the speaker's own body; see Note on Yōga, § 9. Cf. verse 77.

11.

tanth^{a}*r gali töy manth*^{a}*r mŏtsē*
manth^{a}*r gol*^{u} *töy mọtuy tsĕth*
tsĕth gol^{u} *töy kĕ̄h-ti nā kunē*
shū̆ñĕs shū̆ñāh mīlith gauv

[Rājānaka Bhāskara's Sanskrit translation in Stein A.

tantraṁ sarvaṁ līyatē mantra ēva
mantraś cittē līyatē nādamūlaḥ
cittē līnē līyatē sarvam ēva
dṛśyaṁ draṣṭā śiṣyatē citsvarūpaḥ

(MS. *mantraḥ cittē* and *citsurūpaḥ.*)

The following is the text of Stein B :—

तन्त्र् गलि ता मन्त्र् साती
मन्त्र् गलि ता शुचि शून्या ॥
शूल् [read शून्य्] गलि ता अनामय्॥ शुचि
एङ्गय् उपदेश् चिञा ॥ ३६ ॥]

(This is a mixture of Nos. 1 and 11.)

Holy books will disappear, and then only the mystic formula will remain.

When the mystic formula departed, naught but mind was left.

When the mind disappeared naught was left anywhere,

And a void became merged within the Void.

In its general lines, this closely agrees with verse 9. The void is the apparent material world, which is really empty nothingness, and, when final release is attained, its apparent existence disappears in the Great Transcendental Void, regarding which, see Note on Yōga, § 24, verse 1, and the Vocabulary s. v. *shūñ*. Lallā is fond of the expression in the last line, and repeats it in verses 30 and 69.

12.

hĕth karith rājy phēri nā
dith karith trupti nā man
lūba vĕnā zīv mari nā
zīwont^u mari tŏy suy chuy jñān

[Rājānaka Bhāskara's Sanskrit translation in Stein A.

dātur manas tṛpyati nâiva rājyaṁ
dattvā grahītuś ca tad ēva labdhvā
jīvō 'pi lōbhēna na mṛtyum ēti
mṛtasya nâivâsti hi jātu mṛtyuḥ

The following is the text of Stein B :—

हिता कर्ता राज्य् फरि ना
देता कर्ता तृपि ना मन् ॥
विन् लोभा जूव् मरि ना
जूवन्तोय् मरि ता सोये ज्ञानी ॥ २७ ॥]

If thou take and rule a kingdom, even then is there no respite.

And if thou give it to another, still in thy heart is no content.

But the soul that is free from desire will never die.

If, while it is yet alive, it die, then that alone is the true knowledge.

Praise of freedom from desire. The gain or the abandonment of power gives no true respite from care. Only freedom from desire brings content. A man does not grasp the true knowledge till he understand that, even while alive, he should be as one dead (i. e. free from all desire). Cf. verse 87.

13.

yimaṇy shĕh tĕ timaṇy shĕh mĕ
Shyāma-galā! tŏyĕ vĕn tŏṭ^ü s
yuhuy bĕn abēda tĕ ta mĕ
t^a h shĕn swōmī bŏh shĕy^i mush^ü s

[Rājānaka Bhāskara's Sanskrit translation in Stein A.

yad ēva ṣaṭkaṁ tē dēva tad ēva ca mama prabhō
niyōktā tu niyōjyáhaṁ tasyástîty āvayōr bhidā

The following is the text of Stein B:—

एमय् मुचि तीमय् ष मि
श्यामगला चियीविन् तुट्टुस् ॥
एज़्य् भिन्नाभेद् चि ता मि ॥
चू षन् स्वामी भु षय् मूठूस् ॥ १ ॥]

God of the dark blue throat! As Thou hast the six, so the same six have I.

And yet, estranged from Thee, into misery have I fallen.

Only this discord was there, that, though betwixt Thee and me there was no difference,

Thou wast the Lord of six, while I by six was led astray.

Śiva is said to have a dark blue throat from the legend of the churning by which the gods extracted immortality-giving nectar from the ocean. The first to come up in the churning was the deadly Kālakūṭa poison, which was swallowed by Śiva to prevent its doing any further harm. The poison dyed his neck dark blue.

Hindū philosophy has numerous groups of six. The Supreme Deity has six attributes, viz. omniscience, contentment, knowledge of the past from eternity, absolute self-sufficiency, irreducible potency, and omnipotence. Lallā exclaims that, though she knew it not, she, as really one with Him, also had these six. But, in her ignorance, while the Supreme was ever master of these six, she was misled by another six. This other six is capable of various interpretations. They may be the six 'enemies', viz. sexual desire, wrath, desire, arrogance, delusion, and jealousy; or they may be the six human infirmities, or the six periods of human life, or the six changes in life, for all of which see the Vocabulary, s. v. *shĕh.*

14.

Shiv gur[u] *töy Kēshĕv palānas*
Brahmā pāyirĕn wölasĕs
yōgī yōga-kali parzānĕs
*kus dēv ashwawār pĕṭh cēḍĕs**

* V. l. *cērĕs*

15.

anāhath kha-swarūph shūñālay
yĕs nāv na war[a]*n na guth*[a]*r ta rūph*
aham-vimarshĕ nāda-binduy yĕs won[u]
*suy dēv ashwawār pĕṭh cēḍĕs**

* V. l. *cērĕs*

[Rājānaka Bhāskara's Sanskrit translation of 14 and 15 in Stein A.

śivō 'śvaḥ kēśavas tasya paryāṇam ātmabhūs tathā
pādayantraṁ tatra yōgyaḥ sādī ka iti mē vada
anāhataḥ khasvarūpaḥ śūnyasthō vigatāmayaḥ
anāmarūpavarṇō 'jō nādavindvātmakō 'pi saḥ

(MS. has *anāmâvarṇō jō rūpō.* We follow the printed edition.)

The following is the text of 14 and 15 in Stein B :—

शिव् घोळो केशव् ॥ पलानि ॥
ब्रह्मा ति पायळ्यन् विलसोस्
योगी योगकलि पर्जानि
अश्ववार् ॥ कुसो पिट्ठ् खथोस् ॥ १९ ॥

अनाहत् ॥ खस्वरूप् ॥ शून्यालय् ॥
यस् ॥ नाव् ॥ ना रूप् ॥ वर्ण ना गोत्र् ॥
अङ्गनिह् ॥ नादबिन्द् ॥ तयवानो ॥
एङ्गय् ॥ देव् तस् ॥ पिट्ठ खथोस् ॥ २० ॥]

14. Śiva is the horse. Zealously employed upon the saddle is Viṣṇu, and, upon the stirrup, Brahmā.

The Yōgī, by the art of his yōga, will recognize who is the god that will mount upon him as the rider.

15. The ever-unobstructed sound, the principle of absolute vacuity, whose abode is the Void,

Which hath no name, nor colour, nor lineage, nor form,

Which they declare to be (successively transformed into) the Sound and the Dot by its own reflection on itself,—

That alone is the god that will mount upon him.

Siva here is not, like Viṣṇu and Brahmā, the personal deity. He is the 'Śiva-tattva', the first phase of the Supreme in the universe. The Yōgī understands that this is but a manifestation of a deeper Reality of the Absolute Spirit. He is, as it were, but the horse upon which the Supreme rides. The Supreme is described under various mystical names in verse 15. He is the unobstructed sound,—the sacred syllable *ōṁ*,—which, once uttered, vibrates in perpetuity (see Vocabulary, s. v. *anāhath*). His essence is the *kha*, or sky, i.e. ethereality (cf. verse 1), whose home is in the Void conceived to exist in the *Sahasrâra* in the sinus of the forehead of the microcosm (cf. again verse 1, and also note on Yōga, §§ 20, 24); nothing whatever can be predicated concerning Him. The 'Sound and the Dot' refer to the theory regarding the first stage of enlightenment. The Supreme resides in a man's subtile body in the form of a minute dot of light, surrounded by coils of His *Parā Śakti*, or the Supreme Energy. When by yōga, or intense abstract meditation on the Ego, the man gets his first glimpse of this dot, the latter is set in motion, and the *Parā Śakti* is roused, and awakes with a loud cry. For further particulars, see note on Yōga, §§ 23, 24, 25.

The commentator quotes the following lines on the sacred syllable *ōṁ*, which illustrates what is said above:—

uktō ya ēṣa uccāras tatra yō 'sau sphuran sthitaḥ ।
avyaktânukṛti-prāyō dhwanir varṇaḥ sa kathyatē ॥
nâsyôccāraỵitā kaścit pratihantā na vidyatē ।
swayam uccaratē dēvaḥ prâṇinām urasi sthitaḥ ॥
ēkō nādâtmakō varṇaḥ sarva-varṇâvibhāga-vān ।
sō 'n-astam-ita-rūpatwād anāhata ihôditaḥ ॥

That spoken utterance which continues vibrating there (i.e. at the point of utterance), a sound that mostly has the semblance of inarticulateness, is the syllable (*ōṁ*).

There is no one who causes it to be uttered, and no one who checks it. The God dwelling in the human breast utters it Himself.

This one syllable consisting of the Nāda and containing all syllables without distinction, is here called 'unobstructed' because its nature is imperishable.

16.

tūri salil khoṭ[u] *töy tūrē*
himi tr[a]*h gay bĕn abĕn vimarshā*
ċaitanyĕ-rav bāti sab samē
Shiwa-may ċarāċar zag pashyā

[Rājānaka Bhāskara's Sanskrit translation in Stein A.

māyājāḍyaṁ taj jaḍaṁ bōdhanīyaṁ
saṁsṛtyākhyaṁ tad ghanatvaṁ himaṁ ca
citsūryō 'smin prōditō trīṇi sadyō
jāḍyān muktaṁ nīram ādyaṁ śivākhyam

(The printed edition has *bōdha-nīraṁ*)

The following is the text of Stein B :—

तूठि सलिल् ॥ खटो ता तूरू ॥
हिम्मि त्रि गय् ॥ भिन्नो भिन्नो विमर्शा
चेतन् ॥ रव् नारौ बाति ॥ सब् सम्मे
शिवमैं चराचर् जग् पश्शा ॥१३॥]

When cold hath obtained the mastery over water, the water becometh ice;

Or, again, it may be turned to snow. Thus there are three different things; but, on reflection, we see that they are not different.

When the sun of the Supreme Consciousness shineth forth, the three will become the same.

Lo! By it all things, whether with life or without it, the universe itself, are seen as only Śiva.

Just as the sun reduces ice and snow to identity with water, so the sun of true knowlege makes the soul recognize not only its identity with the Supreme, but also that the whole universe is one, conjured forth out of the Absolute by the divine Māyā. See Note on Yōga, § 24.

17.

dēv waṭā diwor^{u} waṭā
pēṭha bōna chuy yēka wāṭh
pūz kas karakh, hōṭā baṭā!
kar manas ta pawanas sangāṭh

[Rājānaka Bhāskara's Sanskrit translation in Stein A.

caityaṁ dēvō nirmitau dvau tvayā yau
pūjāhētōs tau śilātō na bhinnau
dēvō 'mēyaṁ citsvarūpaṁ vidhēyaṁ
tadvyāptyarthaṁ prāṇacittāikyam ēva

(MS. has *dēvaḥ*, and *tadvāptyartha*. Printed edition has *dēvō 'mēyaś citsvarūpō.*)

The following is the text of Stein B:—

देव् वट्टा देवरो वट्टा
पिट्ठ बुन् छ्योय् एक वाट् ॥
पूज् कस् करिक् होट्टा बट्टा
कर् मनस् त पवनस् ॥ सङ्गाट् ॥ ७ ॥]

An idol is but a lump of stone, a temple is but a lump of stone.

From crown to sole each is of but the one stuff.

O learned Paṇḍit! what is this to which thou offerest worship?

Bring thou together a determined mind and thy vital airs.

Idol-worship is vain. In lieu of worshipping stocks and stones, thou shouldst perform the Yōgic *prāṇāgnihōtra*, a spiritual offering of the vital breaths; i.e. practise yōga by bringing thy vital airs under control. See Vocabulary, s.vv. *nāḍi* and *prān*, 2, and note on Yōga, §§ 5, 21.

18.

ösā bōl pàr^{i}nĕm sāsā*
mĕ mani wāsā khīd nā hĕyē
bŏh yid sahaza Shĕnkara-bŭkts^{ü} āsā
makaris sāsā mal kyāh pĕyē

* V. l. *pàḍ^{i}nĕm*

[Rājānaka Bhāskara's Sanskrit translation in Stein A.

avācyānāṁ sahasrāṇi kathayantu na manmanaḥ
mālinyam ēty udāsīnaṁ rajōbhir makurō yathā

The following is the text of Stein B:—

आसा भुल् पळीनिम् ॥ सासा
मि मन्वासा खिद् ना हिय् ॥
सहजे शङ्कर भच्चू आसा ॥
मकुरस् ॥ स्वासा मल् क्या पिय् ॥ २३ ॥]

Let him utter a thousand abuses at me.

But, if I be innately devoted to Śiva (*or* if I be devoted to Śiva the Real and the True) disquiet will find no abode within my heart.

Is a mirror fouled if a few ashes fall upon it?

On the contrary, the ashes serve only to polish the mirror. A reply to her critics.

19.

atshĕn āy ta gatshun gatshē*
pakun gatshē dĕn kyāwu rāth
yōray āy ta tūr^{i} gatshun gatshē
kēh na-ta kēh na-ta kēh na-ta kyāh

* V. l. *atshān*

[Rājānaka Bhāskara's Sanskrit translation in Stein A.

jarāgatā kṣīṇatarō 'dya dēhō
jātō 'vasāyō gamanāya kāryaḥ
samāgatāḥ smō yata ēva tatra
gantavyam ēvēha dṛḍhaṁ na kiṁcit]

They came and came, and then they have to go.
Ever must they, night and day, move on and on.
Whence they came, thither must they go.
What is anything? It is nothing, nothing, nothing.

Or, if we read *aśhān*, the first line means, they came becoming emaciated (i.e. came wearily), and then they have to go.

The weary round of perpetual birth and rebirth. Cf. Koheleth, xii. 8, 'Vanities of vanities, saith the Preacher, all is vanity'.

20.

mūḍ zönith pashith ta kőr[u]
kol[u] *shruta-wőn*[u] *zaḍa-rūp*' *ās*
yus[u] *yih dapiy tas tiy bōl**
yuhuy tattwa-vidis chuh abhyās

* V.l. *bōz*

[Rājānaka Bhāskara's Sanskrit translation in Stein A.

jñātvā sarvaṁ mūḍhavat tiṣṭha svasthaḥ
śrutvā sarvaṁ śrōtrahīnēna bhāvyam
dṛṣṭvā sarvaṁ tūrṇam andhatvam ēhi
tattvábhyāsaḥ kīrtitō 'yaṁ budhéndraiḥ

(MS. has *budhîndraiḥ*. Cf. verse 26.)

The following is the text of Stein B:—

मूढ् जानीत् पश्यीत् कर् कल्लो
श्रुतवनो जडरूपी आस्
योसो यी दपी तस् ती भल्लो
एड़्य् तत्त्वविद् छ्योयी अभ्यास् ॥ ४७ ॥]

Though thou hast knowledge, be thou as a fool; though thou canst see, be thou as he that is one-eyed;
Though thou canst hear, be thou as one dumb; in all things be thou as a non-sentient block.

Whatever any one may say to thee, say thou the same to him (*or*, if we read *bōz*, whatever any one may say to thee, listen thou and agree).

It is this that is the true practice for obtaining the knowledge of the basal truths.

For the basal truths, or fundamental and general factors of which the apparent universe consists, see Vocabulary, s. v. *tattwa*, We may compare Kabīr's famous advice :—

sab-sē hiliyē sab-sē miliyē
sab-kā līјiyē nām
'hā̃ jī', 'hā̃ jī', sab-sē kahiyē
basiyē apnē gām

Meet every one in a friendly way,
Greet every one by name.
Say 'yes Sir', 'yes Sir', to each one who addresses you.
But live in your own village (i.e. stick to your own opinions).

21.

*gāl gȧṇḍⁱnĕm bōl pȧrⁱnĕm**
dȧpⁱnĕm tiy yĕs yih rōtsē
sahaza-kusumav pūz kȧrⁱnĕm
bŏh amalöñ^ü ta kas kyāh mōtsē

* V. l. *pȧḍⁱnĕm*

[Rājānaka Bhāskara's Sanskrit translation in Stein A.

nindantu vā mām athavā stuvantu
kurvantu vārcāṁ vividhaiḥ svapuṣpaiḥ
na harṣam āyāmy athavā viṣādaṁ
viśuddhabōdhāmṛtapānasvasthā

(Printed edition has *supuṣpaiḥ*.)

The following is the text of Stein B :—

गाल् ॥ गण्ड़ेनिम् ॥ भुल् ॥ पंक्रेनिं ॥
दंपेनिं यस् ये रुच्चि ॥
सहज कुसुम पूज् करेनिं ॥
भु अमलान्यो त कस् ॥ क्या मुच्ची ॥ २५ ॥]

Let him bind abuse upon me, let him orate blame against me,

Let each one say to me what pleaseth each.

Yea, let him worship me with the offering of his own soul for the flowers.

Still keep I myself untouched and undefiled by all these; so who getteth what therefrom?

She is callous to the blame or praise of the world. The rendering of *sahaza* in the third line is doubtful. Perhaps we should translate 'let him worship me with flowers of reality, i.e. with real flowers'.

22.

děn ṭhězi ta razan āsē
bhū-tal gaganas-kun vikāsē
ṭạnd[ăr][i] *Rāh grōs*[u] *māwāsē*
Shiwa-pūzan gwāh ṭitta ātmāsē

[Rājānaka Bhāskara's Sanskrit translation in Stein A.

nāśaṁ gatē 'rkē khalu mānasaṁjñē
mēyakṣayākhyā rajanī vibhāti
jīvākhyacandraḥ śivadhāmni līnaḥ
svāhantvarāhuṁ grasatē ca sadyaḥ

The following is the text of Stein B:—

दिन् ॥ छ्यीजि ता रजन् आसि
भूतुल् गगनस् कनो त कासि ॥
चन्द्रे गह् यासो मावस्सि ॥
॰ शिव् ॥ पूजुन् ग्वाहिय् चित्तात्मसि ॥ १८ ॥]

The day will be extinguished, and night will come;

The surface of the earth will become extended to the sky;

On the day of the new moon, the moon swallowed up the demon of eclipse.

The illumination of the Self in the organ of thought is the true worship of Śiva.

Once the mind realizes the true nature of the Self, as one with the Supreme Self, here given the name of Śiva, all things fade into nothingness. There is no distinction between day and night, and the boundaries of the apparently solid earth merge into those of the sky, so that earth and sky become one. Nay, the demon of eclipse is eclipsed himself.

According to Hindū tradition, the moon contains sixteen digits, each containing a certain amount of nectar. Each day the gods drink the nectar in one digit, so that on the sixteenth day only one digit remains. This accounts for the waning of the moon. The nectar of the sixteenth day is that which remains over on the day of the new moon. On the occasion of a solar eclipse, the moon and the sun are together, and the nectar of the sixteenth digit, becoming heated and caused to evaporate by the proximity of the sun, ascends into that luminary. Rāhu, the demon of eclipse, then swallows the sun in order to drink the nectar. So much for the tradition explanatory of the natural phenomenon. Here Lallā describes the process of absorption in the Sahasrâra (see note on Yōga, § 21). To the fully enlightened soul, the day of earthly illusion disappears, and all is night; the apparently solid earth loses its bounds, and becomes merged in the sky; in the illumination of the Self, so far from Rāhu swallowing (the nectar of) the moon, it is the moon in the Sahasrâra that swallows the dark demon of ignorance.

There is also a more mystical side to this verse. Normally there is a distinction between the subject of cognition (*pramātar*), the object of cognition (*pramēya*), and the instrument of cognition (*pramāṇa*). The *pramātar* is here typified by Rāhu, the demon of lunar eclipse, the *pramēya* by the moon, and the *pramāṇa* by the sun.[1] The thinker is able to 'swallow the moon', i. e. to think

[1] *Arkaḥ pramāṇaṁ, sōmas tu mēyaṁ, jñāna-kriyâtmakau |*
Rāhur māyāpramātā syāt tad-ācchādana-kōvidaḥ ||
Verse quoted in the Commentary.

away the phenomenal world into a blank; but he cannot completely dissolve it, for there still exists the triad of *pramātar*, *pramēya*, and *pramāṇa*, until the *Parā Saṁvid*, or Higher Consciousness, is attained, by which all three are fused together and sublimated into a void of infinite Unity. Lallā here refers to the presence of *Parā Saṁvid*. Whereas in ordinary meditation 'Rāhu swallows the moon', i.e. the thinker effaces the phenomenal world, the Higher Consciousness (typified by the moon residing in Sahasrâra; see note on Yōga, §§ 19, 20) absorbs the consciousness of the thinker into itself, entirely sublimating its contents into Void.

23.

manasạy mān bhawa-saras
*chyūr*ᵘ *kūpa nērēs nārüc*ᵘ̈ *chŏkh*
*lĕkā-lĕkh, yud*ᵘ *tulā-kōṭi*
*tuli tūl*ᵘ *ta tul nā kĕ̄h*

[Rājānaka Bhāskara's Sanskrit translation in Stein A.

kruddhaṁ manō vahnisamānarūpaṁ
tiraskṛtaṁ bhāraṇataṁ vibhāti
vicārataḥ sarvavikārahīnaṁ
viśuddhabōdhâikasvarūpam ēva

The following is the text of Stein B:—

मनस् मन् ॥ भवसरस् ॥
क्रोढ्रू कोप् ॥ निरिस् ता नारच्चुक् ॥
लिकान् ॥ लक्ष्य् ॥ तूला कोटू ॥
तुलि तूलो ता तुल् ना अक् ॥ १२ ॥]

Look upon thy mind alone as the ocean of existence.

If thou restrain it not, but let it loose, from its rage will issue angry words, like wounds caused by fire.

Yet, if thou weigh them in the scales of truth, their weight is naught.

According to legend, a terribly destructive fire, named *vaḍavāgni*, is imprisoned at the bottom of the ocean. If it were to burst forth, the whole world would be destroyed. Similarly, if the fire of wrath burst forth from the ocean of the mind, it would leave deadly scars, and yet, to the wise man, it is nothing.

If, instead of *nārüc^u^ chŏkh*, we read *nārats^i^-chŏkh*, which could be spelt in Nāgarī with identically the same letters, we must substitute 'wounds caused by a fishing-spear' for 'wounds caused by fire'. Otherwise the meaning of the verse would be the same.

24.

shīl ta mān chuy pōñ^u^ kranjĕ
mŏchĕ yĕm^i^ roṭ^u^ màll^i^ yud^u^ wāv
host^u^ yus^u^ mast-wāla ganḍĕ
tih yĕs tagi töy suh ada nĕhāl

[Rājānaka Bhāskara's Sanskrit translation in Stein A.

śīlasya mānasya ca rakṣaṇaṁ bhaṭais
tair ēva śakyaṁ nipuṇaṁ vidhātuṁ
vāyuṁ karēṇātha gajaṁ ca tantunā
yaiḥ śakyatē stambhayituṁ sudhīraiḥ]

Integrity and high repute are but water carried in a basket.

If some mighty man can grasp the wind within his fist,

Or if he can tether an elephant with a hair of his head,

Only if one be skilled in such feats as these, will he be successful (in retaining integrity and high repute).

The vanity of earthly repute.

25.

shĕ wan taṭith shĕshi-kal wuz^ü^m
prakrĕth hŏz^ü^m pawana-sötiy
lōlaki nāra wölinj^ü^ buz^ü^m
Shĕnkar lobum tamiy sötiy

[Sanskrit translation in Stein A.

kāmādikaṁ kānanaṣaṭkam ētac
chittvāmṛtaṁ bōdhamayaṁ mayāptam
prāṇādhirōdhāt prakṛtiṁ ca bhaktyā
manaś ca dagdhvā śivadhāma labdham]

By (controlling) my vital airs I cut my way through the six forests, till the digit of the moon awoke for me, and the material world dried up within me.

With the fire of love I parched my heart as a man parcheth grain,

And at that moment did I obtain Śiva.

In the spiritual body of a man there are six *cakras*, or seats of a *śakti*, impelling him to experience the objective universe and to look upon it as real. These must be mastered before true enlightenment is reached, and Lallā compares the process to cutting a way through six forests. A mystical moon, the abode of the Supreme Śiva, is supposed to exist under the frontal sinus, and, once he has mastered the six *cakras*, the devotee becomes cognisant of this moon and is absorbed in the Śiva.

The mastery is effected by control and suppression of the vital airs (see Vocab., s. v. *prān* 2), and the exciting cause is ardent love, or desire, for Śiva. For further particulars, see Vocab., s. vv. *shĕh* and *sōm*, and Note on Yōga, §§ 9 ff. and 21.

26.

ƫitta-turog^u gagàn^i brama-wŏn^u
nimēshĕ aki ƫhanḍi yōzana-lach
ƫētani-wagi bŏd^i raṭith zŏn^u
*prān apān sandörith pakh^ach**

* V. l.

yĕm^i na wagi yih raṭith zŏn^u
prān apān phuṭ^ar^inas pakh^ach

[Rājānaka Bhāskara's Sanskrit translation in Stein A.

cittābhidhaḥ sarvagatis turaṅgaḥ
kṣaṇāntarē yōjanalakṣagāmī
dhāryō budhēndrēṇa vivēkavalgā-
nōdēna vāyudvayapakṣarōdhāt

(MS. has *turaṅga* instead of *turaṅgaḥ*.)]

The steed of my thoughts speedeth over the sky (of my heart).

A hundred thousand leagues traverseth he in the twinkling of an eye.

The wise man knew how to block the wheels (of the chariot) of his outward and inward vital airs, as he seized the horse by the bridle of self-realization.

Or, if we adopt the alternative reading of the last two lines, we must translate them:—

If a man hath not known how to seize the horse by the bridle, the wheels (of the chariot) of his outward and inward vital airs have burst in pieces.

As explained in the notes on the preceding verse, self-realization is obtained by mastering the vital airs. The two principal airs are the outward and the inward, known as *prāṇa* and *apāṇa*. See Vocabulary, s. v. *prān*, 2, and Note on Yōga, §§ 2, 16, 23.

27.

*khĕth ganḍith shĕmi nā mānas**
brānth yimav tröv^ü timạy gay khăs^it^i
shāstra būzith chuh yĕma-bayĕ krūr^u
soh^u nā pŏt^u ta dăñiy lăs^it^i

* V. l. *khĕna ganḍana-nishĕ man thövith dūr^u*

[Rājānaka Bhāskara's Sanskrit translation in Stein A.

khādanād bhūṣaṇād vāpi manō yasya gatabhramaṁ
sa muktō, nōttamarṇād yō gṛhṇāty arthaṁ hi sō 'nṛṇaḥ

The following is the text of Stein B :—

खिना गण्डना निश्रा मन् ॥ दूरो ॥
भ्रान्त् येमु चावू तीमै गै खस्ती ॥
शास्त्र् ॥ भूजीत ॥ ध्यो यमभट्ट ॥ क्रूरो
सहो ना पचो ता दन्या लस्ती ॥ ८ ॥]

By eating and apparelling the mind will not become at peace.

They only have ascended who have abandoned false hopes.

When they have learnt from the scriptures that the fear of Yama is terrible (to him who is in debt to Desire),

And when the lender hath trusted them not (with a loan), then indeed live they blessed and at peace.

Or, if we adopt the alternative reading, the first two lines must be translated :—

They only who have kept their minds from eating and apparel, and who have abandoned false hopes, will ascend.

Yama is the judge of the soul after death. Desire is compared to a money-lender, who gives a loan of fruition, but demands a hard repayment of principal and interest. Happy indeed is the contented soul to whom he refuses to make the loan.

28.

yĕwa tūrü tsali tim ambar hĕtā
kshŏd yĕwa gali tim āhār ann
tsittā ! swa-para-vĕtsāras pĕtā
tsēntan yih dēh wan-kāwan

[Rājānaka Bhāskara's Sanskrit translation in Stein A.

śītárthaṁ vasanaṁ grāhyaṁ kṣudhárthaṁ bhōjanaṁ tathā
manō vivēkitāṁ nēyam alaṁ bhōgánucintanaiḥ

The following is the text of Stein B :—

यवा तूळ् चल्लि ते अम्बुर् ॥ हिता ॥
क्षुध् चलि ते आहार् ॥ अन्न्
चित्ता स्वपरविचारस् पित्ता
चिन्ता देहस् वन् क्यावन् ॥ २६ ॥]

Don but such apparel as will cause the cold to flee.

Eat but so much food as will cause hunger to cease.

O Mind ! devote thyself to discernment of the Self and of the Supreme,

And recognize thy body as but food for forest crows.

29.

sahazas shĕm ta dam nō gatshi
yitshi nō prāwakh mŏkti-dwār
salilas lawan-zan mīlith gatshi
tō-ti chuy durlab sahaza-vĕtsār

[Rājānaka Bhāskara's Sanskrit translation in Stein A.

svabhāvalabdhau na śamō 'sti kāraṇaṁ
tathā damaḥ kiṁtu paraṁ vivēkaḥ
nīrâikarūpaṁ lavaṇaṁ yathā bhavēt
tathâikatáptāv api nâiṣa labhyaḥ]

Quietism and self-command are not required for (the knowledge of) the Self,

Nor by the mere wish wilt thou reach the door of final release.

E'en though a man become absorbed (in his contemplations) as salt is absorbed in water,

Still rarely doth he attain to the discernment of the nature of his Self.

Ordinary ascetism, and even ardent desire, are common enough, but without the knowledge of the true nature of Self, they are of no avail for ultimate release.

30.

lūb mārun sahaz vĕcārun
drọg^u zānun kalpan trāv
nishĕ chuy ta dūr^u mō gārun
shūñĕs shūñāh mīlith gauv

[Rājānaka Bhāskara's Sanskrit translation in Stein A.

lōbhaṁ tyaktvā vaimanasyaṁ ca tadvat
kāryō nityaṁ svasvabhāvāvamarśaḥ
śūnyāśūnyaṁ naiva bhinnaṁ yathaivaṁ
tasmāt tvaṁ tadbhēdabuddhir vṛthaiva]

(Printed edition has *śūnyāc chūnyaṁ.*)

Slay thou desire; meditate thou on the nature of the Self.

Abandon thou thy vain imaginings; for know thou that that knowledge is rare and of great price.

Yet is it near by thee; search for it not afar.

(It is naught but a void); and a void has become merged within the Void.

Cf. verses 11 and 69.

31.

makuras zan mal colum manas
adẹ mĕ lūb^ūm zanas zān
suh yĕli dyūṭhum nishĕ pānas
sŏruy suy ta bŏh nō kĕh

[Rājānaka Bhāskara's Sanskrit translation in Stein A.

cittādarśē nirmalatvaṁ prayātē
prōdbhūtā mē svē janē pratyabhijñā
dṛṣṭō dēvaḥ svasvarūpō mayāsau
nāhaṁ na tvaṁ nāiva cāyaṁ prapañcaḥ]

The foulness of my mind fled from me as foulness from a mirror,
And then among the people did I gain repute (as a devotee).
When I beheld Him, that He was near me,
I saw that all was He, and that I am nothing.

32.

kēh chiy nĕndri-hātiy wudiy
kēban wudĕn nĕsar pĕyĕ
kēh chiy snān karith apūtiy
kēh chiy gēh bazith ti akriy

[Rājānaka Bhāskara's Sanskrit translation in Stein A.

kaścit prasuptō 'pi vibuddha ēva
kaścit prabuddhō 'pi ca suptatulyaḥ
snātō 'pi kaścid aśucir matō mē
bhuktvā striyāṁ cāpy aparaḥ supūtaḥ

(MS. has *svapnatulyaḥ* and *priyaṁ*. We follow the printed edition. The *i* of *kaścid* is apparently lengthened before the cæsura; cf. verses 50 and 56.)]

Some, though they be sound asleep, are yet awake;
On others, though they be awake, hath slumber fallen.
Some, though they bathe in sacred pools, are yet unclean;
Others, though they be full of household cares, are yet free from action.

'Sleep' is the sleep of illusion. 'Uncleanness' is impurity of soul. All action is defilement, and hinders the soul from obtaining final release. But, says Lallā, the real freedom from action is that of the soul. The body may be a slave to duty, and yet the soul may be free.

33.

dwādashānta-mandal yĕs dēwas thajī
nāsika-pawana-dōr[i] anāhata-rav
swayam kalpan àntih[i] ṭsajī
pānay suh dēv ta arṭsun kas

[Rājānaka Bhāskara's Sanskrit translation in Stein A.

yō dvādaśántē svayam ēva kalpitē
sadóditē dēvagṛhē svayaṁ sthitaḥ
saṁprērayan práṇaravim sa śaṁkarō
yasyátmabhūtaḥ sa kam arcayēd budhaḥ

The following is the text of Stein B:—

द्वादशान्त् मण्डल् ॥ यस् ॥ थज्यी
नासिकि पवुन् ॥ अनाहत् रव् ॥
सायम् ॥ अन्तिहि कल्पन् चज्यी
क्यो स्वपमे देवर्चुन करव् ॥ ११ ॥]

He who hath recognized the *Brahma-randhra* as the shrine of the Self-God,

He who hath known the Unobstructed Sound borne upon the breath (that riseth from the heart) unto the nose,

His vain imaginings of themselves have fled far away,

And he himself (recognizeth) himself as the God. To whom else, therefore, should he offer worship?

The 'Unobstructed Sound' is the mystic syllable *ōṁ*, for a full account of which, and for the meaning of this allusion, see the notes on verse 15. *Dwādashānta-manḍal*, or, in Sanskrit *dwādaśānta-manḍala*, is the *Brahma-randhra* (see Note on Yōga, §§ 5, 7, 19, 21, 26). As a technical term it is said at the present day to be a spot or cavity in the anterior fontanelle of the brain, under the frontal sinus. Other authorities identify it with the central canal of the spinal cord. It is closely connected with the *Sahasrāra*, which, in each man, is the abode of the Supreme Śiva, who is to be recognized as one with the Self, i.e. as the Supreme Self. Hence, if a man recognize this, he knows that he himself is the Supreme Self within himself, and that it is unnecessary to worship any other deity.

34.

okuy ōṁ-kār yĕs nābi darē
*kumbuy brahmānḍas sum garē**
akh suy manthᵃr ćĕtas karē
tas sās manthᵃr kyāh karē

* V. l. *sōma-garē*

[Rājānaka Bhāskara's Sanskrit translation in Stein A.

ā brahmānḍaṁ nābhitō yēna nityam
ōṁkārākhyō mantra ēkō dhṛtō 'yam
kṛtvā cittaṁ tadvimarśaikasāraṁ
kiṁ tasyānyair mantravṛndair vidhēyam]

He from whose navel steadfastly proceedeth in its upward course the syllable *ōṁ*, and naught but it,

And for whom the *kumbhaka* exercise formeth a bridge to the *Brahma-randhra*,

He beareth in his mind the one and only mystic spell,

And of what benefit to him are a thousand spells?

Or, if we take the alternative reading of the second line, that line must be translated :—

And whom the *kumbhaka* exercise leadeth into the abode of the moon by the *Brahma-randhra.*

This verse, like the preceding, is in praise of the mystic syllable *ōṁ*, which is here stated to possess all the virtues of all other mystic syllables, or spells, put together. By the 'navel' is meant the *kanda*, or mysterious bulb supposed to exist in the region of the navel and the pudendum. It is the focal centre of all bodily thought and action, and from it radiate the various tubes through which circulate the vital airs. In the true devotee, the syllable is fixed here, and perpetually rises upwards (as stated in the preceding verse) from the heart.

The *kumbhaka* or 'jar' exercise consists in meditation accompanied by 'bottling up' or retaining the breath after inspiration (*pūraka*). The devotee by this suppression blocks up the vital airs circulating through the tubes radiating from the *kanda*, and thereby causes the organ of thought to become absorbed into Śiva represented by the mystical moon supposed to exist in his brain. For further explanation of this extremely recondite theory, see Note on Yōga, §§ 5, 21, and Vocabulary, s. v. *sōm.*

Regarding the *Brahma-randhra*, see the note on the preceding verse. It is situated close to the *Sahasrāra*, which is the abode of the moon (see Note on Yōga, §§ 8, 19).

35.

samsāras āyĕs tapasiy
bōdha-prakāsh lobum sahaz
marĕm na kūh ta mara na kaīsi
mara nēch ta lasa nēch

[Rājānaka Bhāskara's Sanskrit translation in Stein A.

āsādya saṁsāram ahaṁ varākī
prāptā viśuddhaṁ sahajaṁ prabōdham
mriyē na kasyāpi na kō 'pi mē vā
mṛtāmṛtē māṁ prati tulyarūpē

(MS. *varākā.*)]

I came into this universe of birth and rebirth, and through asceticism gained I the self-illuminating light of knowledge.

If any man die, it is naught to me; and if I die it is naught to him.

Good is it if I die, and good is it if I live long.

Praise of perfect contentment. The idiom of *marĕm na kūh* is worth noting. Literally it is 'no one will die for me', or, as we should say in Ireland 'no one will die on me', i.e. if any one die it will not be my business. The commentary here quotes the following verse of Utpala Dēva [*Śiva-stōtrāvalī*, xiii. 3] as to the point:—

tāvakē vapuṣi viśwa-nirbharē
cit-sudhārasa-mayē niratyayē
tiṣṭhataḥ satatam arcataḥ Prabhuṁ
jīvitaṁ mṛtam athānyad astu mē

As I stand in thy imperishable body, which is composed of the cosmos, and is of the nectar of pure spirit, and as I everlastingly worship the Lord, let me have life or let me have death (for it matters not).

36.

prathuy tīrthan gaċhān sannyās
gwārani swa-darshĕna-myūlᵘ
ċittā! parith mau nishpath ās
dēshĕkh dūrē dramun nyūlᵘ

[Rājānaka Bhāskara's Sanskrit translation in Stein A.

yatnēna mōkṣâikadhiyā sadāmī
saṁnyāsinas tīrthavarān prayānti
cittâikasādhyō na sa labhyatē tair
dūrvāsthalaṁ bhāty atinīlam ārāt

(Printed edition has *mōkṣâikadhiyaḥ*.)

The following is the text of Stein B:—

पृथिवून् ॥ तीर्था गमनिय् ॥ सन्नस्ति
ग्वारहा सुरदर्शन् ता मीलो ॥
चित्ता पत्तोत् ॥ मौ निष्पत्त् अस्ति
दिशिह् दूर्या द्रमुन् नीलो ॥ ६ ॥]

An ascetic wandereth from holy place to holy place,

To seek the union brought about by (visiting a god, and yet he is but) visiting himself.

O my soul! study thou (the mystery that God is thy Self) and be not unbelieving.

The farther thou wilt look (from thy Self), the more green will seem the heap of grass.

The uselessness of seeking God by long pilgrimages, when He is really the Self of the seeker. *Dramun* is the *dub* grass of India. Here, a pile of this grass is used metaphorically to indicate worldly pursuits. The further a man's thoughts wander from the consideration of the identity of the Supreme and the Self, the more tempting will these worldly pursuits appear.

37.

pawan pūrith yus[u] ani wagi
tas bŏna sparshi na bŏcha ta trēsh
tih yĕs karun ȧntih[i] tagi
samsāras suy zĕyi nēch

[Rājānaka Bhāskara's Sanskrit translation in Stein A.

yaḥ pūrakēṇa cittaṁ svaṁ rōdhayēt kṣuttṛḍādikaṁ
na pīḍayati saṁsārē saphalaṁ cāsya jīvitam

(MS. has *kṣuṭṭṛḍācikam.*)]

He who rightly inhaleth his vital airs, and bringeth them under the bridle,

Him, verily, nor hunger nor thirst will touch.

He who is skilled in doing this unto the end,

Fortunate in this universe will he be born.

Pūraka, or inhalation of the breath, is one of the methods employed to encompass *prāṇāyāma*, or restraint of the vital airs, a necessary process for the obtainment of complete *yōga*, or union with the Supreme. See Note on Yōga, §§ 2, 21, 23, and Vocabulary, s. vv. *nāḍi*

and *prān* 2. By these *yōga*-processes, when a man is reborn into the world, he will be able in it to effect this union. With the second line the commentary compares *Bhagavad Gītā*, ii. 14, 15:—

mātrā-sparśās tu, Kauntēya, śītōṣṇa-sukha-duḥkha-dāḥ ।
āgamápāyinō 'nityās tā̃s titikṣaswa, Bhārata ॥
yaṁ hi na vyathayanty ētē puruṣaṁ, puruṣarṣabha ।
sama-duḥkha-sukhaṁ dhīraṁ sō 'mṛtatwāya kalpatē ॥

It is the touchings of the senses' instruments, O Kuntī's son, that beget cold and heat, pleasure and pain; it is they that come and go, that abide not; bear with them, O thou of Bharata's race.

Verily the man whom these disturb not, indifferent alike to pain and pleasure, and wise, is meet for immortality, O chief of men. (*Barnett's Translation.*)

38.

zal thamawun hutawah t[a]*ranāwun*
wūrdhwa-gaman pairiv ċarith
kāṭha-dhēni dōd shramāwun
ȧntih[i] *sakol*[u] *kapaṭa-ċarith*

[Rājānaka Bhāskara's Sanskrit translation in Stein A.

nīrastambhō vahniśaityaṁ tathâiva
pādais tadvad vyōmayānaṁ hy aśakyam
dōhō dhēnōḥ kāṣṭhamayyās tathâiva
sarvaṁ câitaj jṛmbhitaṁ kaitavasya

(MS. has *dhēnō kāṣṭha*° and *câita*. The printed edition omits *hy*.)]

To stop a flowing stream, to cool a raging fire,
To walk on one's feet in the sky,
To labour at milking a wooden cow,—
All these, in the end, are but base jugglery.

By means of intense *yōga*, or concentration of the mind, it is quite possible to achieve magical powers (*vibhūti*: see note on Yōga, § 2), and to perform apparently impossible actions; but this is nothing but the art of a conjurer. The true *yōgī* disdains such miraculous powers. The *yōga* to which he devotes himself is union with the Supreme Self, by acquiring the knowledge of his own Self.

39.

kus^{u} push^{u} ta kŏssa pushȫñī
kam kusum lȫg^{i}zēs pūzē
kawa goḍ^{u} dizĕs zalaci dȫñī
kawa-sana mantra Shĕnkar-swātma wuzē

40.

man push^{u} tȫy yiʦh pushȫñī
bāwȧk^{i} kusum lȫg^{i}zēs pūzē
shĕshi-rasa goḍ^{u} dizĕs zalaci dȫñī
ʦhŏpi-mantra Shĕnkar-swātma wuzē

[Rājānaka Bhāskara's Sanskrit translation of 39 and 40 in Stein A.

kaḥ pauṣpikaḥ kā́pi ca tasya patnī
puṣpaiś ca kair dēvavarasya pūjā
kāryā, tathā kiṁ gaḍukaṁ vidhēyaṁ
mantraś ca kas tatra vada prayōjyaḥ

icchāmanōbhyāṁ nanu pauṣpikābhyām
ādāya puṣpaṁ dṛḍhabhāvanā́khyam
svā́nandapūrair gaḍukaṁ ca dattrā
maunā́khyamantrēṇa samarcayēśam

The following is the text of 39 and 40 in Stein B:—

कुसो पूषी त़ कुसा पूषान्यी
कुसो कुसुम् ॥ लागोंजिस् ॥ पूजि ॥
कव गड्य दीजिस् जल् धान्यी
कवा मन्त्रा शङ्कुर् ॥ श्रोजि ॥ ९ ॥

मन् ॥ पूषी ता इच्छ् पूषाण्यी
भावकुसुम् ॥ लागोजिस् ॥ पूजि ॥
शशिरस दोजिस् ॥ गड्य जल् धान्यी
छुपि मन्त्रा निन्द्रि श्रोजि ॥ १० ॥]

39. Who is the man, and who the woman, that bringeth wreaths?

What flowers shouldst thou offer in His worship?

What stream of water wilt thou pour over His image?

By what mystic formula will the Śiva-Self become manifest?

40. The mind is the man, and pure desire is the woman, that bringeth wreaths.

Offer thou the flowers of devotion in His worship.

Nectar of the moon, for ritual, shalt thou make to stream over Him.

By the mystic formula of silence will the Śiva-Self become manifest.

A plea for spiritual, as against formal worship. The nectar from the moon refers to the mystic moon in the *sahasrāra* (cf. verse 33) said to abide under the frontal sinus. From this moon a mystic nectar passes into the spiritual frame of the devotee, and enables him to become master of himself. For further particulars, see Note on Yōga, §§ 5, 8, 19, 20, 21, and Vocabulary, s. v. *sōm*.

The mystic formula, or *mantra*, of silence is the so-called *ajapa mantra*, in which the devotee utters no sound, but simply performs various exhalations and inhalations. It is also called *haṁsaḥ* (cf. verse 65), in which word the *anusvāra* or *bindu* represents Puruṣa, and the *visarga* Prakṛti. The *Tāntrika-abhidhāna* (s. v.) defines *ajapā* as *haṁsa*, or inspiration + expiration (*śvāsa-praśvāsa*), saying that 60 *śvāsas* = 1 *prāṇa*, 60 *prāṇas* = 1 *nāḍī*, 60 *nāḍīs* = 1 *ahōrātra* (day and night). Thus in one day-night there are 21,600 *śvāsa-praśvāsas*, or *haṁsa-japas*.

41.

āyĕs kami dishi ta kami watē
gaṭsha kami dishi kawa zāna wath
ȧntihʻ dāy lagimay tatē
chĕnis phŏkas kā̃ṭsh-ti nō sath

[Rājānaka Bhāskara's Sanskrit translation in Stein A.

kayā diśā kēna pathágatáham
paścād gamiṣyāmi kayátha kēna
ittham gatim vēdmi nijām na tasmād
ucchvāsamātrēṇa dhṛtim bhajāmi

(Printed edition has *pathâtha kēna.*)

The following is the text of Stein B :—

योजि कव दिशी कव जाना
गक्षीजि कव दिशी कम् सत् ॥
अष्टदल् (sic) कमल् ॥ वसवाना
छ्यनीस् ॥ फुक्कस् कांछ्य् ना सत् ॥ ४६ ॥]

From what quarter did I come, and by what road?

To what quarter shall I go? and how shall I know the road?

In the end, if I gain the good counsel (it is well),

For there is no substance in an empty breath.

'Reason thus with life, a breath thou art.' Lallā knows not whence she came or whither she will go. Life is but an empty breath. The one thing that is worth grasping is the teaching of the identity of the Self with the Supreme Self.

42.

gagan ts^{a}y bhū-tal ts^{a}y
ts^{a}y chukh dĕn pawan ta rāth
arg tsandan pōsh pöñ^{i} ts^{a}y
ts^{a}y chukh sóruy ta lög^{i}ziy kyāh

[Rājānaka Bhāskara's Sanskrit translation in Stein A.

ākāśō bhūr vāyur āpō 'nilaś ca
rātriś cáhaś céti sarvam tvam ēva
tatkāryatvāt puṣpam arghádi ca tvam
tvatpūjártham nâiva kimcil labhē 'ham]

Thou alone art the heavens, and Thou alone art the earth.

Thou alone art the day, the air, the night.

Thou alone art the meal-offering, the sandal inunction, the flowers, the water of aspersion.

Thou alone art all that is. What, therefore, can I offer thee?

Another plea for spiritual, as against formal worship. The whole creation is but an emanation from the Supreme. Any offering made by man can only be an offering of Himself to Himself.

43.

yem[i] lūb manmath mad tsūr mọ́run
wata-nösh[i] mörith ta lốgun dās
tȧmiy sahaz Yīshwar gốrun
tȧmiy sốruy vyondun swās

[Rājānaka Bhāskara's Sanskrit translation in Stein A.

kāmō lōbhō 'haṁkṛtiś céti yēna
yatnāt pūrvaṁ māritā mārgacaurāḥ
tēnâivâikēnâiṣvaraṁ dhāma labdhvā
sarvaṁ tyaktvā bhasmavad bhāvajātam

(MS. has °*cauraḥ* and *bhāvajānuṁ*. Printed edition *câiva yēna.*)]

He who hath slain the thieves—desire, lust, and pride—

When he hath slain these highway robbers, he hath thereby made himself the servant (of all).

He hath searched out Him who is the real and true Lord.

He hath meditated and found that all that is is ashes.

The true saint is the servant of all, by his humility and loving kindliness.

44.

pānas lögith rūdukh mĕ tsᵃh
mĕ tsĕ tshāḍān lūstum dŏh
pānas-manz yĕli ḍyūkhukh mĕ tsᵃh
mĕ tsĕ ta pānas dyutum tshŏh

[Rājānaka Bhāskara's Sanskrit translation in Stein A.

dēhādiṣaṭkōśapidhānatas tvām
aprāpya khinnāsmi ciraṁ mahēśa
upādhinirmuktavibōdharūpaṁ
jñātvādya viśrāntim upāgatā tvām

(MS. has *dēhâpi°*, *upâgatatvāt.*)]

(This verse has throughout a double meaning. The first meaning is:—)

Absorbed within Thyself, Thou remainedst hidden from me.

The livelong day I passed seeking for 'me' and 'Thee'.

When I beheld Thee in my Self,

I gave to Thee and to my Self the unrestrained rapture of (our union).

(In the second meaning, the two words *mĕ* and *tsĕ*, 'I Thee', are taken as one word *mĕtsĕ*, which means 'earth', and we get the following translation:—)

My body befouled I with mud, and Thou remainedst hidden from me.

The livelong day I passed seeking for mud.

When I beheld the mud upon my body,

I gave my body the unrestrained rapture (of union) with the mud.

In the first version, Lallā tells us how, in the days of her ignorance, she imagined that she could distinguish between her Self and the Supreme Self, and then, how, when she had discovered their identity, she was filled with the rapture of union. Moreover, as the Supreme Self was identical with her Self, He also was filled with the same rapture.

In the second version she sarcastically compares earthly possessions and desires to the mud with which an ascetic daubs his body. He who cares for these has all the joys of possession, ignorant of the truth that they are worthless as mud.

45.

kush pōsh tēl dīph zal nā gatshē
sadbhāwa gŏra-kath yus[u] mani hĕyē
Shĕmbhus sŏri nityĕ panañĕ yitshē
sāda pĕzē sahaza akriy nā zĕyē

[Rājānaka Bhāskara's Sanskrit translation in Stein A.

puṣpâdikaṁ dravyam idaṁ na tasya
pūjāsu, prājñā, upayōgi kiṁcit
gurūpadēśād dṛḍhayā ca bhaktyā
smṛtyârcyatē yēna viśuddha ātmā

(By poetic licence the *u* of *pūjāsu* is shortened before *pr*. Printed edition has *pūjāsu sarvam upayōgi* in which the second *a* of *sarvam* is lengthened before the cæsura; cf. verse 32.)]

Kuśa-grass, flowers, sesame-seed, water,—all the paraphernalia of worship—are wanted not

By him who taketh into heart with honest faith his teacher's word.

In his own loving longing he will ever meditate upon Śambhu.

He will sink into the true joyance; and so, becoming in his nature free from action, he will not be born again.

Action—works, desire—is the great enemy of absorption into the Supreme, and causes perpetual rebirth. By recognizing the identity of the Self with the Supreme, as taught by the *guru*, or spiritual teacher, a man becomes free from the bond of action.

Śambhu is a name of Śiva.

46.

asi pŏndi zŏsi zāmi
nĕthạy snān kari tīrthan
wȧh^{a}r'-wah^{a}ras nonuy āsi
nishĕ chuy ta parzāntan

[Rājānaka Bhāskara's Sanskrit translation in Stein A.

snātaṁ hasantaṁ vividhaṁ vidhēyaṁ
kurvantam ētatparajātam antam
paśyâtmatattvaṁ nijadēha ēva
kṛtapradēśântaramārgaṇēna

(Printed edition has *ētatpura ēva santam*, *paśyâtmadēvaṁ*, and *kṛtaṁ*.)

The following is the text of Stein B :—

अस्ति पुन्दि जामि चास्ति ॥
नितुह् स्नान् करि ता तीर्थन् ॥
वह्री वह्रस् नन्नोय् आसि
निशि छ्योयी ता पर्जन्तान् ॥ ३ ॥]

He it is who laugheth, who sneezeth, who cougheth, who yawneth.

He it is who ceaselessly batheth in holy pools.

He it is who is an ascetic, naked from year's end to year's end.

Recognize thou that verily He is nigh to thee.

'The Kingdom of heaven is within you.'

The ascetic wanders about to holy places and torments his body in his search for God. He knows not that all the time He is the ascetic's Self, and is hence ever close at hand. When the ascetic performs the most trivial action, it is really not he who does it, but the Supreme, Who is identical with his Self.

47.

yĕth saras sär^{i}-phol^{u} nā vĕtsiy
tath sari sakaliy pōñ^{u} cĕn
mrag srugāl gänḍ^{i} zala-hästiy
zĕn nā zĕn ta totuy pĕn

[Rājānaka Bhāskara's Sanskrit translation in Stein A.

sarōvarē yatra na sarṣapasya
kaṇō 'pi mäty ēva vicitram ētat
vivardhatē tatpayasā samastaṁ
bhūtaṁ sthitaṁ bhāvi ca dēhijātam

(Printed edition has the last line *yāvat pramāṇaṁ khalu dēhijātam.*)

The following is the text of Stein B:—

यत् सर् सर्षपफलो ना विचि
तत् सर् सकलीय् ॥ पून्नो च्चिन्
मृग् स्रगाल् ॥ गण्डी जल्हस्ती
जिन् ना जिन् ता ततोय् पिन् ॥४॥]

It is a lake so tiny that in it a mustard seed findeth no room.

Yet from that lake doth every one drink water.

And into it do deer, jackals, rhinoceroses, and sea-elephants

Keep falling, falling, almost before they have time to become born.

The real insignificance of the universe. As compared with the Universal Self it is of no account; yet foolish mortals look upon it as something wonderful, and enjoy it. Life, too, is but a momentary breath, as compared with eternity; and, in reality, an unsaved soul, in whatever form it may be born, has no time to live, but, from the point of view of Eternity, lives for but an instant, and dies and dies, and is born and reborn, again and again.

48.

Lal bŏh lūshᵘs shāḍan ta gwāran
hal mĕ korᵘmas rasa-nishĕ ti
wuchun hyotᵘmas tŏḍⁱ ḍīṭhⁱmas baran*
mĕ-ti kal ganĕyĕ zi zŏgᵘmas tàtⁱ

* V. l. *tŏrⁱ*

49.

mal wŏndi zŏlum
zigar mŏrum
tĕli Lal nāv drām
yĕli dàlⁱ trŏvⁱmas tàtⁱ

[Rājānaka Bhāskara's Sanskrit translation of 48 and 49 in Stein A.

draṣṭuṁ vibhuṁ tīrthavarān gatāhaṁ
śrāntā sthitā tadguṇakīrtanēṣu
tatō 'pi khinnásmi ca mānasēna
svántar niviṣṭā khalu tadvimarśē

(MS. has *khinnā ca mānasēna.*)

tatō 'tra dṛṣṭvávaraṇāni bhūyō
jñātaṁ mayátrâiva bhaviṣyatíti
bhaktyā yadā tāni ca [saṁpra]viṣṭā
lalléti lōkē prathitā tadáham. *Yugmam*

(MS. *dṛṣṭāvaruṇā°*. For the emendation, compare verse 63. The MS. is partly defaced in the third line. Judging from the remains of the characters, the missing syllables seem to have been those put between brackets. Printed edition bears out the above emendations. It also has *bhaṅktvā* for *bhaktyā.*)]

48. I, Lallā, wearied myself seeking for Him and searching.

I laboured and strove even beyond my strength.

I began to look for Him, and, lo, I saw that bolts were on His door,

And even in me, as I was, did longing for Him become fixed; and there, where I was, I gazed upon Him.

49. Foulness burnt I from my soul.
My heart (with its desires) did I slay.
And then did my name of Lallā spread abroad,
When I sat, just there, with bended knee.

48. Ineffectual human efforts. In her unregenerate days Lallā had striven to find God. Then, by God's grace, she was permitted to see that the door of approach to Him was barred to all human effort, and that no strivings of hers were of avail. So she stood there, outside the door, full of naught but longing love, and He revealed Himself to her, for she found Him in her Self.

49. A continuation of the preceding verse. When she had given up effort, and, having cleansed her mind from earthly passions, waited in patience with humility; then, and not till then, did she gain the true wisdom, and her reputation as a prophetess became widely spread.

50.

trayi nĕngi sarāh sȧri saras.
aki nĕngi saras arshĕs jāy
Haramŏkha Kaũsara akh sum saras
sati nĕngi saras shũñākār

[Rājānaka Bhāskara's Sanskrit translation.

vāratrayaṁ nīramayaṁ smarāmi
tathâikadâham avakāśahīnam
ākāśam anyāny api câdbhutāni
smarāmi śūnyaṁ khalu saptavāram

(From the printed edition. The last syllable of *tathâikadâham* is lengthened before the cæsura; cf. verses 32 and 56.)]

Three times do I remember a lake overflowing.
Once do I remember seeing in the firmament the only existing place.

Once do I remember seeing a bridge from Haramukh to Kaũsar.

Seven times do I remember seeing the whole world a void.

As a result of her having achieved the perfect knowledge, not only, as told in the preceding verse, has she gained a great reputation, but she has become endued with the power of remembering the occurrences of her former lives.

At intervals of a *kalpa* (i.e. a day of Brahmā, or 432 million years) the universe incurs a partial dissolution (*khaṇḍa-pralaya*). A hundred years of Brahmā—each year being made up of these *kalpas*, or days of Brahmā—constitutes a *mahā-kalpa*, or great kalpa. At the end of this vast period of time there is a 'great dissolution' (*mahā-pralaya*) in which not only is our universe destroyed, but all the worlds of the gods with their inhabitants, and even Brahmā himself.

The lake mentioned by Lallā is, as in verse 47, the universe. By its overflow is meant a partial dissolution, three of which she remembers experiencing. When the only place that exists is the firmament, it is a great dissolution, and she remembers seeing one of these.

Between the peak of Haramukh to the North and the mountain lake of Kaũsar to the South, lies the Valley of Kashmīr. At the beginning of the *kalpa* now current this Valley is said to have been a lake called Satīsaras, and across this lake, from Haramukh to Kaũsar, she remembers a bridge.[1]

Seven times altogether she remembers seeing the world becoming absorbed into the Void (cf. Note to Verse 1).

Lallā's object in mentioning these experiences over such enormous periods of time is to emphasize the eternal pre-existence of the soul, and its perpetual birth and rebirth unless released by the true knowledge.

Cf. Verses 93 and 95.

[1] Cf. *Rāja-taraṅgiṇī*, i. 25. 'Formerly, since the beginning of the Kalpa, the land in the womb of the *Himālaya* was filled with water during the periods of the [first] six Manus [and formed] the 'Lake of Satī' (*Satīsaras*). Afterwards . . . Kaśyapa . . . created the land known by the name of *Kaśmīr* in the space [previously occupied by] the lake.' *Stein's Translation.*

51.

zanañĕ zāyāy r$^{\dot{a}}$t^{i} töy k$^{\dot{a}}$tiy
karith wŏḍaras bahu klēsh
phīrith dwār bazani wöt^{i} tȧtiy
Shiv chuy krūṭh^{u} ta tsēn wŏpadēsh

52.

yŏsay shēl pīṭhis ta paṭas
sŏy shēl chĕy pruthi-wŏn^{u} dēsh
sŏy shēl shūba-wönis graṭas
Shiv chuy krūṭh^{u} ta tsēn wŏpadēsh

53.

rav mata thali-thali töp^{i}tan
töp^{i}tan wŏttom^{u} wŏttom^{u} dēsh
Warun mata lūka-garu ȧts^{i}tan
Shiv chuy krūṭh^{u} töy tsēn wŏpadēsh

54.

yihay matru-rūp^{i} pay diyē
yihay bhāryĕ-rūp^{i} kari vishēsh
yihay māyĕ-rūp^{i} ȧnt^{i} zuv hĕyē
Shiv chuy krūṭh^{u} ta tsēn wŏpadēsh

[Rājānaka Bhāskara's Sanskrit translation of 51-54.

prasūdaraṁ klēśayutaṁ vinīya
jātō malāktō 'py anuyāti saṁtatam
yatprēritaḥ saukhyadhiyā naraḥ strīṁ
kaṣṭēna labhyaṁ śṛṇu taṁ gurōḥ śivam

yathā śilaikaiva svajātibhēdāt
pīṭhādinānāvidharūpabhāginī
tathaiva yō 'nantatayā vibhāti
kaṣṭēna labhyaṁ śṛṇu taṁ gurōḥ śivam

sthalē sthalē svaiḥ kiraṇair yathā raviḥ
pataty abhēdēna gṛhēṣu vābhriyam
jalaṁ tathā sarvajagadgṛhēṣu
kaṣṭēna labhyaṁ śṛṇu taṁ gurōḥ śivam

mātṛsvarūpēṇa payaḥpradā nu
bhāryāsvarūpēṇa vilāsakāriṇī
yac chaktir antē mṛtirūpam ēti ca
kaṣṭēna labhyaṁ śṛṇu taṁ gurōḥ śivam

(From the printed edition.)

The following is the text of 52, 53, and 54 in Stein B :—

यसै शिल् पीठस् ॥ ता वट्टस्
सयी शिल् पृथिवानीस् देशा ॥
सै शिल् शोभवानी यट्टस् ॥
शिव् छ्योयी कष्टो त चिन् ॥ उपदेशा ॥ ३३ ॥

रव् मत आत्मथलि तापीतन् ॥
तापीतन् ॥ उत्तमि देशा ॥
वर्ण् मत लोटो गृह् अचीतन् ॥
शिव् छ्योय् कष्टो त चिन् उपदेशा ॥ ३५ ॥

एहिय् मातृरूपी पय् दीयिय् ॥
एहिय् ॥ भार्यरूपी विशेषा ॥
एहिय् ॥ मायिरूपी जीवू हियिय् ॥
शिव् छ्योयी कष्टो त चिन् ॥ उपदेशा ॥ ३२ ॥]

51. Comely and full of sap were they born from the mother,
After causing many a pang to her womb.
Again and again thither did they come, and waited at that door.
Hardly, in sooth, is Śiva to be found. Meditate therefore on the doctrine.

52. The same rock that serveth for a pedestal or for a pavement
Really is but (part of) a district of the earth.
Or the same rock may become (a millstone) for a handsome mill.
Hardly, in sooth, is Śiva to be found. Meditate therefore on the doctrine.

53. Doth not the sun cause (everything) to glow in every region?

Doth it cause only each good land to glow?

Doth not Varuṇa enter into every house?

Hardly, in sooth, is Śiva to be found. Meditate therefore on the doctrine.

54. The same woman is a mother, and giveth milk unto her babe.

The same woman, as a wife, hath her special character.

The same woman, as a deceiver, endeth by taking thy life.

Hardly, in sooth, is Śiva to be found. Meditate therefore on the doctrine.

A group of verses linked together by their fourth lines, which are identical in each. Verse 80 belongs also to this group.

51. The soul, while still in the womb of its mother, remembers its former births, and determines to seek release from future transmigration as soon as it is born. But directly it is born it forgets all this, and, becoming entangled in worldly desires, is condemned to visit wombs again and again, and to wait at their doors for admission again into the world. Cf. Verse 87.

As the attainment of Śiva is thus hard for a mortal once he is born, Lallā entreats him to heed her doctrine, and thus to obtain release.

52. All things are but forms of the Supreme. She uses as a parable the fact that though a pedestal, a pavement, a tract of land, or a millstone, may all differ widely in appearance, at bottom they are all the same—only stone.

53. Another parable showing the universality of the Supreme. He is everywhere without exception, just as the sun shines impartially on every spot in the earth, and just as Varuṇa, the god of water, is found in every house, and not only in the houses of the good. The facts described are those mentioned in Matt. v. 45, but the application is different.

54. Another parable to the same effect. The infinite variety of a woman, as a mother, as a wife, or as a Delilah. Yet she is, throughout all, the same—a woman. The Sanskrit translation makes the Delilah to be the *śakti*, which misleads people from the truth, appearing at one time as a mother, and at another as a wife, but always a misleader.

55.

kandĕv gĕh tĕzi kandĕv wan-wās
vĕpholu man nā raṭith ta wās
dĕn rāth gaṇzarith panunu shwās
yuthuy chukh ta tyuthuy ās

[Rājānaka Bhāskara's Sanskrit translation.

gṛhē nivāsō na vimōkṣahētur
vanē 'thavā yōgivaraiḥ pradiṣṭaḥ
divāniśaṁ svātmavimarśanāḍhyō
yathā sthitas tvaṁ paramō 'sty upāyaḥ

(From the printed edition.)]

Some have abandoned home, some have abandoned hermitage;
But fruitless is every abiding-place, if thou hast not thy mind under subjection.
Day and night counting each breath,
As thou art, so there abide.

Some, in the hope of salvation, have abandoned house and home for a hermit's life, and others, in a like hope, have given up such a life, and have become ordinary householders. But it matters not where one lives, so long as one applies oneself to learning the mysteries of Self. The devotee should practise restraining his breath—one of the chief means of securing emancipation. See Verses 37 and 40 and Vocabulary s. vv. *nāḍi* and *prān* 2.

'Caelum non animum mutant qui trans mare currunt.'

56.

yē gŏrā Paramēshwarā!
bāvtam tĕ chuy antar vyod[u]
dŏshĕway wŏpadān kandā-purā
h[a]*h kawa t*[a]*run*[u] *ta hāh kawa tot*[u]

57.

nābi-sthāna chĕy prakrĕth zalawȧñī
hiḍis tām yĕti prān wata-got[u]
brahmāṇḍa pĕṭha sūt[i] *nadi wahawañī*
h[a]*h tawa t*[a]*run*[u] *ta hāh tawa tot*[u]

[Rājānaka Bhāskara's Sanskrit translation of 56 and 57.

gurō! mamâitam upadēśam ēkaṁ
kuruṣva bōdhâptikaraṁ dayātaḥ
hāh-hūh imau staḥ samam āsyajâtāv
uṣṇō 'sti hāh kim atha hūh suśītaḥ

nābhyutthitō hāh jaṭharâgnitaptō
hūh dvādaśântāc chiśirāt samutthaḥ
hāh prâṇabhūtō 'sty atha hūh apânaḥ
siddhânta ēvaṁ munibhiḥ pradiṣṭaḥ

(From the printed edition. The *a* of *mamâitam* and *i* of *kim* are lengthened before the cæsura; cf. verses 32 and 50.)

The following is the text of 56 and 57 in Stein B:—

ये गुरा परमेसुरा
दपुम् अन्तुर् वित्तो ॥
द्वनवै उपन्याय कन्दपुरा
हह् ॥ कव तूळरो (sic) हाह् ॥ कव ततो ॥ ४४ ॥

नाभिस्थान् ॥ छियी प्रकत् (sic) जलवन्यी
हीळीस् ताँ छ्योयी ईसुर् सुतो ॥
मानसमण्ड़ल् ॥ नद् वहवन्यी ॥
हह् तव तूळनो (sic) हाह ॥ तव ततो ॥ ४५ ॥]

56. O my Teacher! Thou who art as God to me!

Explain thou to me the inner meaning; for it is known to thee.

Two breathings are there, both taking their rise in the City of the Bulb.

Why then is *h^a^h* cold, and *hāh* hot?

57. The region of the navel is by nature fiery hot.

Thence proceedeth thy vital air, rising to thy throat, (and issueth from thy mouth as *hāh*).

When it meeteth the river flowing from the *Brahma-randhra* (it issueth from thy mouth as *h^a^h*),

And therefore *h^a^h* is cold, and *hāh* is hot.

These two verses refer to the practice of *prāṇāyāma*, or suppressing the breath in order to obtain *yōga*, or union with the Supreme. Expiration and inhalation are carefully watched and controlled by the *yōgī*. Lallā notices that some of her expirations, which she names *h^a^h*, are cool, while others, which she calls *hāh*, are hot. She addresses her *guru*, or spiritual teacher, whom she has been taught, like all devotees, to recognize as the representative to her of God.

In order to understand the reply, it must be explained that, according to Śaiva teaching, situated within the body, between the pudendum and the navel, is a *kanda*, or bulb, the focus of all bodily action, from which radiate the various *nāḍis*, or tubes, through which circulate the *prāṇas*, or vital airs. This *kanda* is called *kandă-pură*, or 'City of the Bulb', in verse 56, and *năbi-sthăn*, or that which has its position near the navel, in verse 57. One of the vital airs—called the *prāṇa* κατ' ἐξοχήν—rises directly from the *kanda* through the windpipe, and is expired through the mouth. Hence it is hot. For further particulars, see the Note on Yōga, § 5, and the Vocabulary, s. vv. *kandă-pură*, *nāḍi*, and *prān*, 2. So much for the hot air.

The *Brahma-randhra* is the anterior fontanelle in the upper part of the head (§§ 5, 27). Near this is the *sahasrāra* (§§ 19, 20, 21, 27), a spot which is the upper extremity of the tube called the *suṣumnā nāḍi*, the other extremity of which is the *kanda* already mentioned.

This *sahasrāra* is considered to be the abode of that emanation of the Supreme Śiva which is the man's Self, and which is mystically spoken of as the moon. The moon is universally looked upon as the source of coldness, and hence the vital air passing down the *suṣumnā nāḍi* is cold. When this meets the hot air, *prāṇa*, coming upwards from the *kanda* (close to which is the microcosmic sun, §§ 5, 8, 9, 21), this *prāṇa* is deprived of its heat by contact with the down-flowing stream, and hence, in this case, the expired air is cold. For further particulars, see the Vocabulary, s. v. *sōm*.

H^{a}*h* is a short abrupt expiration, and *hāh* is a prolonged one; and at the bottom of the teacher's explanation lies the idea that in the short expiration the hot upward current of air suddenly meets the downward current of cold air, and is checked by it. Hence it is cooled. On the other hand, a prolonged expiration has time to recover itself and to regain its heat. The sun is located in the pelvis, and so the upward breath is hot; and the moon is at the brain, and its currents are downwards and cold.

58.

yih yih karm korum suh artsun
  yih rasani wŏtsorum tiy manth^{a}*r*
yuhuy log^{u}*mō dihas partsun*
  suy yih parama-Shiwun^{u} *tanth*^{a}*r*

[Rājānaka Bhāskara's Sanskrit translation.

karōmi yat karma tad ēva pūjā
  vadāmi yac cāpi tad ēva mantraḥ
yad ēva cāyāti tathāiva yōgād
  dravyaṁ tad ēvāsti mamātra tantram

(From the printed edition.)

The following is the text of Stein B:—

यो यी कम्म् करमो ॥ अर्चुंय् ॥
  रसनि उच्चरि तेमै मन्त्र् ॥
एङ्गय् ॥ लगों देहस ॥ पर्चुय् ॥
  सोयी परमशिवानो तन्त्र् ॥ २४ ॥]

Whate'er work I did, that was worship.

Whate'er I uttered with my tongue, that was a mystic formula.

This recognition, and this alone, became one with my body,

That this alone is the essence of the scriptures of the Supreme Śiva.

Laborare est orare; but the labour, it is understood, must be dedicated to the Supreme. When all that one does, and all that one says is dedicated to Him, this is equal to all burnt offerings and sacrifices.

59.

ts^a^h nā bŏh ṇā dhyĕy nā dhyān
gauv pānay Sarwa-kriy mashith
anyau ḍyūṭhukh kĕtsh nā anway
gay sath lüy^i^ par pashith

[Rājānaka Bhāskara's Sanskrit translation.

nāhaṁ na ca tvaṁ na ca kāpi carcā
dhyānasya yōgyātra padē 'tiśāntē
kō 'py anvayaś cātra na bhāti tasmād
vismārya līnaṁ svam ivātra sadbhiḥ

(From the printed edition.)]

There is no 'Thou', no 'I', no object of contemplation, not even contemplation.

It is only the All-Creator, who Himself became lost in forgetfulness.

The blind folk saw not any meaning in this,

But when they saw the Supreme, the seven worlds became lost in nothingness.

All that exists is but the Supreme in one or other of His manifestations. When, therefore, an untaught man knows not the unity of Self and all creation with the

Supreme Self, and imagines that there is a difference between 'I' and 'thou', or between contemplation and its object, it is really the Supreme, temporarily blinded by His own illusive power, Who is lost in this ignorance. This paradox, and the logical inference to be derived from it cannot be understood by the blind, i. e. those who are sunk in ignorance of the nature of things. But when a man has once grasped the facts, the whole universe disappears for him, and he gains release.

The last line may also be translated, 'but good men become absorbed in Him, when once they gain sight of the Supreme.' So interpreted by Rājānaka Bhāskara.

60.

tshāḍān lūtsh^{ü}*s pönī-pānas*
tshĕpith gyānas wŏtum na kũtsh
lay kür^{ü}*mas ta wöts*^{ü}*s al-thānas*
bár^{i} *bár*^{i} *bāna ta cĕwān na kũh*

[Rājānaka Bhāskara's Sanskrit translation.

svātmánvēṣaṇayatnamātraniratā śrāntā tatō 'haṁ sthitā
tajjñānáikamahāpadē 'tivijanē práṇádirōdhāt tataḥ
labdhvánandasurāgṛhaṁ ca tad anu dṛṣṭvātra bhāṇḍāny alaṁ
pūrṇāny ēva tathápi tatra vimukhaḥ práptō janaḥ śōcitaḥ

(From the printed edition. The third half-line does not scan, the metre being Śārdūlavikrīḍita. The *u* of *anu* should be long. As it falls on the cæsura, possibly the author intended it to be long by metrical licence. There are similar cases in his translations of verses 32, 50, and 56; cf. also verse 45.)]

I searched for myself, and wearied myself in vain,
For no one hath, I ween, e'er by such efforts reached the hidden knowledge.
Then absorbed I myself in It, and straightway reached the abode of nectar,
Where there are many filled jars, but no one drinketh from them.

No human efforts can gain the perfect knowledge. This is obtained only by quietism and the grace of the Supreme. 'It' in which Lallā became absorbed is the *tat* of the famous Upaniṣadic formula *tat tvam asi*, 'thou art It', the essence of the Śaiva doctrines. Once she had grasped the identity of her Self with the Supreme Self, she reached the *Al-thān*. This word means literally 'the abode of wine', i.e. nectar. The abode of nectar is the moon, in which nectar is produced month by month. As explained under verses 56, 57, and in the Note on Yōga, § 19, a mystic moon, representing the Supreme, exists in the spot in the brain called the *sahasrāra*. By practising *yōga*, a devotee is finally absorbed microcosmically into the *sahasrāra*, and macrocosmically into the Supreme. Lallā laments that so few avail themselves of this means of salvation. The wine of salvation is there, but few there be that drink of it.

The pronominal suffix *m* in *wŏtum* is a kind of *dativus commodi*, and means 'in my opinion'.

Al-thān is also explained as a contraction of *alaṁ-sthāna*, the place of 'enough', where everything is exactly balanced, and which can only be described by negation of all qualifications, '*nēti, nēti*', i.e. the Supreme. In either interpretation the resultant meaning is the same.

61.

yuh^{u} *yih karm kara pĕtarun pānas*
arzun barzun biyis kyut^{u}
àntih^{i} *lāgi-rost*^{u} *pushĕrun swātmas*
ada yūr^{i} *gatsha ta tūr*^{i} *chum hyot*^{u}

[The following is the text of Stein B :—

यो यो कम्म् करि सो पानस् ॥
मि जानो जि बियीस् ॥ कीवूस् ॥
अन्ते अन्त हारीयि प्राणस्
यौठी गच्छ ता तौठी छ्योस् ॥२२॥]

Whatever work I may do, the burden of the completion thereof lieth on myself,

But the earnings and the collecting of the fruits thereof are another's.

If in the end, without thought for their fruits,
I lay these works as an offering before the Supreme Self,
Then, where'er I may go, there is it well for me.

The vanity of human wishes. The ordinary worldling performs actions for the sake of what he may gain by them; but these gains cannot follow him to another world. They are left behind to his 'laughing heirs'.

The true believer, without thought of reward, does his duty, and offers all that he does to God; and it is he who after death reaps the full fruit of his actions in the shape of final release. This is one of the fundamental doctrines of the *Bhagavad Gītā*. If a man engages in worldly affairs for the lusts of the flesh, he damns his soul; if he takes them up without regard to their fruits, solely from the sense of duty (*karma-yōga*) and the love of God (*bhakti-yōga*), he saves his soul.

62.

rājĕs bŏj^i yĕm^i kartal tyŏj^i
swargas bŏj^i chuy taph tŏy dān
sahazas bŏj^i yĕm^i gŏra-kath pŏj^i
pāpa-pŏñĕ-bŏj^i chuy panunuy pān

He who gaineth a kingdom is he who hath wielded a sword.
He who gaineth paradise is he who mortifieth himself and who giveth in charity.
He who hath knowledge of the nature of the Self, is he who followeth the Guru's teaching.
That which reapeth the fruit of virtue and of vice is a man's own Self.

Every action has its fruit. The exercise of worldly activity produces worldly prosperity. If a man pursues a formal religion, he reaps the fruit in paradise, which is transient, and from which, when the fruits of his pious actions have been exhausted, he will be subject to rebirth.

The one hope of ultimate release is the acquirement of the true knowledge of the Self, and this can only be acquired from the teaching of a Śaiva Guru, or spiritual preceptor.

63.

jñāna-mārg chĕy hāka-wör^{ü}
dizĕs shĕma-dama-kriyĕ-pūñ^{ü}
lāmā-tsakra-posh^{u} *pröñ*^{ü} *kriy dör*^{ü}
khĕna khĕna mötsiy wör^{ü}*y chĕñ*^{ü}

The way of knowledge is a garden of herbs.

Thou must enclose it with the hedge of quietism and self-restraint and pious deeds.

Thus will thy former deeds be offered like beasts at the Mothers' sacrifice,

And, by steady eating of its crop, the garden will become empty and bare.

Deeds are of two kinds,—the deeds of former lives, of which the accumulated results still persist, and the deeds done in the present life. Both kinds have results, through the action of the endless chain of cause and effect, and so long as these results continue to exist, ultimate release is impossible.

In the garden of knowledge, the herbs are the deeds of the present life. It must be carefully guarded from outside temptations by the performance of the daily obligatory religious rites and the practice of quietism and self-restraint. In this garden are allowed to browse the goats destined to sacrifice, typifying the works of former lives, the fruits of which are the existing crop—the deeds of the present life. Hemmed in by the hedge of holy works, the goats are compelled to eat this crop, or, in other words, the works of former lives are compelled to render themselves unfruitful. This unfruitfulness is consummated by the sacrifice of the goats, and when that is accomplished the soul becomes assimilated to the Supreme Void, the *Śūnya*. See Vocabulary, s. v. *shūñ*.

A Lāmā is one of the divine Mothers, to whom animals are offered in sacrifice. See Vocabulary, s. v. *lāmā*, for further particulars.

64.

kalan kāla-zöl^{i} *yid*^{a}*way tsĕ gol*^{u}
vĕndiv gih wā vĕndiv wan-wās
zönith sarwa-gath Probh^{u} *amol*^{u}
yuthuy zānĕkh tyuthuy ās

[The following is the text of Stein B :—

कलना कालजाली यिद् ॥ विगलो ॥
कन्दिव् ॥ गेह् ॥ कन्दिव् वनवास् ॥
जानीत् ॥ सर्वगत् ॥ प्रभ् ॥ अमलो ॥
यीथोय् जानक् ॥ तीथोय् आस ॥ ३८ ॥

This is a mixture of Nos. 55 and 64.]

If, in flux of time, thou hast destroyed the whole body of thy desires,
Choose ye a home-life, or choose ye a hermitage.
If thou wilt come to know that the Lord is all-pervading and without taint,
Then, as thou wilt know, so wilt thou be.

Freedom from desire and knowledge of the nature of the Self give ultimate release, whether a man lead the life of a householder or bury himself in a hermitage. The mode of life is immaterial. With this knowledge, his own soul becomes assimilated to his conception of the nature of the Supreme; and he becomes spiritually one with Him.

65.

Shiwa Shiwa karūn hamsa-gath sŏrith
rūzith vĕwahör^{i} *dĕn kyōh rāth*
lāgi-rost^{u} *aduy*^{u} *yus*^{u} *man karith*
tas^{i} *vĕth prason*^{u} *sura-guru-nāth*

[The following is the text of Stein B:—

शिव शिव करान्त यमी लोयो ॥
चज्यीस् ॥ भयु भङ्ग् ॥ ता द्रत् ॥
यमी अद्वय् ॥ मन् ॥ सम्पन्नो
तमी प्रसन्नो सुरगुरुनाथ् ॥ ३० ॥

This is a mixture of Nos. 5 and 65.]

He who ever calleth on the name of Śiva and who beareth in mind the Way of the Swan,

Even if night and day he remain busy with his worldly calling,

And who without thought for fruits maketh his mind non-dualist,

On him alone is ever gracious the Lord of the Chiefest of gods.

The Way of the Swan is a mystic name for the celebrated formula *sō 'ham*, I am He (cf. the *tat tvam asi*, thou art It, of verse 60). In Sanskrit letters, if the words *sō 'ham* be reversed, they become *haṁsaḥ*, a word which means 'swan'. Hence the origin of the term. The devout believer must perform his necessary religious duties, but, as explained under verse 61, without thought of the reward that they may bring. *Haṁsa* is a term often applied to the Supreme Śiva dwelling in the Sahasrâra and identical with the individual soul (see Note on Yōga, § 20). The full title, in this sense, is *Parama-haṁsa*. The word is also used to indicate the *Ajapa mantra*. See verse 40.

The non-dualist mind is that which fully recognizes the identity of the Self with the Supreme Self,—that all is one, not two, or manifold.

66.

tsarmun tsaṭith ditith pȧn^{i} *pānas*
tyuth^{u} *kyāh wavyōth ta phalihiy sṓw*^{u}
mūḍas wŏpadēsh gȧy^{i} *rīnz*^{i} *dumaṭas*
kȧñ^{i} *dā̃das gōr āparith rṓw*^{u}

Thou hast cut up the hide and pegged it down, all for thyself.

Hast thou sown such seed that it will bear abounding fruit?

Fool! teaching proffered to thee is but balls flung at a boundary-pillar.

It is all lost, as though sweet stuff were fed unto a tawny bullock.

Just as a degraded Camār, whose whole occupation is with that which is dead and foul, cares for a hide by cutting it into its intended shape and pegging it out to dry, so the worldly man cherishes his body, which itself is but a hide, and stretches it out over the world of enjoyment with the pegs of desire. On the other hand, the wise man is like a decent husbandman. He sows the living seed that shall spring up and bear the harvest of spiritual blessing.

Instruction given to the foolish worldly man returns to the giver, as a ball in the game of hockey bounds back from one of the goal-pillars.

To give instruction to such a person is as much lost labour as it is to feed a lusty bullock with sweetmeats in the hope of increasing its milk. 'Bullock's milk' is a common phrase used to indicate a hoped-for but impossible result. Here the fool not only believes in its existence but tries to increase its yield. *Gōr*, molasses, is often given to a *cow* to increase her milk. The fool tries it on a bullock.

67.

lalith lalĭth waday bŏ-dŏy
ṭsittā! muhücü pĕyiy māy
rōziy nō pata lŏh-langarücü ṭshāy
niza-swarūph kyāh moṭhuy hāy

Good Sir, for thee will I keep weeping with gentle sound and gentle words.

My Soul! love for the world, begotten of illusion, hath befallen thee.

Not even the shadow of thine iron anchor will survive for thee.

Alas! why hast thou forgotten the nature of thy Self?

Lallā addresses herself as 'Good Sir'.

The iron anchor—a common object in Kashmīr navigable rivers—is worldly possessions that tie a man's soul down to this world. None of these will he carry with him after death.

68.

Lal bŏh ƀāyĕs sŏman-bāga-baras
wuchum Shiwas Shĕk^{a}th mīlith ta wāh
tàt^{i} lay kür^{ü}m amrĕta-saras
zinday maras ta mĕ kari kyāh

I, Lallā, passed in through the door of the jasmine-garden of my soul.

And there, O Joy! saw I Śiva seated united with His Śakti.

There became I absorbed in the lake of nectar.

Now, what can (existence) do unto me? For, even though alive, I shall in it be dead.

The first line contains a paronomasia. The word *sŏman* may be the Persian word meaning 'jasmine', or may be the Indian word meaning 'my own mind' or 'soul'. We have attempted to indicate this in the translation.

Śiva united in one with His Śakti, or energic power, is the highest form of the Supreme Self. The lake of nectar is a metaphor for the bliss of union with the Supreme. Drowned in this, though alive, Lallā is as it were dead, and is certain of release from future birth, life, or death.

69.

ċitta-turogᵘ wagi hěth roṭum
ċělith milavith dashě-nāḍi-wāv
taway shěshi-kal věgalith wüċhᵘm
shūñěs shūñāh mīlith gauv

With a rein did I hold back the steed of my thought.

By ardent practice did I bring together the vital airs of my ten *nāḍis*.

Therefore did the digit of the moon melt and descend unto me,

And a void became merged within the Void.

The rein by which she holds back the steed of her thought is the absence of desire.

The *nāḍis* are the tubes in the body through which the vital airs are believed to circulate, and it is the devotee's object to bring these airs under subjection. See the Vocabulary s. vv. *nāḍi* and *prān*, 2, and Note on Yōga, §§ 5, 21.

The mystic moon in the *sahasrāra* has been explained above under verses 40 and 56, 57. When the devotee has completely blocked the circulation of his vital airs, this moon distils nectar, as there explained. See also Note on Yōga, §§ 8, 19, 21, 22.

For the empty void of matter merging into the great Void, see verse 11.

70.

ċěth amara-pathi thövⁱzi
*tih trövith lagi zūḍě**
tati ċᵃh nō shĩkⁱzi sandörⁱzi
dŏda-shurᵘ ta kŏchě nō mūḍě†

* V. l. *zūrě* † V. l. *mūrě*

[The following is the text of Stein B :—

चित्ता अमरपथि थाविजि
  ते चावीत ता लगिय् ॥ जूठि
तत्या चू कङ्गित् सन्धारिजि
  दद्वो शोठो ता कुछ्यि ता ना मूठि ॥ २८ ॥

The MS. numbers this 19 by error.]

Put thou thy thoughts upon the path of immortality.

If thou leave them without guidance, into evil state will they fall.

There, be thou not fearful, but be thou very courageous.

For they are like unto a suckling child, that tosseth restless on its mother's bosom.

For the literal meaning of the last line, see the Vocabulary, s. v. *mūrun*.

71.

mārukh māra-būth kām krūd lūb
  na-ta kān barith māriněy pān
manay khěn dikh swa-věcāra shěm
  vishěy tihond^u kyāh kyuth^u druw^u zān

[The following is the text in Stein B (in which it has no number) :—

मारुक् मारभूत पाराशुक्
  कान् भरीत् मारिनिय्
मनय् खिन्न् दीस्
  अल्पें आसुव् [—] ऊखिनिस्तशर् कव दीय् ॥

In the fourth line, the MS. is worm-eaten, and one word is destroyed. The whole is corrupt, and is unintelligible as it stands.]

Murder thou the murderous demons, lust, anger, and desire.

Otherwise they will aim their arrows, and destroy thy Self.

With careful thought, by meditation on thy Self, give to them quietism as their only food.

Then wilt thou know what, and how little firm, is their realm of power.

The arrows are temptations to worldliness.

72.

ƫala-ƫitta! wŏndas bhayĕ mō bar
cyöñ^{ü} ƫinth karān pāna Anād
ƫĕ kō-zanañi kshōd hari, kar
kēwal tasonduy tāruk^{u} nād

Ah restless mind! have no fear within thy heart.

The Beginningless One Himself taketh thought for thee,

(And considereth) how hunger may fall from thee.

Utter, therefore, to Him alone the cry of salvation.

Trust in God for the things of this life, and He will provide. No formal rites are required in order to secure his protection. All that is necessary is unceasingly to utter the 'unobstructed cry' (see verses 14, 15), i. e. the mystic syllable *ōṁ*, which properly uttered, and with faith, will secure the presence of the Supreme, Who is everything that man can need.

73.

ṭsāmar chaṭhar rathu simhāsan
hlād nāṭĕ-ras tūla-paryŏkh
kyāh mönith yiti sthir āsawunu
kō-zana kāsiy maranüñü shŏkh

74.

kyāh bŏḍukh muha bhawa-sŏḍari-dārĕ
sŏthu lūrith pĕyiy tama-pŏkh
yĕma-baṭh karinĕy köli chōra-dārĕ
kō-zana kāsiy maranüñü shŏkh

75.

karm zah kāran trah kŏmbith
yĕwa labakh paralōkas ŏkh
wŏth khas sūrya-manḍal ṭsŏmbith
taway ṭsaliy maranüñü shŏkh

76.

jñānȧki ambar pairith tanē
yim pad Lali dȧpi tim hrĕdi ŏkh
kārȧni pranawȧki lay koru Lalē
ṭsĕth-jyōti kösün maranüñü shŏkh

[The following is the text of 73–76 in Stein B :—

चामर् ॥ छ्च् रथ् सिंहासन् ॥
ल्हाद् ॥ तूलय् पर्यङ्क् ॥
क्या मानीत् ॥ स्थिर् ॥ इति आसुन् ॥
कीन् ॥ कासूय् मरणञी शङ्क् ॥ ३९ ॥

क्या बुडोख् ॥ सुत् सोदरि दारि ॥
धारि लोळीत् पिय् भवपङ्क्
यमभट्ट करनिय क्रूरधारि
कीन् कासूय् मरणञी शङ्क् ॥ ४० ॥

कर्म् जू कारण् त्रि कुम्भीत् ॥
यव लभक् ॥ परलोकस् ॥ अङ्क् ॥
उत्थ् खस् ॥ सूर्या मण्डलो चुम्भीत् ॥
तवै चलिय् मर्णञी शङ्क् ॥ ३७ ॥

ज्ञान अम्बर् पैरीम लल्लि
यीम् पद् दपीतीम् हृदि अङ्क् ॥
कारणी प्रोणोकी गरीञि लल्लि
कीन ॥ कासूय् ॥ मरणञी शङ्क् ॥ ४१ ॥]

73. A royal chowry, sunshade, chariot, throne,
Happy revels, the pleasures of the theatre, a bed of cotton down,—
Bethink thee which of these is lasting in this world,
And how can it take from thee the fear of death.

74. In thy illusion why didst thou sink in the stream of the ocean of existence?
When thou hadst destroyed the high-banked road, there came before thee the slough of spiritual darkness.
At the appointed time will Yama's apparitors drag thee off in woful plight.
Who can take from thee the fear of death?

75. Works two are there, and causes three. On them practise thou the *kumbhaka-yōga*.
Then, in another world, wilt thou gain the mark of honour.
Arise, mount, pierce through the sun's disk.
Then will flee from thee the fear of death.

76. Clothe thou thy body in the garb of knowledge.
Brand thou on thy heart the verses that Lallā spake.

With the help of the *praṇava* Lallā absorbed herself
In union with the Soul-light, and so expelled the fear of death.

These four verses form a group.

73. The chowry, or fly-whisk, and the sunshade are emblems of royalty. So strong is this feeling about the sunshade, or, in plain English, the umbrella, that some years ago a serious riot took place in southern India, due to the fact that some low-caste people had taken to going about with cheap cotton umbrellas imported from England. People of such castes had no right to protect themselves from the sun or rain!

74. The high-banked road is the way of truth, by which the Self is enabled to approach the Supreme Self. These high embanked roads across marshy country are common features of a Kāshmīrī landscape.

Yama is the god who rules the land of shades. His apparitors carry off the soul after death for judgement by him, cruelly treating it on the way. *Chōra-dārĕ karun* is the name of a punishment, in which the criminal is dragged along the ground till the blood flows from his body in streams.

75. Works are of two kinds, good and bad. There are three causes of the apparent existence of the material world, which are technically known as *malas* or impurities. These are (1) *āṇava-mala*, or the impurity due to the soul deeming itself to be finite; (2) *māyīya-mala*, or the impurity due to the cognition that one thing is different from another; and (3) *kārma-mala*, resulting in action—the producer of pleasure and pain.

It is the devotee's business to destroy the fruits of all works, whether good or bad, and to destroy these *malas*. This he does by practising *yōga*. One important form of *yōga* is the *kumbhaka-yōga*, in which the breath is entirely suspended. *Kŏmbith* literally means 'bottling up (the breath)'. Cf. verse 34, and see the Vocabulary, s. vv. *kāran* and *kumbᵘ*. The disembodied soul, on its way to emancipation, is said to pass through the sun's orb on its way to union with the Supreme.

76. The *praṇava* is one of the names of the mystic syllable *ōṁ*, for which see verses 14, 15.

77.

mörith pönts būth tim phal-hanḍī
tsĕtana-dāna-wakhur khĕth
taḍạy zānakh paramu pad tsanḍī
hishiy khösh^{i}-khŏr kŏ̃h-ti na khĕth

[The following is the text of Stein B:—

मारीत् पञ्चभूत् तें हण्डे
चेतुन् धान वाखुर् दित् ॥
जानहा परमो पद् यिद् रण्डे
खशे खुर् हशे खुर् कित् ॥ १७ ॥

See remarks on verse 10.]

Ah! thou hasty one, feed thou those fatted rams—the five principles of experience—on the grain and cates of spiritual meditation, and then slay them.

Not till then wilt thou gain the knowledge of the place of the Supreme, and (thou wilt also know that) if thou violate custom it is all the same, and causeth thee no loss.

Lallā is said to have made a practice of going about in a nude condition, 'for', said she, 'he only is a man who fears God, and there are few such about'. See verse 94 and the note to K. Pr., p. 20, below. This verse appears to be an answer of hers to some woman who remonstrated with her for not following the usual customs in regard to female dress.

The five *bhūtas*, or *mahābhūtas*, are the five factors constituting the principles of experience of the sensible universe. They are solidity, liquidity, formativity, aeriality, and vacuity. For further particulars, see the Vocabulary, s. v. *būth*, 2.

Just as a ram fattened on fruits and such like has but the smallest beginning in his mother's womb, and grows to great size and vigour before he is ready for sacrifice, so these principles are developed from earlier, subtile, capacities (*tanmātras*), and under the influence of the chain of cause and effect, which result in illusion (*māyā*), become powerful and conceal from the soul its knowledge of its real Self.

In order to attain to true knowledge, the seeker must first certify to himself the essential nothingness of these five *bhūtas*, and cause them to disappear one by one from his experience, by meditating on, and realizing, the nature of Self. Just as a fatted ram is prepared for sacrifice and death by feeding it on grain and cakes, so these must be prepared for disappearance by this meditation and realization.

The 'violation of custom' is literally 'the left-handed conduct' and there is probably a suggestion of the *vāma-mārga*, or left-handed, Kaula, ritual. Cf. the last line of verse 10.

78.

kus ḍingi ta kus zāgi
kus sar watari tēliy
kus haras pūzi lāgi
kus parama-pad mēliy

79.

man ḍingi ta akŏl zāgi
dŏḍ[i] sar panca-yind[i] watari tēliy
swa-vĕtsāra-pŏñ haras pūzi lāgi
parama-pad tsētana-Shiv mēliy

[The following is the text of 78 and 79 in Stein B (in which they have no number:—

कुसो डङ्गि त कुसो जागि
कुसो सर् वत्रि तिलेया
कुसो हरस् [पूजि लागि]
कुसो परमपद् मिलेया ॥

In this verse the MS. is worm-eaten, and four *akṣaras* are destroyed in the third line. These I have supplied from verse 79. They are enclosed in brackets.

मन् डङ्गि ता अकुल् जागि
  दाडुय् पञ्च् इन्द्रिय् चिलेया (sic)
पुख्वे हरस पूजि लगि (sic)
  एङ्गय् चेतन् शिव् मिलेया ॥]

78. Who is he that is wrapped in sleep, and who is he that is awake?

What lake is that which continually oozeth away?

What is that which a man may offer in worship to Hara?

What is that supreme station to which thou wilt attain?

79. The mind is he who is wrapped in sleep, and when it hath transcended the *kula* it is he who is awake.

The five organs are the lake that continually oozeth away.

That holy thing which a man may offer in worship to Hara is the discrimination of the Self.

That supreme station to which thou wilt attain is the Spirit-Śiva.

78. Hara is a name of Śiva, the personal form of the impersonal Supreme.

79. The *manas*, or mind, is, roughly speaking, the thinking faculty. For a more accurate description, see the Vocabulary, s. v. *man*.

The *kula*, or family, is a group of the following essentials for the experience of the existence of the Self, as distinct from the Supreme Self:—(1) the individual soul; (2) *Prakṛti*, or primal matter,—that on which the individual soul acts, and which reacts on it; (3) space—i.e. the conception of limitation in space; (4) time—i.e. the conception of limitation in time; and (5–9) the five *bhūtas*, or principles of experience, as described under verse 77. When the mind transcends these, and recognizes its Self as one with the limitless Supreme Self, it is in a state of grace, or, as here said, it is awake. The commentary quotes here the following lines; the first is anonymous, and the rest = *Bhagavad Gītā*, ii. 69:—

mana ēva manuṣyāṇāṁ kāraṇaṁ bandha-mōkṣayōḥ ॥
yā niśā sarva-bhūtānāṁ tasyāṁ jāgarti saṁyamī ।
yasyāṁ jāgrati bhūtāni sā niśā paśyatō munēḥ ॥

It is the mind alone that is the cause of men's entanglement and of their release.
In that which to all embodied beings is night, doth the ascetic remain awake,
And that in which they wake, is the night for the saint who hath eyes to see.

The five organs, or principles, of action are those of generation, excretion, locomotion, handling, and expression by voice. The continual exercise of these takes away the power of Self-realization.

80.

zānahö nāḍi-dal mana raṭith
ȼaṭith waṭith, kuṭith klēsh
zānahö ada asta rasāyĕn gaṭith
Shiv chuy krūṭh[u] *ta ȼēn wŏpadēsh*

[The following is the text of Stein B:—

जानिहा नाडीद्‌ला मन् ॥ रट्टीत्
चट्टीत् ॥ वट्टीत् ॥ कुट्टीत् ॥ क्लेश ॥
जानिहा अस्तरसायुन् ॥ घट्टीत् ॥
शिव् छ्योयी कष्टो त चिन् ॥ उपदेश ॥ ३४ ॥]

If I had known how by my mind to bring into subjection my *nāḍis*,
How to cut, how to bind up; then should I have known how to crush sorrow,
And gradually to compound the Great Elixir.
Hardly, in sooth, is Śiva to be found. Meditate therefore on the doctrine.

As previously explained (see Note on Yōga, §§ 5, 21, and verse 69), the *nāḍis* are the tubes through which the vital airs circulate. It is the devotee's business to bring the latter under control. *Tsaṭun waṭun*, cutting and binding up, is the Kāshmīrī term for operative surgery. Lallā implies that this must be performed upon the mind, which must be cut away from the organs of action (see the preceding Verse), and bound up by self-restraint and quietism.

The Elixir of Life is, of course, the knowledge of the Self.

For the final line, compare verses 51–54.

81.

mad pyuwum syundu-zalan yaitu
rangan līlàm[i] kiyĕm kaitsa
kait[i] khyēm manushĕ-māmsàk[i] nalī
sŏy bŏh Lal ta gauv mĕ kyāh

[The following is the text of Stein B :—

(This verse is given twice in the MS. with slightly differing readings.)

मद् पिवूं सिन्धजलनि यातो
रङ्गन् लीलकीय दिन् त रात् ॥
मांस् चर्वण ॥ भक्षों कातो
सयी भु लल्ल् त गौ मि क्यात् ॥ ४२ ॥

मद् पीवूम् सिन्धुजलनि यातो ॥
रङ्गन् लीलमि कीयम् ॥ काच ॥
कैती खियम् ॥ मनुषमांसकी नली ॥
सयी भु लल्ल ता गौ मि क्यात् ॥ ४३ ॥]

However oft I quaffed that wine—the water of the Sindhu,

However many parts I played upon the stage,

However many lumps of human flesh I ate,

Still I am the same Lallā, and what profit was it all to me?

She had been born again and again, but in former births she had not known the Self. The Sindhu is one of the chief rivers of Kashmīr, famous for its excellent water. She had been born in various forms, divine, human, bestial, as a worm, or what not, and each time had drunk the water of the Sindhu, playing many parts on the stage of human existence. She had been born over and over again as a human being, so to speak eating, i.e. experiencing, human flesh, and now at length she has recognized that it has been the one Self all the time, and that all these existences in ignorance had been profitless.

82.

ōṁ-kār yĕli layĕ onum
 wuhī korum panun^{u} *pān*
sh^{ĕ}*wot*^{u} *trövith ta sath mārg roṭum*
 tĕli Lal bŏh wöts^{ü}*s prakāshĕ-sthān*

When by concentration of my thoughts I brought the *praṇava* under my control,
 I made my body like a blazing coal.
The six paths I traversed and gained the seventh,
 And then did I, Lallā, reach the place of illumination.

The *praṇava* is the mystic syllable *ōṁ*, and here may be taken as indicating any vital formula, such, for instance, as *tat tvam asi* (see verse 60). She brought this under control, i.e. she mastered it, and thus became imbued with the truth. She then became able to suppress her vital airs (see Note on Yōga, § 21 and Vocabulary s. vv. *nāḍi* and *prān*, 2), and thereby entered into a state of grace. By this suppression her frame became suffused with a holy fire.

The six ways are the six *cakras*, or seats of the six subordinate *Śaktis* that urge a man to action. They are supposed to be located along what corresponds to the spinal cord of a man's subtile body. The devotee has to master these one by one, and then attains to the seventh and highest station, or *sahasrāra cakra*, by meditating on which he obtains final release. The whole process is explained in greater detail in the Note on Yōga, §§ 9–21, and Vocabulary, s. vv. *shĕh* and *sōm*.

The word *sath-mārg* may mean either the seventh path or the true path, in either case indicating the *sahasrāra cakra*.

83.

gāṭulwāh akh wuchum bŏcha-sūty marān
pan zan harān puhani wāwa lah
nĕshĕbŏdu akh wuchum wāzas mārān
tana Lal bŏh prārān ƫhĕnĕm-nā prah

A wise man saw I a-dying of hunger,

As the leaves fall with even a gentle wind in the wintry month of Pauṣa.

And saw I also a fool beating his cook.

Since then have I, Lallā, been waiting for the day when love for the world will be cut from me.

She has seen the injustice of this world, and longs for freedom from the desire for existence. A man's wisdom will not save him from starvation, or from liability to death from even the slightest cause; and a fool may be rich and prosperous, whose only sorrow is that his cook now and then does not sufficiently spice his food, and who securely acts as a tyrant to him in consequence.

84.

yih kyāh ösith yih kyuthu rang gōm
cang gōm ƫaṭith huda-hudañĕy dagay
sārĕniy padan kunuy wakhun pyōm
Lali mĕ trāg gōm laga kami shāṭhay

85.

yih kyāh ösith yih kyuthu rang gōm
bĕrongu karith gōm laga kami shāṭhay
tālav-rāzadāñĕ abakh chān pyōm
jān gōm zānĕm pān panunuy

84. What is this that hath happened? What kind hath bechanced me?

* * * * * * * * *

In all these verses but one tale hath fallen to my lot.

I, Lallā, have happened on a lake, and know not on what sand-bank I shall run aground.

85. What is this that hath happened? What kind hath bechanced me?

I made all things out of order, on what sand-bank shall I run aground?

* * * * * * * * *

It turned out well for me, for I myself will learn to know (my Self).

These are two of Lallā's hard sayings which are unintelligible at the present day, although there is no dispute as to the text.

84. The meaning of the word *huda-hudañĕy* in the second line of this verse is unknown to modern Kāshmīrīs, and without knowing their meaning, there is no clue to the sense of the rest of the line. The remaining words of the line in the modern language might mean, 'my claw has been cut (?) by a blow', but whether they bore this meaning in Lallā's time is doubtful.

The latter half of the verse is fairly plain. The one plaint of all her verses is the miserable uncertainty of human existence in this world, till a man has known the Supreme.

85. In this verse it is the third line that is devoid of meaning to Kāshmīrīs of the present day. The actual words might mean 'for plastering my ceiling I got a clumsy carpenter', but it is not likely that this is what Lallā originally intended, or wrote. The word *abakh* is not used nowadays, and there is no tradition as to its meaning, but there is a word *abakhwārĕñ* which means 'clumsy'.

86.

rāza-hams ösith sapodukh koluy
kus-tām ťoluy kyāh-tām hěth
graṭa gauv band töy graṭan hyotᵘ goluy
graṭa-wōlᵘ ťoluy phal-pholᵘ hěth

Once wast thou a swan, and now thou hast become mute.

Some one, I know not who, hath run off with something of thine.

As soon as the mill became stopped, the grain channel became choked,

And away ran the miller with the grain.

This is another of Lallā's hard sayings, the true interpretation of which is unknown. The swan is fabled to have a very melodious voice, and (Lallā is addressing herself) she whose voice was once like that of a swan has now become dumb.

When a mill-stone stops revolving, the orifice in the upper stone, through which the grain is fed on its way to being ground, becomes blocked up and hidden under a pile of grain. The meaning of the metaphor, and who is represented by the miller, is uncertain. The verse has a curious echo of Ecclesiastes xii. 3–4. Perhaps Lallā means that she has now found salvation, and is in a state of silent rapture. Formerly she had preached volubly (cf. verse 89); but now that she sees God she is silent. God is the miller, who turns the mill of worldly experience in order to grind out the grain of the chastened soul. Now He has finished His work. The mill is still, the channel blocked by the husks, and the Miller has taken to Himself the grain. But it must be understood that this is entirely our own attempted interpretation, and has no Kāshmīrī authority.

87.

niyěm karyōth garbā
ťětas kar-bā pěyiy
marana brōṭhay mar-bā
marith ta martaba hᵃriy

88.

atha ma-bā trāwun khar-bā!
lūka-hünz[ü] *kŏng-wŏr*[ü] *khĕyiy*
tati kus-bā dāriy thar-bā!
yĕli nanis kartal pĕyiy

87. Even while in thy mother's womb thou madest a vow.

When, Sir, will that vow come to thy remembrance?

Die, Sir, even before thy death,

Then, when thy death cometh, great honour will increase for thee.

88. Let not the ass loose to stray from thy guiding hand,

Or, of a surety, will it devour thy neighbour's saffron-garden.

Who then will there be there to offer his back to thee to mount,

Where the sword will fall upon thy naked form?

87. It is believed that while a child is in its mother's womb it remembers all its former births, and resolves in its coming life to act so as to acquire release from further transmigration. But directly it is born, recollection of these previous existences disappears and it loses all memory of its resolution. The same idea is developed in verse 51.

Here Lallā reproaches an unbeliever with this act of forgetfulness. She advises him, while yet alive, to become as one dead (cf. verse 12), by destroying the six enemies—lust, wrath, desire, arrogance, delusion, and jealousy (see Vocabulary s. v. *lūb*)—and thus acquiring complete indifference to worldly temptations. The resultant honour is, of course, absorption into the Supreme Self—contrasted with the objects of the worldly ambition practised by her auditor.

The commentator here quotes the following apposite lines from the *Bhagavad Gītā* (v. 23):—

śaknōtīhaiva yaḥ sōḍhuṁ prāk śarīra-vimōkṣaṇāt ।
kāma-krōdhōdbhavaṁ vēgaṁ sa yuktaḥ sa sukhī naraḥ ॥

He who has strength to bear here ere release from the body the passion born of love and wrath, is of the Rule, he is a happy man. (*Barnett's Translation.*)

88. The ass is the mind. Keep it under control, or it will wander forth into strange heresies, and will suffer in consequence.

The saffron-gardens are the most valuable cultivated land in Kāshmīr. An ass loose in one might do incalculable damage, and would suffer accordingly. Apparently, in Lallā's metaphor, the ass's owner, in such a case, would be liable to the extreme penalty of the law.

In the second half of the verse, if the mind is not controlled, and does not recognize the nature of Self, it can give no help when its owner is at the point of death, under the sword of Yama.

The commentator quotes as apposite the following lines from the *Bhagavad Gītā* (ii. 60–63):—

yatatō hy api Kauntēya puruṣasya vipaścitaḥ ।
indriyāṇi pramāthīni haranti prasabhaṁ manaḥ ॥
tāni sarvāṇi saṁyamya yukta āsīta mat-paraḥ ।
vaśē hi yasyēndriyāṇi tasya prajñā pratiṣṭhitā ॥
dhyāyatō viṣayān puṁsaḥ saṁgas tēṣūpajāyatē ।
saṁgāt saṁjāyatē kāmaḥ kāmāt krōdhō 'bhijāyatē ॥
krōdhād bhavati saṁmōhaḥ saṁmōhāt smṛti-vibhramaḥ ।
smṛti-bhraṁśād buddhi-nāśō buddhi-nāśāt praṇaśyati ॥

For though the prudent man strive, O son of Kuntī, his froward instruments of sense carry away his mind perforce.

Let him hold all these in constraint and sit under the Rule, given over to Me; for he who has his sense-instruments under his sway has wisdom abidingly set.

In the man whose thoughts dwell on the ranges of sense arises attachment to them; from attachment is born love; from love springs wrath.

From wrath is confusion born; from confusion wandering of memory; from breaking of memory wreck ot understanding; from wreck of understanding a man is lost. (*Barnett's Translation.*)

89.

lācāri bicāri prawād korum
nador^u chuwa ta hĕyiv mā
phīrith dubāra jān kyāh wonum
prān ta ruhun hĕyiv mā

90.

prān ta ruhun kunuy zônum
prān bazith labi na sād
prān bazith kĕh-ti nō khĕzē
taway lobum 'sō-'ham' sād

[In these verses a number of words have double meanings, so that the whole has two different interpretations. Compare verse 101. The first interpretation is :—]

89. Helpless and wretched made I my cry in the market,
'Here for you be lotus-stalks. Will ye not buy?'
Then again I returned, and, behold, how well I cried,
'Onions and garlic will ye not buy?'

90. I came to know that onion and garlic are the same.
If a man fry onion he will have no tasty dish.
If a man fry onion, let him not eat a scrap thereof.
Therefore found I the flavour of 'I am He'.

89. Lotus-stalks stewed with meat are freely eaten in Kashmīr, and are sold in the markets.

90. Onions fried by themselves make only an evil-smelling mess, of no use as food. The above is the exoteric interpretation of the two verses. The sense is not very great, and, unless there is some double meaning in the words *sō-'ham*, which we have not discovered, the *double entente* breaks down in the last line of the second verse.

[The second, esoteric interpretation is :—]

89. Helpless and wretched made I my cry in the world,

'Here be a thing of no worth. Will ye not therefore take it?'

Then again returning (to my senses), behold, how well I cried,

'The breathing body and the soul will ye not take (under your control)?'

90. I came to know that the breathing body and the soul are one.

That if a man cherish his body, the flavour (of true bliss) he will not gain.

That if he cherish his body, therefrom will he reap no true joy.

And so I gained for myself the flavour of 'I am He'.

89. In her early days, before she had reached a knowledge of her Self, she had been offering worthless teaching to the people, and had urged them to accept it. Then, again, when she had learnt the truth, she came and urged them to practise *yōga* by controlling their vital breaths (see Vocabulary, s. vv. *nāḍi* and *prān*, 2) and by mastering a knowledge of the nature of the soul. The word *prān*, vital breath, is here used to indicate the body, which exists by breathing.

90. Cherishing the body and devoting oneself to worldly enjoyments give no profit. The word 'to eat' also means 'to eat the good things of this life', 'to enjoy oneself', and this gives the double meaning to the third line. Cherishing the body may give apparent temporary pleasure, but even this is mixed with pain, and in the end there is no profit—only ceaseless soul-wandering. Lallā grasps the fact, and thereby discovers the rapture of the great truth contained in the formula 'I am He', or *tat tvam asi*, 'thou art It', for which see verse 60.

91.

Siddha-Māli! Siddhō! sĕda kathan kan thāv
ts^{a}*h dŏh path-kāli sŏran kyāh*
bālakō! tŏh^{i} *kĕthō dĕn rāth bariv*
kāl āv kuṭhān ta kariv kyāh

92.

brō̃ṭh-kōl^{i} *āsan tithiy kēran*
ṭang tsū̃ṭh^{i} *papan tsēran-sūt*^{i}
mājĕ-kōrĕ atha-wās karith ta nēran
dŏh-dĕn baran paradĕn-sūt^{i}

91. O Honoured Saint! O Saint! Heedfully lend thou ear unto my words.

Dost thou remember the days of yore?

O Children! How will ye pass the days and nights?

Harder and harder becometh the age, and what will ye do?

92. In the coming days so malformed will be natures,

That pears and apples will ripen with the apricots.

Hand in hand, from the house will go forth mother and daughter,

And with strange men will they consort day after day.

91. A wail over the evil times in store. Even holy men have no memory of past times and of past existences, to profit by it. So then what chance have the children,—the coming generation,—in this evil *Kali* age?

92. Times will become more and more evil, and there is none to warn or to guide to the true knowledge.

Human nature itself will change for the worse, as if pears and apples, whose ripening time is the late autumn, were to change and ripen with the apricots in the height of the rainy season. All women will be unchaste. Mother and daughter, hand in hand,—i. e. pimping for each other,—will go abroad in search of strange men.

The main idea of this verse has survived in a familiar Kāshmīrī proverb,—*tĕli, hā māli, āsan kiyāmatȧk*[i] *kēran, yĕli ťsũṭh*[i] *papan ťsēran-sũt*[i]. When apples ripen at the same time as apricots, then, O father, will come the day of resurrection, i. e. it will come on a day and at an hour when men look not for it. Cf. K. Pr. 214.

93.

ťsĕth nowuy ťsọnd[a]*rama nowuy*
zalamay ḍyūṭhum nawam-nowuy
yĕna pĕṭha Lali mĕ tan man nówuy
tana Lal bŏh nawam-nüw[ü]*y chĕs*

The soul is ever new and new; the moon is ever new and new.

So saw I the waste of waters ever new and new.

But since I, Lallā, scoured my body and my mind,

I, Lallā, am ever new and new.

The human soul, subject to illusion and worldly desires, is ever changing in its outward appearance, from birth to birth, although it is always the same; just as the moon is always the same moon, though perpetually waxing and waning.

The universe itself, though the same throughout, at stated intervals undergoes dissolution into a waste of waters, and is afterwards re-formed again; and Lallā herself remembers seeing this in former births (cf. verses 50 and 96).

Then at length Lallā scours illusion from her mind, and she becomes a new creature, for now she knows her Self.

94.

gŏran won^{u}nam kunuy watsun
nẹ̆b^{a}ra dop^{u}nam ạnd^{a}rạy atsun
suy gauv Lali mĕ wākh ta watsun
taway mĕ hyotum nangay natsun

My teacher spake to me but one precept.

He said unto me, 'from without enter thou the inmost part'.

That to me became a rule and a precept,

And therefore naked began I to dance.

The *Guru*, or spiritual preceptor, confides to his disciple the mysteries of religion. Lallā's account is that he taught her to recognize the external world as naught but an illusion, and to restrict her thoughts to meditation on her inner Self. When she had grasped the identity of her Self with the Supreme Self, she learnt to appreciate all externals at their true value. So she abandoned even her dress, and took to going about naked.

With this may be compared the concluding lines of verse 77, and the note to K. Pr. 20. The wandering of Lallā in a nude condition is the subject of more than one story in Kashmīr. Here she says that she danced in this state. Filled with the supreme rapture, she behaved like a madwoman.

The dance, called *tāṇḍava,* of the naked devotee is supposed to be a copy of the dance of Śiva, typifying the course of the cosmos under the god's rule. It implies that the devotee has wholly surrendered the world, and become united with Śiva.

95.

kyāh kara pöntsan dahan ta kāhan
wŏkh-shun yith lĕjĕ karith yim gaiy
söriy samahön yith razi lamahön
ada kyāzi rāvihē kāhan gāv

What shall I do to the five, to the ten, to the eleven,
Who scraped out this pot and departed?
Had they all united and pulled upon this rope,
Then how should the cow of the eleven owners have been lost?

The 'five' are the five *bhūtas*, or principles of experience of the material world (see verse 77 and Vocabulary, s. v. *būth*, 2). The 'ten' are the ten principal and secondary vital airs (see Vocabulary, s. v. *prān*, 2). The 'eleven' are the five organs (*indriya*) of sense (*jñānêndriya*), and the five organs of action (*karmêndriya*) (see Vocabulary s. v. *yund*^{u}), together with the thinking faculty or *manas* (see Vocabulary, s. v. *man*) which rules them, as the eleventh.

If all these could be controlled, and were all united in the one endeavour to compass Self-realization, there would have been a chance of success; but they all pull in different directions, one misdirecting the soul hither, and another thither, to the soul's ruin. It is like a cow owned by eleven masters, each of whom holds it by a separate rope, and each of whom pulls it in a different direction. The result is the loss, i. e. the destruction, of the cow.

The 'pot' which they have scraped out is the soul. Just as people take a pot of food, and ladle out its contents, scraping out the last dregs; so these have taken the last dregs of worldly enjoyment out of the soul for their own purposes, and have then gone away and left it helpless. They themselves have gained only temporary joys, while the soul has lost its opportunity of union with the Supreme.

96.

dàmiy ḍīṭh^{ü}*m nad wahawüñ*^{ü}*y*
dàmiy ḍyūṭhum sum na ta tār
dàmiy ḍīṭh^{ü}*m thür*^{ü} *phŏlawüñ*^{ü}*y*
dàmiy ḍyūṭhum gul na ta khār

97.

ḍȧmiy ḍīṭh[ü]*m güj*[ü] *dazawüñ*[ü]*y*
ḍȧmiy ḍyūṭhum ḍ[a]*h na ta nār*
ḍȧmiy ḍīṭh[ü]*m pānḍawan-hünz*[ü] *möjī*
ḍȧmiy ḍīṭh[ü]*m kröjiy mās*

96\. For a moment saw I a river flowing.
For a moment saw I no bridge or means of crossing.
For a moment saw I a bush all flowers.
For a moment saw I nor rose nor thorn.

97\. For a moment saw I a cooking-hearth ablaze.
For a moment saw I nor fire nor smoke.
For a moment saw I the mother of the Pāṇḍavas.
For a moment saw I an aunt of a potter's wife.

These two verses form one of Lallā's best known sayings. Another version will be found in K. Pr. 47. The subject is the impermanence of everything material.

'But pleasures are like poppies spread,
You seize the flower, its bloom is shed;
Or, like the snow-fall in the river,
A moment white, then melts for ever.'

96\. The river is a stream confined within bounds. The next thing seen is the infinite waste of waters at a general dissolution of the universe. Cf. verses 50 and 93.

97\. The Pāṇḍavas, the famous heroes of the Mahābhārata, were kings, and their mother, Kuntī, was a queen. Yet, through treachery, they were all at one time reduced to the direst misery, and wandered hungry and thirsty till they came to the city of King Drupada. Here, with their mother, the Pāṇḍavas, disguised as mendicant Brāhmaṇas, found refuge in the hut of a potter, and supported themselves by begging. Lallā adds that the potter's wife, or her children, called Kuntī their aunt. This is contrary to the Mahābhārata story, for it would make out that the Pāṇḍavas and their mother posed as potters, not as Brāhmaṇas. It is a curious fact that the stories of the great Indian epics, as told in Kashmīr, sometimes differ widely from the Sanskrit texts current in India proper. For instance, in a Kāshmīrī Rāmāyaṇa, Sītā is represented as the daughter of Mandōdarī, the wife of Rāvaṇa.

98.

āyĕs watē gayĕs na watē
suman-sŏthi-manz lūstum dŏh*
candas wuchum ta hār na athē†
nāwa-tāras dima kyāh bŏh

* V. l. *swa-mana-sŏthi-manz*
† V. l. *Har-nāv na athē.* Also *atē*

By a way I came, but I went not by the way.

While I was yet on the midst of the embankment with its crazy bridges, the day failed for me.

I looked within my poke, and not a cowry came to hand (or, *atē*, was there).

What shall I give for the ferry-fee?

Or, if we adopt the alternative readings, we must translate:—

By a way I came, but I went not by the way.

While I was yet on the midst of the embankment of my own mind, the day failed for me.

I looked within my poke, and found not Hara's name.

What shall I give for a ferry-fee?

Another of Lallā's most popular sayings, current in many forms besides the two quoted above. Another version will be found in K. Pr. 18. Both the readings given above are probably correct, and the verse has thus a double meaning.

By 'way' is meant a highway, as distinct from an uncertain track. This highway is birth as a human being capable of gaining salvation, and it was Lallā's good fortune to come into the world by it. But she did not avail herself of the opportunity; and so, when she died, she left the highway of salvation, and was compelled to be born and reborn.

If, in the third line, we take the reading '*hār*', or 'cowry', the allusion is to the belief that when a person dies his soul has to cross the river Vaitaraṇī, and passes through many dangers in the course of its traverse. If a small piece of money is placed in his mouth at the time of death, he can use it to pay for a ferry-boat to bring him across. For further particulars see the note to K. Pr. 18. A *sum* is a crazy bridge of one or two planks or sticks thrown across a gap in an embankment.

If, however, we take the other reading '*Har*', i.e. Hara or Śiva, instead of *hār*, we get Lallā's esoteric meaning. It is not the literal cowry that she missed, but the name of Śiva, which she found not in the pocket of her mind. The pronunciation of *suman* (plural dative of *sum*) is, in Kāshmīrī, practically the same as that of *swa-man* or *sŏman*, one's own mind; so that, as read out or recited without regard to spelling, the verse has a double meaning. When she died, she found that in her lifetime she had not stored up a knowledge of the Supreme Śiva, i.e. of the Supreme Self, in her intellect; and therefore on her deathbed found no saving grace, or, as she expresses it, she found herself in the dark on some crazy bridge over a fathomless abyss, and had nothing available to pay for the boat of salvation to ferry her across.

The moral is that, inasmuch as birth in a human body is the only chance that a soul has of being saved, when it is fortunate enough to obtain such a birth it should spend its lifetime in gaining a knowledge of the Supreme Self.

99.

gŏphilō! h^{a}ka kadam tul
wuñĕ chĕy sul ta ṭhāḍun yār
par kar paida parwāz tul
wuñe chĕy sul ta ṭhāḍun yār

100.

daman-basti ditō dam
tithay yitha daman-khār
shęstᵃras sōn gaṭshiy hōsil
wuñē chĕy sul ta ṭshāḍun yār

99. O Heedless One! speedily lift up thy foot (and set forth upon thy journey).

Now is it dawn. Seek thou for the Friend.

Make to thyself wings. Lift thou up the winged (feet).

Now is it dawn. Seek thou for the Friend.

100. Give thou breath to the bellows,
Even as doth the blacksmith.
Then will thine iron turn to gold.
Now is it dawn. Seek thou for the Friend.

Two more very popular verses of Lallā's. Another version will be found in K. Pr. 46. Lallā is addressing herself.

99. She has begun to receive instruction, and urges herself to go forward. The desire of knowledge has come to her, and she must seek for the Friend—the Supreme Self.

100. Just as a blacksmith controls the pipe of his bellows, and with the air thus controlled, turns his rough iron into what he desires; so must she control the vital airs circulating through her pipes or *nāḍis*, and thus convert the crude iron of her soul into the gold of the Supreme Self. See Note on Yōga, §§ 5, 21, and Vocabulary, s. vv. *nāḍi* and *prān*, 2.

As for the meaning of *dam dyunᵘ* see the next verse.

101.

dēhacĕ larĕ dārĕ bar trọpᵃrim
prāna-ṭsūr roṭum ta dyutᵘmas dam
hrĕdayĕcĕ kūṭhᵃrĕ-andar gonḍum
ōmaki cōbạka tulᵘmas bam

[This verse is capable of a double interpretation, depending on the two meanings of the word *prān*, as 'onion', and as 'vital air'. Cf. verses 89, 90. The first interpretation is:—]

I locked the doors and windows of my body.
I seized the thief of my onions, and called for help.
I bound him tightly in the closet of my heart,
And with the whip of the *praṇava* did I flay him.

[The second, esoteric, interpretation is as follows:—]

I locked the doors and windows of my body.
I seized the thief of my vital airs, and controlled my breath.
I bound him tightly in the closet of my heart,
And with the whip of the *praṇava* did I flay him.

It is necessary to explain that the expression *dam dyun*^{u}, to give breath, is used in three senses. It may mean 'to give breath' (e.g. to a bellows), as in the preceding verse. Or it may mean 'to give forth breath', i.e. 'to cry out'. Or it may mean—also as in the preceding verse—'to control the breath' by the *yōga* exercise called *prāṇāyāma* (see Note on Yōga, §§ 2, 23, and Vocabulary, s.v. *nāḍi*). The thief of the vital airs is the worldly temptations that interfere with their proper control.

The *praṇava* is the mystic syllable *ōṁ*, regarding which see verses 15, 33, and 34.

102.

Lal bŏh drāyĕs kapasi-pōshĕcĕ süts^{ü}*y*
kōḍ^{i} *ta dūn*^{i} *kür*^{ü}*nam yüts*^{ü}*y lath*
^{a}*yĕ yĕli khārĕnam zöyijĕ t*^{a}*yĕ*
bōw$^{\dot{a}}$*r*^{i}*-wāna gayĕm alönz*^{ü} *lath*

103.

dŏbi yĕli chövünas dŏbi-kañĕ-pĕṭhạy*
saz ta sāban müṭshünam yüṭsüy
säṭsi yĕli phirünam hani-hani köṭsüy
ada Lali mĕ prövüm parama-gath

* V. l. *yĕli phirünas*

102. I, Lallā, went forth in the hope of (blooming like) a cotton-flower.

Many a kick did the cleaner and the carder give me.

Gossamer made from me did the spinning woman lift from the wheel,

And a hanging kick did I receive in the weaver's work-room.

103. When the washerman dashed me (or turned me over) on the washing-stone,

He rubbed me much with fuller's earth and soap.

When the tailor worked his scissors on me, piece by piece,

Then did I, Lallā, obtain the way of the Supreme.

These two verses form another of Lallā's hard sayings which Kāshmīrīs of the present day do not profess to be able to explain. The general meaning is clear enough. Lallā describes her progress to true knowledge through the metaphor of a cotton-pod. The cotton is first roughly treated by the cleaner and the carder. It is next spun into fine thread, and then hung up in misery as the warp on a weaver's loom. The finished cloth is then dashed by the washerman on his stone, and otherwise severely treated in order to whiten it; and, finally, the tailor cuts it up and makes out of it a finished garment. The various stages towards the attainment of knowledge are thus metaphorically indicated, but the explanation of each separate metaphor is unknown. Very possibly, each stage in the manufacture of the cloth represents, not a stage in a single life, but a separate existence in Lallā's progress from birth to birth.

The word *lath*, occurring twice in verse 102, means 'a kick', and is used in the sense of general violent treatment—once under the cotton-carder's bow, and again when the threads are hung up and strained tight in the loom. The word *t*^{a}*y* has two meanings. In the first place, it indicates a woman whose profession it is to spin a particular kind of gossamer thread; and in the second place, it indicates the particular thread itself. The being drawn out to this extreme fineness is one of the hardships to which the cotton is subjected.

The procedure of an Indian washerman is well known. He has, half submerged on the bank of a pond or river, a large flat stone. On this he dashes with great force the garment to be washed, which has been previously soaked in soap and water. It is a most effective method of driving out all dirt, and also, incidentally, of ruining the texture of the cloth.

104.

süts^{ü}*sas na sātas püts*^{ü}*sas na rumas*
suh mas mĕ Lali cyauv panunuy wākh
ạnd^{a}*rim*^{ü} *gaṭakāh raṭith ta wȍlum*
tsaṭith ta dyut^{u}*mas tatiy cākh*

I hoped not in it for a moment, I trusted it not by a hair.

Still I, Lallā, drank the wine of mine own sayings.

Yet, then did I seize an inner darkness and bring it down,

And tear it, and cut it to pieces.

Another hard saying, the full meaning of which is doubtful. Apparently it means that when Lallā first began to utter her sayings, as she calls her verses and as they are still called (*Lallā-vākyāni*), though they intoxicated her like wine, she had no conception that they would have any permanent effect upon her. Yet she found that by their help she became enabled to dissipate the inner darkness of her soul. Or perhaps 'it' is the vanities of the world. Feeling distrustful and fearful of the dark mysterious world of phenomena, she drank the wine of her verses to give herself courage to fight against it, and thus was emboldened to knock down its phantasmagoria.

105.

pot^{u} *zūni wŏthith mot*^{u} *bōlanówum*
dag lalanöv^{ü}*m dayĕ-sanzĕ prahē*
Làl^{i}*-Làl*^{i} *karān Lāla wuzanówum*
mīlith tas man shrōtsyōm dahē

At the end of moonlight to the mad one did I call,
And soothe his pain with the Love of God.
Crying 'It is I, Lallā—it is I, Lallā', the Beloved I awakened.
I became one with Him, and my mind lost the defilement of the ten.

The end of moonlight is the early dawn,—hence the conclusion of the night of ignorance referred to in the preceding verse. The mad one is the mind intoxicated and maddened by worldly illusion. The Beloved whom Lallā awoke was her own Self, which she roused to the knowledge of its identity with the Supreme Self. The ten are the five organs of sense and the five organs of action—the chief impediments to the acceptance of the Great Truth. See Vocabulary, s. v. *yund*^{u}. *Dah*, ten, also means 'a lake'. Thus, by a paronomasia, the last line may also be translated, 'I became one with him, and my mind lost its defilement, as in a lake (of crystal-clear water).'

106.

āmi pana sọd^{a}*ras nāvi chĕs lamān*
kati bōzi Day myṓn^{u} *mĕ-ti diyi tār*
ūmĕn ṭākĕn pṓñ^{u} *zan shĕmān*
zuv chum bramān gara gatshahö

With a rope of untwisted thread am I towing a boat upon the ocean.

Where will my God hear? Will He carry even me over?

Like water in goblets of unbaked clay, do I slowly waste away.

My soul is in a dizzy whirl. Fain would I reach my home.

The cry of the helpless to God. She has tried formal religion, but found it as little helpful as if she had tried to tow the ship of her soul across the ocean of existence with a rope of untwisted thread.

107.

hā manashĕ! kyāzi chukh wuṭhān sĕki-lawar
ami r^{a}*khi*, hamāli! pakiy na nāv*
lyūkhuy yih Nārōn^{i} *karmañĕ r*^{a}*khi*
tih, māli! hĕkiy na phirith kãh

* V. l. *ami raṭi*

To the Unbeliever.

Man! why dost thou twist a rope of sand?

With such a line, O Burden-bearer! the ship will not progress for thee.

That which Nārāyaṇa wrote for thee in the line of fate,

That, Good Sir! none can reverse for thee.

The rope of sand is the belief in formal religion and the desire for worldly joys. The accomplishment of such desires is beyond the reach of any man. He can only attain to that which is written by Nārāyaṇa, i.e. God, as his fate. No effort of his will can alter that.

The conclusion of the whole matter is that the only method of escaping fate is to effect the union of the Self with the Supreme.

There are various interpretations of some of the words in this verse. *Ami r*^{a}*khi*, by means of this (weak) line, i.e. the rope of sand, may also be translated 'on this (thin) line', i.e. along the narrow track, or towing-path, on the bank of a river. Another reading is *ami raṭi*, by grasping it, *sc.* the rope of sand. The word *hamāli*, O Burden-bearer, may also be read as *ha māli*, O Father, here a polite form of address, equivalent to 'Good Sir'. A 'burden-bearer' is a labouring man accustomed to lifting heavy weights, and, as such, would be employed on the heavy work of pulling a tow-rope. This method of taking a ship up-stream is a common sight on Kashmīr rivers.

108.

nābȧd^{i}*-bāras aṭa-ganḍ ḍyol*^{u} *gōm*
dĕn-kār hol^{u} *gōm hĕka kahyū*
gŏra-sond^{u} *wanun rāwan-tyol*^{u} *pyōm*
pahāli-rost^{u} *khyol*^{u} *gōm hĕka kahyū*

The sling of the load of candy hath become loose upon my (shoulder).

Crooked for me hath become my day's work. How can I succeed?

The words of my teacher have fallen upon me like a blister of loss.

My flock hath lost its shepherd. How can I succeed?

Another of Lallā's hard sayings. Its meaning is apparently as follows:—

Like Christian in *The Pilgrim's Progress*, she has been bearing on her back a burden of worldly illusions and pleasures, compared to a load of sugar-candy, and the knot of the porter's sling that supports it has become loose and galls her. In other words, she has found that such a burden produces only toil and pain. Her wasted life in this workaday world has become a weariness, and she is in despair.

She has recourse to her *Guru*, or spiritual teacher. His words cause her intolerable pain—a pain such as that experienced by the loss of some loved object (the worldly illusion which she must abandon), and she learns that the whole flock of factors that make up her sentient existence have lost their proper ruler, the mind; for it is steeped in ignorance of Self.

109.

ạnd^{a}*riy āyĕs tsạnd*^{a}*riy gārān*
gārān āyĕs hihĕn hih^{i}
ts^{a}*y, hē Nārān! ts*^{a}*y, hē Nārān!*
ts^{a}*y, hē Nārān! yim kam vih*^{i}

Searching and seeking came I from my inner soul into the moonlight.

Searching and seeking came I to know that like are joined to like.

This All is only Thou, O Nārāyaṇa, only Thou.

Only Thou. What are all these Thy sports?

For the comparison of the moonlight to true knowledge, see the Vocabulary, s. v. *sōm*.

'Like joined to like': i. e. the Self is the same as the Supreme Self, and must become absorbed in it.

Nārāyaṇa is generally the name for the Supreme employed by Vaiṣṇavas. Here it is employed by the Śaiva Lallā. The expression 'sport' is a well-known technical term for the changes apparently undergone by the Deity, by which He manifests Himself in creation.

Lallā asks, What are these manifestations? The answer, of course, being that they are all unreal illusion.

APPENDIX I

VERSES BY LALLĀ IN KNOWLES'S DICTIONARY OF KASHMIRI PROVERBS

Mr. Hinton Knowles's valuable *Dictionary of Kashmiri Proverbs and Sayings* (Bombay, 1885) contains a number of verses attributed to Lallā. With Mr. Knowles's kind permission, I have excerpted them and give them in the following appendix. The spelling of the Kāshmīrī quotations has necessarily been changed to agree with the system of transliteration adopted for the preceding pages, and here and there I have had occasion to modify the translations. But, save for a few verbal alterations, Mr. Knowles's valuable notes have been left untouched.

These verses are quoted by the abbreviation K. Pr. with the number of the page of the original work. [G. A. G.]

K. Pr. 18.

Āyĕs watē ta gayĕs ti watē ;
Swamana[1]*-sŏthi lūstum dŏh ;*
Wuchum candas ta hār na athē.
Nāwa-tāras kyāh dima bŏh ?

(Cf. No. 98 above.)

I came by a way (i. e. I was born) and I also went by a way (i. e. I died).

When I was on the embankment of (the illusions of) my own mind (i. e. when my spirit was between the two worlds), the day failed.

I looked in my pocket, but not a cowry came to hand.

What shall I give for crossing the ferry ?

[1] Original has *sĕmanz*. Cf. L. V. 98.

A saying of Lal Dĕd, who was a very holy Hindū woman.

The Kāshmīrī Hindū belief is that during the sixth month after death the spirit of the deceased has to cross the waters of the Vaitaraṇī; but it is impossible to get to the other side of the river except by special means, as the waters are so deep and stormy and the opposing powers, *prĕta*, *yamadut*, *matsya*, and *kūrma* are so strong. Accordingly about this time the bereaved relations call the family Brāhmaṇ, who repeats to them the portions appointed to be read on this occasion. Among other things the departed spirit is represented as standing on the brink of the river and crying 'Where is my father? Where is my mother? Where are my relations and my friends? Is there no one to help me over this river?' This is sometimes recited with much feeling, and great are the lamentations of the bereaved, who now with sobs and tears present a little boat and paddle, made of gold, or silver, or copper, according to their position, to the Brāhmaṇ; and in the boat they place *ghī*, milk, butter, and rice. The boat is for the conveyance of the spirit across Vaitaraṇī, and the provisions are for the appeasement of the contrary powers, *prĕta*, *matsya*, and others, who will try to turn back the boat, but who on having these, *ghī* and rice, &c., thrown to them, will at once depart their own way.

The Hindūs believe that if this ceremony is performed in a right manner, a boat will be at once present upon the waters, close to that portion of the bank of the river, where the spirit is waiting and praying for it, and that the spirit getting into it will be safely conveyed to the opposite side. The gift-boat, however, is taken home by the Brāhmaṇ, and generally turned into money as soon as possible.

At the moment of death amongst other things a *paisā* is placed within the mouth of the corpse, wherewith to pay the ferry.

K. Pr. 20.

Āyĕ wönis gayĕ kādris.

She came to the baniyā's but arrived at the baker's.

To miss the mark.

This saying has its original in a story well known in Kashmīr. Lal Dĕd, whose name has been mentioned before, used to peregrinate in an almost nude condition, and was constantly saying that 'He only was a man, who feared God, and there were very few such men about.'

One day, Shāh Hamadān, after whom the famous mosque in Śrīnagar is called, met her, and she at once ran away. This was a strange thing for Lal Dĕd to do; but it was soon explained. 'I have seen a man', she said, to the astonished baniyā, into whose shop she had fled for refuge. The baniyā, however, turned her out. Then Lal Dĕd rushed to the baker's house and jumped into the oven, which at that time was fully heated for baking the bread. When the baker saw this he fell down in a swoon, thinking that, for certain, the king would hear of this and punish him. However, there was no need to fear, as Lal Dĕd presently appeared from the mouth of the oven clad in clothes of gold, and hastened after Shāh Hamadān. Cf. *Panjāb Notes and Queries*, ii. 743.

K. Pr. 46.

Daman-basti ditō dil, damanas yitha daman-khār.
Shĕstᵃras sŏn gatshiy hŏsil; wuñĕ chĕy sul ta tsā̃ḍun yār.
Sŏdᵃras nō labiy sŏhil, na tath sum ta na tath tār.
Par kar paida parwāz tul; wuñĕ chĕy sul ta tsā̃ḍun yār.
Gŏfilō hᵃka ta kadam tul; hushyār rōz trāv pyŏdil.
Trāwakh nay ta chukh jŏhil; wuñĕ chĕy sul ta tshā̃ḍun yār.

(Cf. Nos. 99 and 100 above.)

Give the heart to the bellows, like as the blacksmith gives breath to the bellows,

And your iron will become gold. Now it is early morning, seek out your friend (i.e. God).

(A man) will not find a shore to the sea, neither is there a bridge over it, nor any other means of crossing.

Make to yourself wings and fly. Now it is early morning, seek out your friend.

O negligent man, speedily step out, take care, and leave off wickedness.

If you will not, then you are a fool. Now while it is early morning, seek out your friend.

A few lines from Lal Dĕd constantly quoted by the Kāshmīrī.

Pyŏdil—the work of a chaprāsī, a bad lot, as he generally makes his money by oppression, lying, and cheating.

K. Pr. 47.

Dàmiy ḍīṭhᵘ̈m nad pakawūñᵘ̈y, dàmiy ḍyūṭhum sum na ta tār.
Dàmiy ḍīṭhᵘ̈m thūrᵘ̈ phŏlawūñᵘ̈y, dàmiy ḍyūṭhum gul na ta khār.
Dàmiy ḍīṭhᵘ̈m pānćan Pāṇḍawan hünzᵘ̈ mōjᵘ̈, dàmiy ḍīṭhᵘ̈m krōjiy mās.

(Cf. Nos. 96, 97 above.)

One moment I saw a little stream flowing, another moment I saw neither a bridge, nor any other means of crossing.

At one time I saw a bush blooming, at another time I saw neither a flower nor a thorn.

At one moment I saw the mother of the five Pāṇḍavas, at another moment I saw a potter's wife's aunt.

'Nothing in this world can last.'

The history of the Pāṇḍavas, and how their mother was reduced by misfortune to profess herself a potter's wife's aunt, are fully explained in the *Mahābhārata*.

K. Pr. 56.

Dilakis bāgas dūrᵘ̈ kar gösil.
Ada dĕwa phŏliy yẹmbᵃrzal bāg.
Marith manganay wumri-hünzᵘ̈ hösil.
Maut chuy pata pata tahsīl-dār.

Keep away dirt from the garden of thy heart.

Then perhaps the Narcissus-garden will blossom for thee.

After death thou wilt be asked for the results of thy life.

Death is after thee like a *tahsīldār* (a tax-collector).

K. Pr. 57.

Diluk[u] khura-khura mĕ, Māli, kāstam, manaki kōtar-marē.
Ňarĕ lōsam lūka-hanzay larĕ ladān.
Yĕli pāna myānuv kaḍith ninanay panani garē,
Pata pata nēri lūka-sāsā narĕ ālawān.
Trövith yinanay manz-maidānas sövith dachiñi lari.

Make far from me longing for the unobtainable, O Father—from the pigeon-hole of my heart.

My arm is wearied from making other people's houses (i.e. from helping others, giving alms, &c.).

When, O my body, they will carry you forth (*ninanay* for *ninay*) from your house,

Afterwards, afterwards, a thousand people will come waving their arms.

They will come and set you in a field, laying you to sleep on your right side.

A verse of Lal Dĕd's constantly quoted in part, or *in toto*, in time of trouble.

Hindūs burn the bodies laying them upon the right side, with their head towards the south, because the gods and good spirits live in that direction, and Yama, the angel of death, also resides there.

K. Pr. 102.

Kĕntsan dit^{i}tham gŏlāla yüts$^{\ddot{u}}$y ;
Kĕntsan zṓn^{u}tham na dĕnas wār ;
Kĕntsan tshuñ$^{\ddot{u}}$tham nöl^{i} brahma-hüts$^{\ddot{u}}$y.
Bagawāna cyāñĕ güts$^{\ddot{u}}$ namaskār.

To some you gave many poppies (i.e. sons);

For some you did not know the fortunate hour of the day (for giving a child), (i.e. have left them childless);

And some you haltered (with a daughter) for murdering a Brāhmaṇ (in some former existence).

O Bhagawān, (the Deity, the Most High), I adore Thy greatness.

Kĕntsan dyut^{u}tham ōray ālav, kĕntsav racyēyĕ nāla Vĕth.
Kĕntsan achĕ lajĕ mas cĕth tālav, kĕ̃h gay wānan phālav dith.

Some Thou (O God) calledst from Thy heaven (lit. from there); some snatched the river Jihlam by the neck of its coat, (i.e. grasped prosperity).

Some have drunk wine and lifted their eyes upwards; some have gone and closed their shops.

Whom God will, God blesses.

Kĕntsan dyut^{u}tham yut^{u} kĕhō tot^{u}, kĕntsan yut^{u} na ta tot^{u} kyāh ?

God has given to some (blessing) here and there (i.e. in both worlds), and He has given to some nothing either here or there.

Kĕntsan rañĕ chĕy shĕhüj$^{\ddot{u}}$ būñ$^{\ddot{u}}$, nērav nĕbar shĕhol^{u} karav.
Kĕntsan rañĕ chĕy bar pĕṭh hųñ$^{\ddot{u}}$, nērav nĕbar ta zang khĕyiwō.
Kĕntsan rañĕ chĕy adal ta wadal; kĕntsan rañē chĕy zadal tshāy.

Some have wives like a shady plane-tree, let us go out under it and cool ourselves.

Some have wives like the bitch at the door, let us go out and get our legs bitten.

Some have wives always in confusion, and some have wives like shade full of holes.

['Shade full of holes', such as that cast by a worn-out thatch.]

K. Pr. 150.

Naphs$^{\ddot{u}}$*ẏy myōn*^{u} *chuy hostuy, ȧm*^{i} *hȧst*^{i} *mong*^{u}*nam gari gari bal;*
Lachĕ-manza sūsa-manza akhāh lūstuy, na-ta hĕt^{i}*nam söriy tal.*

My soul is like an elephant, and that elephant asked me every hour for food;

Out of a lākh and out of a thousand but one is saved; if it hadn't been so, the elephant had crushed all under his feet for me (i. e. in my presence).

One's craving lusts.

K. Pr. 201.

Sirĕs hyuh^{u} *na prakāsh kunē;*
Gangi hyuh^{u} *na tīr*^{a}*th kāh;*
Böyis hyuh^{u} *na bāndav kunē;*
Rañĕ hyuh^{u} *na sukh kāh;*

Achĕn hyuh^{u} *na prakāsh kunē;*
Kŏṭhĕn hyuh^{u} *na tīr*^{a}*th kāh;*
Candas hyuh^{u} *na bāndav kunē;*
Khañi hyuh^{u} *na sukh kāh;*

Māyi hyuh^{u} *na prakāsh kunē;*
Layi hyuh^{u} *na tīr*^{a}*th kāh;*
Dayĕs hyuh^{u} *na bāndav kunē;*
Bayĕs hyuh^{u} *na sukh kāh;*

Sĕd Bāyū was one day, sitting down with his famous female disciple, Lal Dĕd, when the following questions cropped up:—

'Which was the greatest of all lights?' 'Which was the most famous of all pilgrimages?' 'Which was the best of all relations?' 'Which was the best of all manner of ease?' Lal was the first to reply:—

'There is no light like that of the sun;
There is no pilgrimage like Gangā;
There is no relation like a brother;
There is no ease like that of a wife.'

But Sĕd did not quite agree. 'No', said he—

'There is no light like that of the eyes;
There is no pilgrimage like that of the knees;
There is no relation like one's pocket;
There is no ease like that of a blanket.'

Then Lal Dĕd, determining not to be outwitted by her master, again replied:—

'There is no light like that of the knowledge of God;

There is no pilgrimage like that of an ardent love;

There is no relation to be compared with the Deity;

There is no ease like that got from the fear of God.'

I have seen something like a part of the above lines in the Rev. C. Swynnerton's *Adventures of Rājā Rasālū*, but not having the book at hand I cannot say in what connexion they occur there.[1]

Gangā or *Gangābal* is one of the great Hindū places of pilgrimage. Hither go all those Paṇḍits, who have had relations die during the year, carrying some small bones, which they had picked from the ashes at the time of the burning of the dead bodies. These bones are thrown into the sacred waters of Gangābal with money and sweetmeats. The pilgrimage takes place about the 8th day of the Hindū month Bādarpĕt (August 20th *cir.*). Cf. Vigne's *Travels in Kashmīr*, &c., vol. ii, pp. 151, 152.

[[1] See Swynnerton, *Romantic Tales from the Panjâb*, pp. 198 ff.]

APPENDIX II

ON LALLĀ'S LANGUAGE

[By Sir George Grierson.]

Lallā lived in the fourteenth century. These songs have been handed down by word of mouth, and it has been pointed out in the Introduction how in the course of centuries, as the colloquial language changed, the language in which they were originally composed insensibly changed too.[1] We cannot therefore be surprised at finding that the verses as here published are, on the whole, in the Kāshmīrī spoken at the present day. A certain number of archaic forms have, however, survived; some, on account of their very strangeness, which marked them as old-fashioned, and others, because the language of poetry, with its unvarying laws of metre, always changes more slowly than does that of colloquial speech. In this latter respect the compositions of Lallā are not alone in Kashmīr, and all the poetry of her country, even that written in the last century, contains many archaic forms. We therefore find scattered through these verses several examples of words and of idioms which throw light on the history of the Kāshmīrī language, and no apology is needed for drawing attention to the more important. It should be understood that these examples as quoted do not illustrate the general language of the songs, which is much more modern than would be gathered from the mere perusal of this Appendix. Throughout it is assumed that the reader has an elementary acquaintance with modern Kāshmīrī.

Metrical requirements often demand a long syllable at the

[1] So also the Vedic hymns were for centuries handed down by word of mouth, and Lallā's songs give a valuable example of the manner in which their language must have changed from generation to generation before their text was finally established.

end of a line, and we frequently find in this position a long, where the modern language would employ a short, vowel. I have noted all these instances because a number of cases of apparent lengthening also occurs when the vowel is not final in a line, and is not required by the metre to be long. We are therefore not justified in assuming that such long vowels at the end of a line have been lengthened merely for the sake of metre.

Vocabulary.—There are a few words of which the meaning is doubtful, and two or three of which the meaning is altogether unknown at the present day. Such are *līlåmⁱ* (81) and (all in 84–5) *huda-hudañĕy*, *rūza-dāñĕ*, and *abakh*. The first is said to mean 'sports' (cf. Skr. *līlā*), but I have found no tradition as to the meaning of the others. I may note here that in other Kāshmīrī literature which, like Lallā's songs, is preserved by memory and not in writing, such words are not uncommon, and that the reciters, and, when consulted, even Paṇḍits, are never ashamed to confess ignorance of their meaning. As to the genuineness of these unknown words, and as to the general correctness of texts so preserved, the reader is referred to the remarks on pp. 3 ff. of the Introduction.

In this connexion we may note a termination *-wŏnᵘ*, forming nouns of agency or possession, which I have not noted in the modern language. It occurs in the words *shruta-wŏnᵘ*, a hearer; *brama-wŏnᵘ*, a wanderer; *pruthi-wŏnᵘ*, of, or belonging to, the earth; and *shūba-wŏnᵘ*, beautiful. It runs parallel with the modern termination *-wŏlᵘ* (= Hindī *-wālā*), but I am inclined to look upon it rather as directly derived from the Sanskrit termination *-vān*, perhaps influenced as to its form by the analogy of *-wŏlᵘ*. Cf. Skr. *śruta-vān*, *bhrama-vān*, *pṛthvī-mān*, and *śōbhā-vān*.

Occasionally we find *tatsama* forms employed where the modern language employs semi-*tatsamas*. Thus, we have *snān* (mod. *shrān*), bathing; *sūrya* (mod. *sirĕ*), the sun; *sarwa* (mod. *sŏrᵘ*), all. We may note that, for this last word, the Hindī form *sab* also occurs. So, we have *pyuwum* (for *piwum*), compared with Hindī *piyā*, but Modern Kāshmīrī *cyōm*, I drank; *ḍyūkhukh* (for *ḍēkhukh*), compared with H. *dēkhā*, but Mod. K. *ḍyūṭhukh* (for *ḍēṭhukh*), saw thee; *kiyĕm*, compared with H. *kiyā*, but Mod. K. *karĕm*, I made (f. pl. object).

The ordinary word for the numeral 'one' is *akh* or *ok*ᵘ, but Lallā also has *yĕk*ᵘ, which may be compared with the Hindī *ĕk*.

Other miscellaneous instances of unusual vocabulary are *vyuh*ᵘ (Mod. *vih*), appearance; *yund*ᵘ, an organ (*indriya*); *kond*ᵘ, some one, any one (in pl. ag. *kandĕv*); *kyōh* or *kyāwu* (Mod. *kyāh*), or, as well as; *kō-zana* or *kō-zanañi*, by what means?; *pushĕrun* (Mod. *pushĕrun*), to make over; *nā*, *nō* (Mod. *na*), not; and *mau* or *mō* (Mod. *ma*), prohibitive particle.

Phonetics.—*Vowels.*—As in Modern Kāshmīrī, *a* following *c*, *ch*, or *sh* becomes *ĕ*, though as often as not written *a*. No examples have been found of the written change after *c*, but for *ch* we have *lachĕ*, for *lacha*, the oblique form singular of *lach*, a hundred thousand, and there are numerous examples of the change after *sh*, of which *shĕnkar*, for *shankar*, Śaṅkara, will suffice. It is, of course, a commonplace of Kāshmīrī that *i* and *ĕ* are interchangeable, and that the ordinary speaker is unable to distinguish between the two sounds. It thus follows that after *ch*, *a*, *ĕ*, and *i* are all written interchangeably for the same sound—*ĕ*. Thus, *bŏchi-sūty*, (dying) of hunger, is indifferently written with *bŏcha*, *bŏchĕ*, or *bŏchi*. In verse 83, we have *bŏcha*, although the sound of *bŏchi* is certainly intended.

Similarly in the modern language interchange of *ē* and *ī* is equally universal. Lallā goes further, in that she has both *gēh* and *gih*, a house; and *dēh* and *dih*, the body. We may judge from this that she pronounced *gēh* as *gĕh*, and *dēh* as *dĕh*.

In the modern language *ai* (which is interchangeable with *ō*) generally becomes *ū* when followed by *u*-mātrā, and becomes *ǖ* when followed by *i*-mātrā or *ü*-mātrā. Thus, the base *yait-*, or *yōt-*, as much (as), has its nominative singular masculine *yūt*ᵘ, its nominative plural masculine *yǖt*ⁱ, and its nominative singular feminine *yǖċ*ᵘ̈. Similarly, there is a modern Kāshmīrī word *pūr*[u], a foot, for which Lallā gives the plural ablative as *pairiv*, showing that the base of the word is *pair-*. No instance occurs of the form which she would give to the nominative singular of this word, but she would probably have used *pairu*, for, in the place of the modern Kāshmīrī *yūt*[u], she uses *yaitu*, and, in the place of modern *kūt*[i] (nom. pl. masc.), how many?, she has *kait*[i]. In other words, in Lallā's time, *ai* preserved its sound before *u*-mātrā and *i*-mātrā, and probably also before *ü*-mātrā, and the epenthetic change to *ū* and *ǖ* seems to have come into the language since her days. This is borne out by the very fluctuating methods employed in indicating these changes in writing at the present time.

Consonants.—As in the modern language, there are no sonant aspirates. They are occasionally written in *tatsamas*, but even here there is no consistency, and when a sonant aspirate is written we may be sure that the fact is of no importance. On the other hand, we must not reject the possibility that the customary omission of the aspiration of sonant aspirates is not original, but has been introduced during the process of handing down the text by word of mouth. In other words, we can judge nothing from the presence or the omission of the aspiration.

We are, however, on surer ground when we approach the second great law of Kāshmīrī pronunciation—that a final surd is always aspirated. These are regularly aspirated throughout the whole text, and this is original, and is not due to modern pronunciation. Thus in verse 5, *rāth*, night, rhymes with *nāth*, a lord. Now, the *th* of *nāth* is original, and owes nothing to the special Kāshmīrī rule, but the original form of *rāth* is *rāṭ*, and the *t* has been aspirated under the special rule. The fact that *rāt* would not rhyme with *nāth* shows that Lallā pronounced the word as *rāth*, and that consequently she did aspirate her final surds.

Modern Kāshmīrī has a very weak feeling of the difference between cerebrals and often interchanges them, and also commonly, in village dialect, interchanges a cerebral *ṭ* or *ḍ* with a dental *r*. So, Lallā has *död*[i], for modern *ḍöḍ*[i], thoroughly, continually (compare Sanskrit *dārḍhya-*); *dēshun* or *ḍēshun*, to see (**dṛśyati*); *cēḍun* or *cērun*, to mount; *gaṭun* or *garun*, to form; *hyuḍ*^{u} (mod. *hyur*^{u}), the gullet; *mūḍun* or *mūrun*, to triturate; *paḍun* or *parun* to recite; *zūḍ*^{u} or *zūr*^{u}, bad habits.

Here also we may draw attention to the well-known fact that Kāshmīrī has no cerebral *ṇ*. A dental *n* is always substituted for it. Thus, Skr. *kāṇa-*, one-eyed, is represented by Ksh. *kồn*^{u}. This *n*, representing an original *ṇ*, Lallā has changed to a dental *r* in the form *kồr*^{u}. Finally, in this connexion, we have a modern dental *l* represented by Lallā's dental *r* in her *chōr*, for *chūl*, a waterfall.

The modern language shows a tendency to insert a *w* before a long *ā* in the first syllable of a word. So, Lallā has *gwāh* (modern *gāh*), illumination; *gārun* or *gwārun*, to search; and *sās* or *swās*, ashes.

We have interchange of *d* and *z* in *wudun* or *wuzun*, to awake from sleep.[1]

Declension.—*Substantives and Adjectives.*—Kāshmīrī has four declensions, viz. (1) a masculine *a*-declension; (2) a masculine *i*-declension; (3) a feminine *i*-declension; and (4) a feminine *a*-declension. This is the general explanation of the forms involved, and is a good representation of the present state of affairs, but from the point of view of origin it is not quite accurate. The true grouping would be to class the second and third declensions as *ka*-suffix-declensions, and the first and fourth as non-*ka*-suffix declensions. All nouns in the first and second declensions are masculine, and all those in the third and fourth are feminine. Some of the nouns of the fourth declension have really *i*-bases, and what distinguishes them from nouns of the third declension is not that they follow an *a*-declension—which they do not—but that they had no original *ka*-suffix.

For the sake of simplicity, I take the non-*ka*-suffix nouns first, and begin with the first, or masculine, declension. This

[1] The letter *dh* becomes *z* before *y*. *Wuzi* probably < *budhyatē*, while *bōzi*, he hears, < *bōdhyatē*.

is quite correctly described as an *a*-declension. Even the few surviving *i*- and *u*-bases follow it. Thus, the word *gös*ᵘ, a grass-seller, follows this declension, although it must be referred to a Sanskrit *i*-base **ghāsin-*. The typical declension in the modern language is as follows:—

	Singular.	Plural.
Nom.	*ṭsūr*, a thief.	*ṭsūr*.
Dat.	*ṭsūras*.	*ṭsūran*.
Instr. and Ag.	(*ṭsūr*ⁱ), *ṭsūran*.	*ṭsūrav*.
Abl.	(*ṭsūri*), *ṭsūra*.	*ṭsūrav*.

It will be observed that, as in Prakrit, the dative is represented by the old genitive (*cōrasya*, *cōrassa*; *cōrāṇām*, *cōrāṇa*). The forms in brackets given for the instr. and abl. singular are nowadays described as 'old forms' and occur only in special words and idioms. The *i*-termination is to be referred to the Prakrit *-hi*. The instrumental and agent case is everywhere only a special form of the case which I call the ablative. The latter is used in many senses, and its use closely corresponds to that of the Latin ablative. Like that, it is frequently governed by a postposition corresponding to the Latin preposition. In such circumstances it corresponds to the general oblique case of Hindī nouns, and may, itself, also be called the 'oblique case', as is occasionally done in these pages.

In the old Apabhraṁśa dialect current in Kashmīr before the birth of Kāshmīrī the nominative and accusative singular of *a*-bases, masculine and neuter, ended in *-u*. Thus, in the first two verses of the ancient Kashmīr Apabhraṁśa work entitled the *Mahártha-prakāśa*, we have *paru* for *param*; *ghasmaru* for *ghasmaraḥ*; *bhairu* for *bhairavaḥ*; and *cakku* for *cakram*. This termination survived into Lallā's time, for she has *paramu* for *paramaḥ* in v. 77.

We have interesting survivals of the oldest form of the modern dative singular. In v. 22, Lallā treats the word *ātmā*, self, as an *a*-base, and gives it a genitive *ātmāsĕ* (m. c. for *ātmāsi*), which I explain as a contraction of **ātmassa*, with a survival of the original *y* of **ātmasya*,—Kāshmīrī pronunciation **ātmāsĕ*,—in the final *i*; or possibly she may have unconsciously endeavoured to reproduce a quasi-Sanskrit **ātmāsya*. So, again, she has *dēwas* for Prakrit *dēvassa*, of a god, in 33, in which, according to the rule in all the Dardic languages, a vowel is not lengthened in compensation for the simplification of a consonantal group.

In the modern language the ablative generally ends in a short *-a*—a shortening of one of the Prakrit terminations *-āō*, *ā*, or of the Apabhraṁśa *-ahu*. Lallā occasionally has ablatives ending in long *ā*, as in *ōsā* and *sāsā* in 18. Other examples are *trațā* (1) and *vimarshā* (16), but these occur at the end of a line, and the vowel may have been lengthened for the sake of rhyme.

The instrumental-agent in ^{i} and the ablative in *i* may be considered together. They are used in various senses. A locative is very common. For the pure instrumental, we have *abhyōs*^{i} in verse 1. Locatives are *gagàn*^{i}, in the sky (26); *mani*, in the mind (18, 45); and *ànt*^{i} (54) or *àntih*^{i} (33, 37, &c.), in the end. In the last example, the original *hi*-termination has survived. Lallā sometimes substitutes *ē* for the final *i*, as in *athē*, in the hand (10). In other cases the words occur at the end of a line, so that it is possible that the *ē* is here only *i* lengthened for the sake of metre. They are *athē* (98); *garē*, in the house (3, 34); *māwāsē*, on the day of the new moon (22). This termination *i* of the ablative occurs in all declinations, and we shall see that Lallā's change of the *i* to *ē* is very common.

In the modern language the instrumental-ablative plural ends in *-av*, also written *-au*. Perhaps *-au̯* would be the best representation of the true sound. We are at once reminded of the Prakrit termination *-āō*, *-āu*, Apabhraṁśa *-āhũ*, of the ablative plural. In one place (53) Lallā has *garu*, which is to be translated as the locative plural of *gara*, a house. Its origin is evidently the same as that of the form with *-av*.

The other non-*ka*-declension is the fourth, and includes all the feminine nouns of this class. It has two divisions, viz. *a*-bases and *i*-bases. As an example of the modern declension of an *a*-base, we will take *māl* (Skr. *mālā*), a garland.

	Singular.	Plural.
Nom.	*māl.*	*māla.*
Dat.	*māli.*	*mālan.*
Instr.-Abl.	*māli.*	*mālav* (*mālaṷ*).

Which may be compared with the following Prakrit forms:—

	Singular.	Plural.
Nom.	*mālā.*	*mālāō.*
Gen.	*mālāē, mālāi.*	*mālāṇa.*
Abl.	*mālāi*, Ap. *mālahe.*	*mālāu*, Ap. *mālahu.*

It will be observed that Kāshmīrī has throughout lost the distinguishing termination *-ā* of the feminine. So also in Apabhraṁśa (Hc. iv, 330. Cf. Pischel, § 100).

Besides the above, Lallā has other forms. For the dative singular, she has *dārĕ* (74), in the flood, and *watē* (98), on a road. Numerous other instances of datives or agents singular in *-ē* occur at the end of a line, such as *hālē* (4), from *hāl*, a bellows-pipe; *Lalē* (76), by Lallā; *prahē* (105), by love; *tanē* (76), to the body (Pr. *taṇūē*); *watē* (98), on the road; *yitshē* (45), with a wish (*icchā*); *zūnē* (9), to the moonlight (*jyōtsnāyāḥ, joṇhāē*).

The second division, consisting of nouns with *i*-bases, is the so-called irregular fourth declension. In the nominative singular the termination *-i* of the bases is dropped, and the word is otherwise unchanged. But in the other cases, before the old vowel terminations, the *-i-* with the following vowel becomes *ü*-mātrā. This *ü*-mātrā, according to the usual Kāshmīrī phonetic rules, has certain epenthetic effects on the preceding vowel and consonant, for which see the usual grammars. The word *hān* (Skr. *hāni-*), loss, is therefore thus declined:—

	Singular.	Plural.
Nom.	*hān.*	*hȫñ*ü.
Dat.	*hȫñ*ü.	*hȫñ*ü*n.*
Instr.-Abl.	*hȫñ*ü.	*hȫñ*ü*v.*

The corresponding Prakrit declension would be:—

	Singular.	Plural.
Nom.	*hāṇī.*	*hāṇīō*, Ap. *hāṇiu.*
Gen.	*hāṇīi.*	*hāṇīṇa.*
Abl.	*hāṇīi.*	*hāṇīu*, Ap. *hāṇihũ.*

As modern Kāshmīrī *ü*-mātrā represents an original ī̆, it is not surprising that Lallā should use the older form *dö̃ñi*, as the agent case of *dā̃n*, a stream (39, 40), instead of the modern *dö̃ñü*.

Turning now to the *ka*-declensions, these are the second and the third. The second declension consists only of masculine nouns, and the third only of feminine.

In the case of an *a*-base, the original termination of the base, together with the *ka*-suffix, becomes *-aka-*, and in the case of an *i*-base it becomes *-ika-*. I have not yet noted any instance in Kāshmīrī of the *ka*-suffix added to a *u*-base.

In the second declension, an *a*-base is thus declined in the modern language. The noun selected is *wā̃duru*, a monkey:—

	Singular.	Plural.
Nom.	*wā̃duru*, *wā̃dur.*	*wā̃dar.*
Dat.	*wā̃duras.*	*wā̃daran.*
Abl.	*wā̃dara.*	*wā̃darav.*

The corresponding Prakrit forms would be:—

	Singular.	Plural.
Nom.	*vāṇaraō.*	*vāṇaraā.*
Gen.	*vāṇaraassa.*	*vāṇaraāṇa.*
Abl.	*vāṇaraāō*, *vāṇaraā.*	*vāṇaraāō.*

It will be observed that, except in the nominative singular, the Kāshmīrī declension has become exactly the same as in the first—non-*ka*-—declension. The nominative singular is really *wā̃daru*, but, as usual, the final *u*-mātrā epenthetically affects the preceding *a*, and the word becomes *wā̃doru* or *wā̃duru*. As *u*-mātrā is not itself sounded, this is commonly written *wā̃dur*, and words of this group are treated by Kāshmīrī grammarians as exceptional words of the first declension.

For a *ka*-noun with an *i*-base, we have as an example the word *host*^{u}, an elephant. The modern base of this word is *hast-*, but, in the nominative singular, the *a* has become *o* under the influence of the following *u*-mātrā. It is thus declined:—

	Singular.	Plural.
Nom.	*host*^{u}.	*hàst*^{i}.
Dat.	*hastis*.	*hastĕn* (for *hastyan*).
Instr.-Ag.	*hàst*^{i}.	*hastĕv* (for *hastyau̥*).
Abl.	*hasti*.	

The word *host*^{u} represents an earlier *hastikaḥ*, and this would be declined as follows in Prakrit:—

	Singular.	Plural.
Nom.	*hatthiō*, Ap. *hatthiu*.	*hatthiā*.
Gen.	*hatthiassa*.	*hatthiāṇa*.
Abl.	*hatthiāhi*, Ap. *hatthiahe*.	*hatthiāu*, Ap. *hatthiahũ*.

The Kāshmīrī word *host*^{u} is not a *tatsama*. In Kāshmīrī a Prakrit *tth* is not uncommonly represented by *st*. E.g. Skr. *sárthakaḥ*, Pr. *satthaō*, Māgadhī Pr. *śastaē*, Ksh. *sost*^{u}, possessed of.

It is a noteworthy fact that while some Kāshmīrī *a*-bases with the *ka*-suffix are declined like *wădur*^{u}, the great majority have changed their base-forms, and are treated as if they were *i*-bases. For instance, the word *gur*^{u}, a horse (sg. dat. *guris*, abl. *guri*, and so on) follows *host*^{u}, an *i*-base, although the Sanskrit original is *ghōṭakaḥ*, Pr. *ghōḍaō*, which is an *a*-base. This peculiarity certainly goes back as far as Lallā's time. She gives us *hàt*^{i} (32) as the plural nominative of *hot*^{u} (*hatakaḥ*), struck, and *mŏkh*^{a}*t*^{i} (6), the plural nominative of *mŏkh*^{o}*t*^{u} (*muktakaḥ*), released, and so many others. In one case she hesitates between the two forms. She takes the word *makor*^{u} or *makur*^{u}, a mirror, and gives its dative singular as *makuras* (*a*-base) in 31, and as *makaris* (*i*-base) in 18.

I suggest that the origin of the treatment of *a*-bases as if they were *i*-bases is of a complex character. In the first place, when the intervocalic *k* of the *ka*-suffix is elided, a *y* may or may not be substituted for it. If no *y* is inserted, the word remains an *a*-base, and there is an end of the matter. But if a *y* is inserted, a word such as *ghōṭakaḥ* becomes *ghōḍayō*, from which the transition to **guriu*, *gur^u* is easy. Then, again, the fact of the analogy of feminine *ka*-bases must be taken into account. Practically all these end in *-ika-*, and in Kāshmīrī must be treated as *i*-bases. Finally, we know that in dialectic Prakrit *-ika-* was sometimes substituted for *-aka-* (Pischel, § 598). I believe that all these three causes contributed to the change of *a*-bases to *i*-bases in Kāshmīrī.

We have seen that in modern Kāshmīrī the sg. abl. of an *i*-base in this declension ends in *-i*, as in *hasti*. Lallā occasionally makes it end in *-ē*, and this is quite in accordance with the Prakrit form. Thus, from *dūr^u*, far, she has *dūrē* (36), for modern *dūri*; and from *mör^u*, a hut, she has *marē* (K. Pr. 57), for mod. *mari*. The latter word occurs at the end of a line, and the termination may be due to metrical exigencies.

The pl. nom. ends in ^{i}, as in *håst^i*. Lallā on three occasions lengthens this ^{i}, when at the end of a line, to *ī* or *ē*, viz. in *haṇḍī*, rams (77); *nalī*, cowry-shells (81); and *samē*, alike (16).

She makes the plural ablative end in *-iv* in *pairiv*, from *pūr^u*, a foot (38). This, however, is little more than a matter of spelling.

The third, or feminine *ka*-declension appears in the following form in the modern language. The word taken as an example is *gur^ü* a mare.

	Singular.	Plural.
Nom.	*gur^ü*.	*gurĕ* (for *gurya*).
Dat.	*gurĕ* (for *gurya*).	*gurĕn* (for *guryan*).
Instr.-Abl.	*guri*.	*gurĕv* (for *guryau̯*).

The corresponding Prakrit forms would be:—

	Singular.	Plural.
Nom.	*ghōḍiā*.	*ghōḍiā*.
Gen.	*ghōḍiāē*, *ghōḍiāi*.	*ghōḍiāṇa*.
Abl.	*ghōḍiāē*, Ap. *ghōḍiahe*.	*ghōḍiāu*, Ap. *ghōḍiahu*.

As *ĕ* and *i* are interchangeable in Kāshmīrī, the difference between the singular dative and ablative is only one of spelling, and as a matter of custom the two forms are often interchanged even by the most careful writers. The spelling given here is that of Īśvara-kaula.

It should be remembered that *ü*-mātrā in Kāshmīrī represents an original *ĭ*, so that the older form of *gur*[ü] would be *gurĭ*. So Lallā has *hishi* for *hish*[ü], like, in 10 and 77; *möji* (97, end of line), for *möj*[ü], a mother; *pushöñī* (39, 49, end of line), for *pushöñ*[ü], a florist; *thajī* (33, end of line), for *thüj*[ü], a shrine.

So, for the singular dative, we have *wahawañī*, for *wahawañĕ*, flowing (57, end of line).

The Genitive Case.—Lallā's use of the genitive differs somewhat from that customary in modern Kāshmīrī. Nowadays there are three suffixes of the genitive, with sharply distinguished functions. These are *-uk*[u], *-un*[u], and *-hond*[u]. The suffix *-uk*[u] is used with all singular masculine nouns without life. In this case Lallā follows the modern custom.

The suffix *-un*[u] (fem. *-üñ*[ü]) is used only with singular male proper names, as in *rāmun*[u], of Rāma. Lallā uses it with other nouns also, as in *samsārun*[u], of the universe (6); *maranüñ*[ü] (fem.), of dying (73–6); *puhun*[u], of the month of Pauṣa (83); *huda-hudüñ*[ü] (84) (fem.), of unknown meaning; and *karmüñ*[ü] (fem.), of fate (107).

In the modern language *-hond*[u] is used:—

(1) With all feminine nouns, singular or plural.

(2) With all masculine plural nouns.

(3) With all animate masculine singular nouns, except proper names.

It governs the dative case, and as the dative singular of all masculine nouns ends in *s*, we get forms such as *ṭsūras-hond*[u], of the thief; *hastis-hond*[u], of the elephant. In such cases, the *h* of *-hond*[u] is dropped after the *s*, and the form for animate masculine singular nouns becomes as in *ṭsūra-sond*[u], *häst*[i]*-sond*[u]. In two passages (88, K. Pr. 57) Lallā makes *-hond*[u] govern the ablative, in *lūka-hond*[u], not *lūka-sond*[u], of people. Possibly this is for *lūkan-hond*[u], in the plural, with the *n* elided. The word *lūk-* is employed both in the singular and in the plural to mean 'people'.

Adjectives.—Only the numerals call for remarks. The word

for 'three' is *tr^{a}h*, instead of the modern *trĕh* or *trih*. It is treated as a singular, with an ablative *trayi*, in verse 50, as compared with the modern ablative plural *trĕyav*. For 'five', besides the modern *pānts*, we have the tatsama *panca* (79). Other numerals, e.g. *shĕh*, six, are treated as plurals. Cf. pl. dat. *shĕn* (13).

Pronouns.—The pronoun of the first person calls for no remarks. For the second person, the singular dative is not only the modern *ṭĕ*, but also (13) *tŏyĕ*, a form not used in modern Kāshmīrī. In the modern language, whenever the pronoun of the second person appears in a sentence, it must always also appear attached to the verb, as a pronominal suffix. For instance, we must say *ṭĕ golu-th*, not *ṭĕ gol^{u}*, destroyed by thee, i.e. thou destroyedst. But in one case (64), Lallā omits the suffix and has *ṭĕ gol^{u}*.

The modern word for 'this' is *yih*. Lallā also has an older form *yuh^{u}* (for *yih^{u}*) (1, 20, 58), with a feminine *yiha* (54).

The modern nominative masculine of the relative pronoun *yih* is *yus*, who. That this is derived from an older *yis^{u}* is shown by Lallā's *yus^{u}* (i.e. *yis^{u}*) (20, 24, &c.). The feminine is *yŏsa* (52), mod. *yŏssa*.

In addition to the usual indefinite pronoun *kĕ̃h*, some one, any one, Lallā has (55) a plural agent *kandĕv*, from which we can deduce a nominative singular *kond^{u}*, unknown to the modern language.

Under the head of phonetics, attention has been called to the form *yaitu*, for modern *yūt^{u}*, as much as.

Conjugation.—In the modern language the conjunctive participle ends in *-it(h)*, derived from the Sanskrit *-tya*, as in *mörit(h)*, having killed, corresponding to a quasi-Sanskrit **māritya*. In Kāshmīrī poetry and in village talk this form is sometimes used as a past participle. Thus, in the Śiva-pariṇaya, 1630, we have *chus bŏh khasith*, I am ascended, lit. I am having ascended. In two passages Lallā gives this participle an older form, more nearly approaching the original. In 27, she has *khàs^{i}t^{i}*, having ascended, and in the same verse she has *làs^{i}t^{i}* (in the sense of the past participle), they lived long. In the modern language, the word *kĕth* is often pleonastically added, as in *dith kĕth*, having given; *hĕth kĕth*, having taken. In the 12th verse, Lallā gives instead of these forms *dith karith* and *hĕth karith*, which show the origin of this *kĕth*. In these Dardic languages the elision of a medial single *r* is common. *Karith* is itself the conjunctive participle of *karun*, to do, and its use is exactly paralleled by the Hindī use of *kar-kē* added pleonastically to a conjunctive participle in that language.

The present participle in the modern language ends in *-ān*, as in *karān*, doing; but in poetry and in village-speech it often ends in *-an*, as in *karan*. So, Lallā has (48) *tshāḍan*, seeking, and *gwāran*, searching.

The verb *lōsun*, to become weary, is irregular in the modern language, making its past participle *lūs*^{u}, with a feminine *lūs*^{ü} or *lūtsh*^{ü}. Lallā (3, 44, &c.) gives the past participle masculine as *lūst*^{u}, of which the feminine form would be, quite regularly, the modern *lūtsh*^{ü}, which she also employs.

The Sanskrit present has become a future in modern Kāshmīrī. Besides this customary sense it is also used where we should employ a present subjunctive, and, occasionally, in its original sense of a present indicative. For our present purposes we can call this Kāshmīrī tense with its threefold meanings the 'Old Present'. It is thus conjugated in the modern language, taking *tsalun*, to flee, as our sample verb:—

	Singular.	Plural.
1.	*tsala.*	*tsalav.*
2.	*tsalakh.*	*tsaliv.*
3.	*tsali.*	*tsalan.*

Corresponding to the Prakrit:—

	Singular.	Plural.
1.	*calāmi, calaũ.*	*calāmō, calahũ.*
2.	*calasi, calahi.*	*calaha, calahu.*
3.	*calaï.*	*calanti, calahĩ.*

It may be added that the terminations of the Kāshmīrī second person are evidently modern pronominal suffixes, which, as explained under the head of pronouns, must, in the case of this person, always be added to the verb.

Lallā more nearly approaches the original form of the first

person singular in *āsā*, I may be (18), which, however, comes at the end of a line. We see traces of the original *i* of the second person singular in *zānĕkh* (64), for *zānakh*, thou wilt know. In the third person singular she has, over and over again, a final *ē* instead of the final *i*. A few examples are *mŏtsē* (11), *tūrē* (16), *pĕyē* (18), *gatshē* (19, 45), *rōtsē* (21), *āsē* (22), and so many others. In the modern language, this *i* usually becomes *ĕ* before pronominal suffixes.

When pronominal suffixes are added to this tense, Lallā now and then does not follow the usual modern practice. Thus, she has *lagi-m*, mod. *lagĕ-m*, it will be attached to me (41); *khĕyi-wō*, mod. *khĕyi-wa*, he will eat for you (K. Pr. 102); *ninan-ay*, mod. *nin-ay*, they will carry thee (K. Pr. 57); *karin-ĕy*, mod. *karan-ay*, they will make for thee (74); *mārin-ĕy*, mod. *māran-ay*, they will kill for thee (71). In the last two cases, the forms of the 3rd person plural would, in the modern language, belong to the present imperative, and not to this tense.

The past tense is formed from the past participle, which, in the masculine singular, ends in *u*-mātrā. Lallā lengthens this to *ū* at the end of a line in *mŏtū*, for *mọtᵘ* (1). It will be observed that, unlike *u*-mātrā, the long *ū* does not epenthetically affect the preceding vowel. The feminine singular of this participle ends in *ü*-mātrā, but, in *tyōjⁱ* and *pōjⁱ* (both in 62), Lallā makes it end in *i*-mātrā. As already stated, *ü*-mātrā always represents an older *ī̆*.

A second form of the past tense, in the case of some verbs, ends in *au*(*v*) or *ō*(*v*), as in *gau*(*v*), (m. pl. *gay*), gone; *pyau*(*v*) (f. sg. *pĕyĕ*), fallen. For the masculine plural of *gauv*, Lallā once has an older form *gàyⁱ* (66), written *gaiy* in 95; and, for the feminine of *pyauv*, she has, with the suffix of the second person singular, *pĕyi-y*, for modern *pĕyĕ-y*, fell to thee.

The past tenses of two verbs require special notice. In the modern language, the past tense of *karun*, to do, to make, runs as follows:—m. sg. *koru-m*, pl. *kàri-m*; fem. sg. *kürü-m*, pl. *karĕ-m*, I made, and so on for the other persons. In 81, Lallā has *kiyĕ-m* instead of *karĕ-m*, a form quite unknown to the modern language, but reminding us of the Hindī *kiyā*. The other verb is *ḍēshun*, to see, modern past participle *dyūṭhᵘ*. In the modern language, this verb always has a cerebral *ḍ*, but Lallā has it, as has been pointed out under the head of phonetics, both cerebral and dental. Moreover, not only does she use the modern past participle *ḍyūṭhᵘ*, but she also uses another past participle *ḍyūkhᵘ* (for *ḍēkhᵘ*) (44), which may be compared with the Hindī *dēkhnā*.

The third person (singular or plural) of the imperative ends in *-in*, as in *karin*, let him or them do or make. With the suffix of the first person singular it becomes *kärⁱn-am*, let him or them make me. Lallā changes the *a* of the suffix to *ĕ* in *dàpⁱn-ĕm*, let him or them say to me (21); *gàndⁱn-ĕm*, let him or them bind on me (21); *kàrⁱn-ĕm*, let him or them make for me (21); *pàḍⁱn-ĕm*, let him or them recite for me (18, 21). It will be remembered that there was a similar change of *a* to *ĕ* in the second person singular of the old present. There was also a similar change in the case of suffixes added to the third person plural of the same tense, in which the same person also took the form of the imperative.

The polite imperative is formed by adding *ta* to the simple imperative. At the end of a line Lallā lengthens this in *hĕtā* and *pĕtā*, both in 28. The second person plural is *ditō*, modern *diyⁱtav*, please give ye (100).

The future imperative is made by adding *zi* to the simple imperative. Lallā changes this to *zē* in *pĕzē*, he must fall (45). A similar change occurs in *khĕzē*, he must eat (90), but here it is at the end of a line.

Indeclinables.—These call for but few remarks. A final *i* becomes *ē* at the end of a line in *atē*, there (2, 98); *tatē*, there (41); and *kunē*, anywhere (9, 11; K. Pr. 201).

The adverb and conjunction *ta* appears in a strengthened form as *töy* in several places; and similarly *na*, not, is strengthened to *nā* or *nō*, and the prohibitive particle *ma* to *mō* or *mau*. For all these see the Vocabulary.

The emphatic suffix *-y* is added in scores of instances without giving any emphasis at all, and apparently merely for the sake of metre. It is hence often difficult to say whether emphasis is intended or not. It often appears as an *i*-mātrā, and then seems to be always emphatic, as in *tàsⁱ*, to him only (65); *làlⁱ*, it is I, even I, Lallā (105); *tūrⁱ*, there verily (19, 61); *yūrⁱ*, in the very place where (61); *sadöyⁱ* (from *sadā*), always (7).

APPENDIX III

ON LALLĀ'S METRES

[BY SIR GEORGE GRIERSON]

THE subject of Kāshmīrī prosody has never been investigated, and hardly anything is known about it. The following remarks may therefore be found of interest.

We may say that, in Kashmīr, two distinct metrical systems are known and cultivated. The first is that used for formal works, such as epic poems and the like. Here Persian metres, with many irregularities and licences, are employed. Numerous examples will be found in the edition of Maḥmūd Gāmī's *Yūsuf Zulaikhā* published by the late K. F. Burkhard in the 'Zeitschrift der Deutschen Morgenländischen Gesellschaft', vols. xlix and liii. In that case we have a poem written by a Muslim in the Persian character, and the use of Persian metres is to be expected, but we find the same system in epics written by Hindūs. For instance, a great portion of the *Śiva-pariṇaya* of Kṛṣṇa Rāzdān is in the well-known *hazaj* metre, and the same is employed in the narrative portions of the *Śrīrāmâvatāra-carita* of Dēvâkara-prasāda Bhaṭṭa, a writer of the eighteenth century. As an example of the latter, I may quote a couple of lines: —

gŏbur ŏsus-na ṡanṡal ŏs^u tamis man
tithay yitha sūrĕ pöñis manz chuh kŏpan

He had no son, and his mind was agitated,
Just as (the reflection of) the sun trembles in the water.

If, with the customary licence, we read the words *ŏs^u* and *yitha* each as one long syllable, we have at once a complete *hazaj*:—

◡ – – –, ◡ – – –, ◡ – –
◡ – – –, ◡ – – –, ◡ – –

The other metrical system is used in songs, and is by no means so simple a matter. I regret that, during my own stay in Kashmīr, I neglected to study it, and when, after my return to this country, I endeavoured to ascertain from native sources what rules were followed in such compositions, I failed to obtain any definite information. All that I could gather was that a poet scanned his verses by ear. A long and minute examination of scores of songs led me to no certain conclusion beyond the fact that a stress-accent seemed to play an important part. Here and there I came across traces of well-known metres, but nowhere, even allowing for the fullest licence, did they extend over more than a few lines at a time. In the year 1917, Sir Aurel Stein had occasion to visit Kashmīr, and with his ever inexhaustible kindness, undertook to investigate the question. With the help of Paṇḍit Nityânanda Śāstrī and a *Śrāvakā*, or professional reciter, he ascertained definitely that in songs the metre depends solely on the stress-accent. In Lallā's verses, four stresses go to each *pāda*, or line. Thus, if we mark the stressed syllables each with a perpendicular stroke, the first two songs would be read as follows:—

1.

abhyōs^{i} *savikās layĕ wŏthū*
gaganas sagun myūl^{u} *sami ŧraṭū*
shūñ gol^{u} *ta anāmay mŏtū*
yuhuy wŏpadēsh chuy baṭā

2.

wākh mānas kŏl-akŏl nā atē
ŧhŏpi mudri ati nā pravēsh
rōzan shiwa-shĕk^{a}*th nā atē*
mọt^{u}*yĕy kūh ta suy wŏpadēsh*

So far as I am aware, this is not paralleled by any similar metric system in Persia or Northern India; but it is interesting to note that, although stress is the sole criterion of the metre, some of the songs give forth distant echoes of well-known Indian methods of scansion. Take, for instance, the second verse quoted above. It will not scan according to Indian rules, but nevertheless its lilt is strongly suggestive of the Indian *dōhā*. The dōhā is a metre based on instants, each of which is the time occupied in uttering one short syllable, one long syllable counting as two instants. Each half-verse is divided into the following groups of instants:—6 + 4 + 3, 6 + 4 + 1. The group of 3 is generally an iambus (◡ –), and the second half-line generally ends in a trochee (– ◡). The opening verse of the *Sat-saiyā* of Vihārī is a good Hindī example:—

6 4 3
mērī bhava|-bādhā | harau

6 4 1
Rādhā nā|gari sō|i

6 4 3
jā tana kī | jhā̃ī | paḍai

6 4 1
Śyāma harita | duti hō|i

It will be noticed that in Lallā's second verse, as in a dōhā, the first and third lines end in a strongly marked iambus. So, again, the second and fourth lines end in a heavy long closed syllable, which, with the inherent vowel, not pronounced, of the final consonant, is really a trochee, as in the above dōhā. But this is not all. In Lallā's verse, if we read the unstressed *mu* of *mudri,* and the word *nā* as short, thus:—

6 4 1
ṭhŏpi mudri ati | na pravē|sh(a)

it would scan, like the second section of a dōhā in instants:—6 + 4 + 1.

In the same way, other songs that I have examined show traces of other well-known metres, Persian or Indian, and it is evident that the rude village compositions which developed into the verses of Lallā were originally intended to be based on some standard metre, but that in the mouths of the rustics stress became substituted for quantity.

So far as my experience goes, no such development has taken place in Hindōstān or the Panjāb. Here the rules of prosody depending on the quantity of each syllable are everywhere followed, although, of course, in the ruder songs, great metrical licence prevails. We observe a similar state of affairs in Southern India. A series of Kanarese Ballads was published in the *Indian Antiquary* by the late Dr. Fleet, and regarding them he observes[1] that they follow the principle of Kanarese metre consisting of feet of four instants each. 'But no absolute metrical precision is aimed at; and—though the principle of construction is distinctly recognizable—in carrying it out by scanning or in adapting the words to the airs, short syllables have been drawn out long and long syllables clipped short, *ad libitum*. . . . The rhythm of the songs can only be learned by actually hearing them sung.'

I believe that the only Indo-Aryan language that shows a tendency to substitute, as in Kāshmīrī, stress for quantity is Bengali. It will have been observed that in Lallā's verses quoted above there is a stress on the first syllable of every line. Similarly, Mr. J. D. Anderson[2] has shown that in Bengali verse, although quantity is sometimes nominally observed, the metre is conditioned by a strong phrasal stress-accent falling on the beginning of each line and on the first syllable after each cæsura. Usually the verse consists of a fixed number of syllables, wholly independent of quantity; and this number, regulated and controlled by the stress-accents, constitutes the metre. Mr. Anderson—and I am entirely of his opinion—is inclined to see Tibeto-Burman influence in this metrical system of Bengal. Could we be justified in suggesting a similar foreign influence in Kashmīr? The population of the Happy Valley is far from being homogeneous. Local tradition compels us to consider it as very probable that, although the upper classes are probably of the same stock as that of North-Western India, a substratum of the inhabitants is connected with non-Indian tribes whose original home was Central Asia, and this is borne out by the

[1] Vol. xiv (1883), p 294

[2] JRAS, 1914, pp. 1046 ff.

results of philological inquiries. It was in this substratum, not amongst the learned Paṇḍits of Kashmīr, that the rude songs which developed into Lallā's verses and into the songs of modern Kashmīr took their rise.

A well-known parallel to Lallā's abandonment of quantity in exchange for stress-accent is to be found in mediaeval Greek and Latin poetry. Here, of course, there can be no question of mutual influence, although we find just the same state of affairs. The accentual poems of Gregory of Nazianzen bear much the same relation to the other poems composed by him and by the writers of classical times that the verses of Lallā bear to the *amiaṁ pāuakavvaṁ* of Hāla and of the older Indian poets whose quatrains are preserved in his anthology.

G. A. G.

APPENDIX IV

CONCORDANCE OF THE VERSES IN MS. STEIN B AND IN THE PRESENT EDITION

No. of Verse in Stein B.	No of Verse in present edition.	Remarks.
1	13	
2	8	
3	46	
4	47	
5	7	
6	36	
7	17	
8	27	
9	39	
10	40	
11	33	
12	23	
13	16	
14	2	
15	1	
16	10	
17	77	
18	22	
19	14	
20	15	
21	9	
22	61	
23	18	
24	58	
25	21	
26	28	
27	12	
28	70	Wrongly numbered 19 in MS.
29	5	Wrongly numbered 20 in MS.
30	65	A mixture of 5 and 65 in MS.
31	6	
32	54	
33	52	
34	80	
35	53	
36	11	A mixture of 11 and 1 in MS.
37	75	
38	64	With borrowing from 55.
39	73	
40	74	
41	76	
42, 43	81	Stein B 42 and 43 are variants of the same verse.
44	56	
45	57	
46	41	
47	20	
—	71	These verses do not form part of the collection in Stein B, but are scribbled in at the end as a kind of appendix, and are not numbered.
—	78	
—	79	

VOCABULARY

THIS vocabulary contains every word in the foregoing verses of Lallā, with a reference to each place in which it occurs. The order of words is that adopted by Sir George Grierson in other works on Kāshmīrī, the arrangement being based on the English alphabetical order of the consonants, without regard to the vowels. The latter come into consideration only in cases in which the same consonant is followed, or the same consonants are separated by different vowels. Thus, the different words containing the consonants *tr* will be found in the succession *tăr*, *tŏr*, *tŏr*^{u}, *tūr*^{i}, and *tūr*^{ü}. All words beginning with vowels are arranged together at the commencement, their mutual order being determined by the consonants. Long and nasalized vowels are not differentiated from short ones, except in cases where the difference between two words depends only on such variations. A similar principle has been followed in the case of diacritical marks. For instance, *piṭhis* precedes *pĕtarum*, because *h* precedes *r*, the difference between *ṭ* and *t* being ignored. The letter *ṫ* follows *t* (and *ṭ*). As the consonants *v* and *w* merely represent different phases of the same sound, they are treated, for the purposes of alphabetical order, as the same letter.

In Kāshmīrī the sonant aspirates *gh*, *ḍh*, *dh*, and *bh*[1] lose their aspiration, although, in the case of *tatsamas*, the aspiration is sometimes retained in writing. Even in this latter respect there is no uniform custom, the same word being written indiscriminately with or without the aspiration. At one time a man will write *abhyās*, and at another time he will write *abyās*. Similarly, Lallā writes *bhāryā*, a wife, with *bh*, but *būt*(*h*) (Sanskrit *bhūta*), a principle of creation, with *b*. The latter is a Śaiva technical term, and, of all words, we should have expected it to be spelt in the Sanskrit fashion. To avoid confusion, I have therefore, for the purposes of alphabetical order, treated each of these sonant aspirates as identical with its corresponding unaspirated letter. That is to say, *gh* will be found in the place allotted to *g*, *ḍh* in that allotted to *ḍ*, *dh* in that allotted to *d*, and *bh* in that allotted to *b*.

G. A. G.

[1] The sonant aspirate *jh* does not occur.

WORDS BEGINNING WITH VOWELS

ā, interj. added to *pashi* (see *pashun*) m. c., and with it forming *pashyā*, 16.

abēd, m. absence of difference, identity; sg. abl. *abēda*, while, or although, there is identity (of the soul with the Supreme), 13.

abŏdᵘ, adj. one who has no knowledge, a fool, i.e. one who has no knowledge of himself; pl. nom. *abŏdⁱ*, 6.

abakh, a word of doubtful meaning; perhaps = clumsy, stupid, 85, q.v.

abal, adj. c. g. without strength, weak, weak from sickness; f. sg. abl. *abali*, used as subst., 8.

abĕn, adj. c. g. not different, identical; *abĕn vimarshā*, (they are) identical, (as one can see) on reflection, 16.

abhyās, m. repeated practice, esp. of *yōga* or of meditation on the identity of the Self with the Supreme, 1; habitual practice of a course of conduct, 20; sg. ag. *abhyö̆sⁱ*, 1.

achⁱ, f. the eye; *achĕ lagañĕ tālav*, the eyes to be turned upwards, K. Pr. 102; *achĕn hyuhᵘ*, like the eyes, K. Pr. 201.

ada, adv. then, at that time, 24, 31, 61, 80, 95, 103, K. Pr. 56.

adal ta wadal, m. interchange, confusion, K. Pr. 102.

aduyᵘ, adj. non-dual; (of the mind) convinced of the non-duality or identity of the Self with the Supreme, 5, 65.

aham, I, the ego; *aham-vimarshĕ*, by reflection on the nature of the ego, 15.

āhārun, to eat food; impve. sg. 2, *āhār*, 28.

okᵘ, card. one; with emph. *y*, *okuy*, one only, the only one, the unique, 34; m. sg. abl. *aki nĕngi*, at one time, on one occasion, 50; *nimēshĕ aki*, in a single twinkle of the eye, 26. Cf. *yēka*.

akh, card. one, 34; as indefinite article, a, 50, 83 (bis); *akhāh*, one, a single one, K. Pr. 150. Cf. *yēka*.

ŏkh, m. a mark, a sign impressed upon anything; esp. a mark indicating eminence or excellence, 75. Cf. the next.

ŏkhun, to make a mark: to impress a mark upon anything, to brand anything; impve. sg. 2, *ŏkh*, 76.

akhĕr, m. a syllable, such as the syllable *ōm*, or the like, 10.

akŏl, m. that which transcends the *kula*, i.e. the sphere of the Absolute, or of Transcendental Being, 79; *kŏl-akŏl*, the totality of all creation, 2. See *kŏl*, and Note on Yōga, § 19.

akriy, adj. c. g. not acting, free from work; hence, in a religious sense, free from the bond of works as an impediment to salvation, in a state of salvation, 32, 45.

al, m. wine (offered to a god), 10 (cf. *pal*); the wine of bliss or nectar of bliss, said to flow from the digits of the moon (see *sōm*); *al-thān*, the place of this nectar, the abode of bliss, i.e. union with the Supreme, 60. *Al-thān*, however, may also be explained as equivalent to the Sanskrit *alaṁ-sthāna*, i.e. the place regarding which only '*nêti nêti*' can be said, or which can be described by no epithet, the highest place (*anuttara pada*), i.e. also, union with the Supreme.

alônd^{u}, adj. (f. *alönz*^{ü}), pendant, hanging, 102 (f. sg. nom.).

ālav, m. a call, a cry;—*dyun*^{u}, to summon, K. Pr. 102.

ālawun, to wave, move up and down; pres. part. *ālawān*, K. Pr. 57.

àm^{i}, *ami*, see *ath*.

ōṁ, the mystic syllable *ōṁ*, the *praṇava*; sg. gen. *ōmaki cōbạka*, with the whip of the *praṇava*, 101; *ōṁ-kār*, the syllable *ōṁ*, 34, 82.

It is believed that the syllable *ōṁ* contains altogether five elements, viz. *a*, *u*, *m*, and the *Bindu* and *Nāda*, on which see Note on Yōga, §§ 23, 24, and *anāhath*.

ôm^{u}, adj. raw, uncooked; (of an earthen vessel) unbaked, 106; (of a string) not twisted, and hence without strength, 106; m. sg. abl. *āmi*, 106; m. pl. dat. *āmĕn*, 106.

ambar, m. clothing, clothes, garments, 28, 76.

amol^{u}, adj. undefiled, pure, free from all defilement (of the Supreme), 64.

amalôn^{u}, adj. (f. *amalöñ*^{ü}), undefiled, 21 (f. sg. nom.).

amar, m. immortality; *amara-pathi*, on the path (leading) to immortality, i.e. in the path of reflection on the Self or ego, 70.

amrĕth, m. the water of immortality, nectar, *amṛta*; sg. abl. *amrĕta-sar*, the lake of nectar, i.e. of the nectar of bliss (*ānanda*) of union with the Supreme, 68. Regarding the nectar distilled from the microcosmic moon, see Note on Yōga, §§, 8, 19, 21, 22.

on^{u}, adj. blind; m. pl. ag. *anyau*, 59.

anād, adj. c. g. without beginning, existing from eternity, an epithet of the Supreme, 72.

andar, postpos. in, within; *kūṭh*^{a}*rĕ-andar*, in the closet, 101; *ạnd*^{a}*rạy atsun*, one must enter into the very inmost part, 94; *ạnd*^{a}*riy*, from the inmost recesses, 109.

ạnd^{a}*ryum*^{u}, adj. (f. *ạnd*^{a}*rim*^{ü}, 104), belonging to the interior, inner, 4, 104.

anāhath, adj. c. g. unobstructed, whose progress is perpetual; (often) that of which the sound is everlasting, the mystic syllable *ōṁ* (15), also called the *anāhath shĕbd*, or (33) *anāhata-rav*. In Sanskrit it is called the *anāhata-dhvani* (Note on Yōga, § 23). It is described as having the semblance of inarticulateness (*avyaktānukṛtiprāya*), to be uttered only by the deity dwelling within the breast of living creatures, and therefore to have no human utterer or obstructor of its sound. It is composed of a portion of all the vowels nasalized, and is called *anāhath* (Skr. *anāhata*), i.e. perpetual, because it never comes to a close but vibrates perpetually (*an-astam-ita-rūpatwāt*). Another explanation of the name is that it is 'sound caused without any percussion', i.e. self-created. It is said (33) to take its rise from the heart and to issue through the nose. In 15, it is described as identical with, or as equivalent to, the Supreme Himself.

As a Śaiva technical term *anāhata* sometimes does not designate *ōṁ*, but is applied to other things. For instance, it is used as the name of the fourth of the mystic *cakras*, or circles. See Note on Yōga, §§ 15, 17, 23, 25, 27.

anāmay, adj. c. g. not bad; *hence*, perfect; that which is perfect and free from all qualities, pure consciousness, the Supreme, 1.

ann, pl. m. food, victuals, 28.

anun, to bring; *wagi anun*, to bring under the rein, to bring into subjection, 37; *layĕ anun*, to bring under subjection by concentration of the mind and breath, 82.

Fut. sg. 3, *ani*, 37; past. part. m. sg. with suff. 1st pers. sg. ag. *onum*, 82.

anth, m. an end; *ànt*[i] (54) or *àntih*[i] (33, 37, 38, 41, 61), adv. in the end, finally, ultimately.

antar, m. the inner meaning, the hidden meaning, mystery (of anything), 56.

anway, m. logical connexion; tenor, drift, purport; the real truth (concerning anything), 59.

apān, m. one of the five vital airs (1, *prāṇa*, 2, *apāna*, 3, *samāna*, 4, *udāna*, 5, *vyāna*). Of these, two (*prāṇa* and *apāna*) are referred to by L. D. See Note on Yōga, § 16 note.

The *apāna* (Ksh. *apān*) is the vital air that goes downwards and out at the anus. The *prāṇa* is that which goes upwards and is exhaled through the mouth and nose. For perfect union with the Supreme, it is necessary to bring these two into absolute control, 26. Cf. Deussen, *Allgemeine Geschichte der Philosophie*, i. 2, p. 248, 3, p. 70. See Note on Yōga, §§ 2, 16, 21, 23, and Articles *nāḍi* and *prān*, 2, for full particulars.

āparun, to put food into another's mouth, to feed from the hand. Conj. part. *āparith*, 66.

apūt[u], adj. unclean, impure, ceremonially unclean; m. pl. nom., with emph. *y*, *apūtiy*, 32.

ōr, adv. there, in that place; *ōra-y*, even from there, K. Pr. 102.

arg, m. an offering of unhusked grain made in worshipping a god (Skr. *argha*, in a slightly different sense), 42.

arsh, m. the sky, the firmament; sg. dat. (in sense of loc.), *arshĕs*, 50.

arćun 1, m. the act of worshipping, worship, 58.

arćun 2, to worship; inf. *arćun*, 10; fut. pass. part. *arćun*, worship is to be done (with dat. of obj.), 33.

arzun, m. the result of labour, earnings, 61.

ōs, m. the mouth; sg. abl. *ōsā* (a form not found in modern Ksh.), 18.

ashwawār, m. a rider (on a horse), 14, 15.

asun, to laugh; fut. (in sense of pres.) sg. 3, *asi*, 46.

āsun, to be, 18, 20, 36, 86, 92; to become, 64; to come into existence, 22; to happen, 84, 85; to be, to remain, to continue, 46, 55; *ōsith*, having been, i.e. whereas thou wast formerly (so and so, now thou hast become such and such), 86.

Conj. part. *ōsith*, 84–6. Fut. ind. and pres. subj. sg. 1, *āsā* (m. c. for *āsa*), 18; 3, *āsi* (in sense of pres.), 46; *āsē* (m. c.) (fut.), 22; pl. 3, *āsan*, 92; impve. sg. 2, *ās*, 20, 36, 55, 64.

asta, adv. slowly, gradually, 80.

āsawun[u], n. ag. one who is or continues; *sthir āsawun*[u], that which is permanent, 73.

aṭa, f. the shoulders; the rope for tying a burden on the shoulders; *aṭa-ganḍ*, the knot by which this rope is tied, 108.

ati, adv. there, in that place, 2; *atē*, m. c. for *ati*, 2 (bis), 98.

ath, pron., that (within sight); adj. sg. ag. m. *ȧm*[i], K. Pr. 150; abl. *ami*, 107.

atha, m. the hand; *atha-wās karun*, (of two persons) to join hand in hand, to hold each other's hand (for mutual confidence), 92; sg. abl. *atha trāwun*, to dismiss from the hand, to let loose, to set free, 88; loc. *athē*, in the hand; (to be) in a person's possession, (to come) to hand, 98, K. Pr. 18; *athē hyon*[u], to carry in the hand, 10.

ātmā, m. the Self; esp. the Self as identical with the Supreme; old. sg. gen. *ātmāsē* (probably m. c. for *ātmāsi*, quasi-Sanskrit **ātmasya*), 22 (see p. 133).

aćhĕn, adv. not torn; hence, uninterruptedly, continuously, 19.

aćhun, to become weak, feeble, emaciated; pres. part. *aćhān*, becoming feeble, hence, wearily, 19.

aṭsun, to enter. Fut. pass. part. m. sg. *aṭsun*, it is to be entered, i.e. you should (or may) enter = 'come in', 94; impve. pol. sg. 3, *mata āṭsⁱtan*, lit. let him not enter (as a question), i.e. he certainly does enter, 53; past f. sg. 1, *ṭsāyĕs*, I (f.) entered, 68.

ār, *āy*, *āyĕ*, *āyĕs*, see *yunᵘ*.

bā, interj. Sir! 87 (bis), 88 (quater).

bhū, in *bhū-tal*, the surface of the earth, the whole earth as opposed to the sky, 22, 42; *bhūr*, id., *bhūr bhuwaḥ swar*, the earth, the atmosphere, and heaven, i.e. the whole visible universe, 9.

bŏcha, f. hunger, 37; abl. *bŏcha-* (for *bŏchi-*) *sūty marun*, to die of hunger, 83.

bicōrᵘ, adj. (f. *bicörᵘ*), without means, without resources, destitute, unfortunate, wretched; f. sg. ag. *bicāri*, 89.

bōdh, perfect intelligence, knowledge of the Self, *svātma-jñāna*; *bōdha-prakāsh*, the enlightenment or illumination of this knowledge, 35.

bọdᵘ, adj. wise, a wise man, one who is intelligent; m. sg. ag. *bŏdⁱ*, 26.

bādun, to afflict, cause pain to; p. p. m. sg. with suff. 1st pers. sg. ag, *bōdum*, 7.

bŏḍun, to sink, be immersed in, be drowned in; past m. sg. 2. *bọḍukh*, 74.

bāg, m. a garden, K. Pr. 56; *swaman-bāga-bar*, the door of the garden of one's soul, or *sōman-bāga-bar*, the door of the jasmine-garden, 68, see art. *swa*; sg. dat. *bāgas*, K. Pr. 56.

bagawān, m. God; sg. voc. *bagawāna*, K. Pr. 102.

bahu, adj. much, many, 51.

bŏh, pron. 1st pers., I, 3, 7 (ter), 13, 18, 21, 31, 48, 59, 68, 81–3, 93, 98, 102; K. Pr. 18; with interjection *döy*, *bŏ-döy*, I, good Sir!

mĕ, me, 44; to me, 68, 81, 84, 94; to me, in my possession (dat. of possession), 13; for me, as regards me (dat. commodi), 8, 18, 44; K. Pr. 57; by me (ag.) 3, 31, 44 (bis), 48, 93–4, 103–4; *mĕ-ti*, me also, 106; to me also, 48.

myōnᵘ, my, 106; K. Pr. 150; m. sg. voc. *myānuv*, K. Pr. 57.

böjⁱ, one who has a share (*bāj*) in anything; hence, one who gets such and such as his allotted share of fate, one who gains possession (of) (the thing obtained being put in the dat., as three times in 62, or compounded with *böjⁱ*, as in *pāpa-pŏñĕ-böjⁱ*, he who obtains (the fruit) of his sins and virtuous acts of a former life, also in 62).

boktu, adj. (f. *bükťü*), full of devotional faith (*bhakti*). *Shĕnkara-boktu*, full of devotional faith to Śaṅkara (i.e. Śiva); f. sg. nom. 18.

bal, m. a religious offering of food to gods, animals, &c.; hence, food generally given to an animal, K. Pr. 150.

bōl, 1, m. speech; *bōl paḍun*, to recite speech; hence, to abuse, blame with abusive language, 18, 21.

bōl, 2, see *bōlun*.

bālukh, a male child, a boy; pl. voc. *bālakō*, 91.

bōlun, to say; impve. sg. 2, *bōl*, 20.

bōlanāwun, to cause to converse, to address, summon, call to; p. p. m. sg. with suff. 1st pers. sg. ag. *bōlanŏwum*, 105.

bam, m. the skin; *bam tulun*, to raise the skin, to raise weals (with a whip), 101.

bān, m. the sun, 9.

bāna, m. a vessel, dish, jar; pl. nom. *bāna*, 60.

bĕn, adj., c. g. different, distinct, 13; a different form, a manner of difference, 16; pl. nom. *bĕn*, 16.

bŏn, adj. and adv. low, below; *pĕṭha bŏna*, from top to bottom, 17.

bŏna, 2, (for 1, see *bŏn*), adv. as it were; used almost as an expletive, 37.

band gaťhun, to become stopped (of a mill at work), 86.

bindu, m. a dot or spot; esp. the dot indicating the sign *anusvāra*, forming the final nasal sound of the syllable *ōṁ*, or, similarly, the dot over the semicircle of *anunāsika* (ँ), of which the semicircle indicates the nasal sound. *Nāda-binduy* (with emph. *y*), 15. For the meaning of this compound, see Note on Yōga, § 25.

bāndav, m. a relation, a person related, K. Pr. 201 (ter).

būñü, f. the 'Chinār', or Oriental Plane-tree, *Platanus orientalis*, K. Pr. 102. It is a fine tree, common in Kashmīr.

bar, m. a door; sg. dat. *ťāyĕs bāga-baras*, I entered the garden door, 68; *bar-* (for *baras-*) *pĕṭh hūñü*, a bitch at the door, K. Pr. 102; pl. nom. *bar trŏpᵃrim*, I shut the doors, 101; pl. dat. *töḍⁱ ḍīṭhⁱmas baran*, I saw (that there were) bolts on His doors, 48.

bār, m. a load; sg. dat. *bāras*, (the knot) of (i.e. that tied) the load, 108.

boru, adj. full; m. pl. nom. *bārⁱ bārⁱ bāna*, (innumerable) dishes all filled (with nectar), 60.

bhūr, see *bhū*.

brahm, a Brāhmaṇ, in *brahma-hüťü*, murder of a Brāhmaṇ, with emph. *y*, K. Pr. 102.

brahmā, name of the first person of the three gods, Brahmā, Viṣṇu, and Śiva, 14.

brahmāṇḍ, m. Brahmā's egg, the universe, the world; used to mean the *Brahma-randhra*, or Brahmā's crevice, one of the sutures in the crown of the head, the anterior fontanelle, 34, 57. It is the upper extremity of the *Suṣumnā Nāḍī*; see Note on Yōga, §§ 5, 7, 19, 21, 27. Sg. dat. *brahmāṇḍas*, 34; abl. *brahmāṇḍa*, 57.

bramun, to wander; hence, to be confused, to be filled with an agitated desire, 106; pres. part. *bramān*, 106.

brama-wŏnᵘ, m. a wanderer, one who roams about, 26.

barun, to fill; used in various idioms; *bhayĕ barun*, to experience fear, to fear (at heart), 72; *dŏh-dĕn barànⁱ*, to pass each day, spend each day, 92; *dĕn-rāth barànⁱ*, to pass day and night, 91; *kūn barun*, to aim an arrow, 71.

Conj. part. *barith*, 71; impve. sg. 2, *bar*, 72; fut. pl. 2, *bariv*, 91; 3, *baran*, 92.

bĕrongᵘ, adj. out of order, deranged, disarranged, 85.

brānth, f. error; hence, false hopes, hope in material things, 27.

brŏ̄ṭh, postpos. governing abl., before; with emph. *y*, *marana brŏ̄ṭhay*, even before (the time appointed for) death, 87; *brŏ̄ṭh-kölⁱ*, in future times, 92.

bhāryā, f. a wife: *bhāryĕ-rūpⁱ*, f. possessing the form of a wife, in the character of a wife, 54.

barzun, a jingle of *arzun*; *arzun barzun*, earnings, the result of labour, the savings gained from one's life-work, 61.

basta, f. a sheepskin, goatskin, or the like; *daman-basta*, f. a smith's bellows; sg. dat. *-basti*, 100 = K. Pr. 46.

baṭa, m. a Brāhmaṇ, a Kāshmīrī Brāhmaṇ; hence, a true Brāhmaṇ, a Brāhmaṇ who seeks salvation, 1, 17; sg. voc. *baṭā*, 1, 17.

baṭh, m. a warrior, a soldier; a servant, a messenger, 74; *yĕma-baṭh*, (pl. nom.), the messengers of Yama, the god of the nether world, who drag the souls of dying men to hell to be judged by Yama, 74.

būth, 1, m. a demon; *māra-būth* (pl. nom.), murderous demons, 71.

būth, 2, m. a technical name in Śaiva philosophy for the group of the five *tattvas*, or factors, of which the apparent universe consists, called in Sanskrit the *bhūtas* or *mahābhūtas*. They are the five factors, or principles, which constitute the materiality of the sensible universe. They are (1) the principle of solidity, technically called *pṛthivī*, or earth; (2) the principle of liquidity, technically *āp*, or water; (3) the principle of formativity, technically *agni*, or fire; (4) the principle of aeriality, technically *vāyu*, or the atmosphere; and (5) the principle of vacuity, technically *ākāśa*, or the sky. See J. C. Chatterji, *Kashmīr Shaivism*, p. 48. Pl. nom. *būth*, 77 (cf. 95).

bhū-tal, see *bhū*.
bātun, (of the sun), to shine forth; fut. sg. 3, *bāti*, 16.
bhav, m. existence, esp. existence in this world of illusion, in contradistinction to union with the Supreme. *bhawa-ruz*, the disease of existence, existence compared to a disease, 8; *bhawa-sọdᵃri-dārĕ*, in the current of the ocean of existence, 74; *bhawa-sar*, the ocean of existence, 23.
bāv, m. devotional love (to a deity); sg. gen. (m. pl. nom.) *bāwàkⁱ*, 40.
bhuwaḥ, the air, atmosphere; *bhūr bhuwaḥ swar*, the earth, the atmosphere, and heaven, i.e. the whole visible universe, 9.
bāwun, to show, explain; pol. impve. sg. 2, with suff. 1st pers. sg. dat., *bāvtam*, please explain to me, 56.
bŏwurᵘ, m. (in modern Ksh. *wŏwurᵘ*), a weaver; *bōwᵃrⁱ-wān*, a weaver's workshop; sg. abl. *-wāna*, 102.
bayĕ (27, K. Pr. 201) or *bhayĕ* (72), m. fear; esp. (K. Pr. 201) the fear of God; *yĕma-bayĕ*, the fear of Yama (the god of death), the fear of death and what follows, 27; *bhayĕ barun*, to experience fear, to feel fear, 72; sg. dat. *bayĕs hyuhᵘ*, (there is no bliss) like the fear of God, K. Pr. 201.
bŏyᵘ, m. a brother; sg. dat. *bŏyis hyuhᵘ*, (there is no relation) like a brother, K. Pr. 201.
byākh, pron. another; sg. dat. *biyis kyutᵘ*, for another (i.e. not for oneself), 61.
biyis, see *byākh*.
bazun, 1, to cook (vegetables or the like) in hot oil, to fry (vegetables); conj. part. *bazith*, 90 (bis) (with pun on the meaning of *bazun*, 2).
bazun, 2, to reverence, serve; hence, *dwār bazun*, to serve a door, to wait at a door, 51; *gĕh bazun*, to serve a house, to be occupied with household affairs, 32; *prān bazun*, to serve one's life, to be devoted to one's own life, to be attached to one's bodily welfare rather than to spiritual things, 90 (bis) (with pun on *prān bazun*, to fry an onion, cf. *bazun*, 1). Inf., dat. of purpose, *bazani*, 51; conj. part. *bazith*, 32, 90 (bis).
bōzun, to hear; to listen to, 106; to hear (from), to learn (from), 27; to attend to, heed, 20.

Conj. part. *būzith*, 27; impve. sg. 2, *bōz*, 20; fut. sg. 3, *bōzi*, 106.
buzun, to parch or roast (grain, &c.); met. to parch (the heart), to purify it, to destroy all evil thoughts from the heart; p. p. sg. f. with suff. 1st pers. sg. ag. *buzüm*, 25.

cŏbukh, m. a whip; sg. abl. *cōbạka*, 101.
cēḍun or *cērun*, to mount (e.g. a horse); *pĕṭh cēḍun*, to mount

and ride on the back (of a horse, &c.), *pĕṭh* being an adv., not a postposition, 14, 15; fut. sg. 3, with suff. 3rd pers. dat. sg., *cēḍĕs* (*cērĕs*), he will mount on it, 14, 15.

chuh, is (m. sg.), 7, 20, 27; *chukh*, thou art (m.), 42 (bis), 55, 107 (aux.), K. Pr, 46; *chum*, is (m.) to or for me, 61, 106; *chĕs*, I (f.) am, 93, 106 (aux.); *chuwa*, is (m.) for you, 89; *chĕy*, is (f.) for thee, 99 (bis), 100, K. Pr. 46 (quater); it (f.) is verily, 52, 57, 63, K. Pr. 102 (quater); *chiy*, they (m.) are verily, 32 (ter); *chuy*, it (m.) is to thee, 30, 56, K. Pr. 56; is (m.) verily, 1, 12, 17, 24, 29, 46, 51–4, 62 (bis), 80, K. Pr. 150.

chŏkh, m. a wound; *nārāċⁱ-chŏkh*, the wound caused by a barbed fish-spear, 23 (comm.).

chān, m. (?) a carpenter, 85, q.v.

chọnᵘ, adj. empty, 63; empty, vain, unsubstantial, having no substance, 41; m. sg. dat. *chĕnis*, 41; f. sg. nom. *chĕñᵘ*, 63.

chōr, in *chōra-dārĕ*, 74, a waterfall (in modern Kāshmīrī *chūl*); *chōra-dār*, the stream of a waterfall, a torrent; hence, *chōra-dārĕ karun*, to make (a person) in a torrent, to make him stream (with blood), the name of a certain punishment, in which a person is dragged along the ground till his body streams with blood.

chōrun, to release, let go; let loose, set free; p. p. m. sg. *chyūrᵘ*, 23.

chaṭhᵃr, m. an umbrella (one of the insignia of royalty), 73.

chāwun, to fling at or to; to dash down (on), 103; p. p. f. sg. with suff. 3rd pers. sg. ag. and 1st pers. sg. nom. *chövᵘnas*, 103.

chyūrᵘ, see *chōrun*.

cākh, m. a tear or rent (in cloth or the like); *cākh dyunᵘ*, to tear or rend, 104 (dat. of obj.).

canda, m. a pocket, esp. a pocket for carrying money, a purse; sg. dat. *candas*, 98 (= K. Pr. 18), K. Pr. 201.

cang, m. a claw, talon, 84.

cērun, see *cēḍun*.

cyonᵘ, to drink; conj. part. *cĕth*, K. Pr. 102; pres. part. *cĕwān*, 60; fut. pl. 3, *cĕn*, 47; p. p. m. sg. *cyauv*, 104.

cyāñĕ, *cyöñᵘ*, see *ċᵃh*.

dọbᵘ, m. a washerman; sg. ag. *dŏbⁱ*, 103; *dŏbⁱ-kūñᵘ*, a washerman's stone (on which he beats the clothes he washes), 103.

dubāra, adv. a second time, again, 89.

dachyunᵘ, adj. right, not left; f. sg. abl. *dachiñi lari*, on the right side (corpses are placed on the funeral pyre lying on the right side) K. Pr. 57.

dãd, m. a bullock; sg. dat. *dãdas*, 66.
dŏd, m. milk, 38; *dŏda-shur*ᵘ, a milk-child, a suckling, 70.
*dŏḍ*ⁱ, adv. continually, always, 79. In modern Kāshmīrī *dŏḍ*ⁱ.
dag, f. a blow, 84; pain of a blow, hence, pain generally; the pangs of love, 105; sg. dat. or pl. nom. with emph. *y*, *dagay*, ? for *dagiy*, 84.
*d*ᵃ*h*, m. smoke, 97.
dah, card. ten; pl. dat. *dahan*, 95; *doh*ᵘ, m. a group of ten, sg. abl. *dahi* m. c. *dahē*, 105. There are ten organs (five of sense, and five of action), see *yund*ᵘ; and ten vital airs, of which five are principal, and five are secondary, see *prān*, 2.
dēh or (58) *dih*, m. a body, the human body (of flesh and blood, as opposed to the spirit), 28, 58, 101; *kŏdēh*, a vile body, 7; sg. dat. *dihas*, 58; gen. (f. sg. dat.) *dēhacĕ*, 101.
dŏh, m. a day, daytime, 44, 98; K. Pr. 18; pl. the days (as in 'the days of yore'), 91; *dŏh lūstum*, the day came to an end for me, the day expired and night fell, 44, 98; K. Pr. 18; *dŏh-dĕn baran*, they will pass the daytime of each day, 92; pl. nom. *dŏh*, 91.
dikh, see *dyun*ᵘ.
dal, m. a group, a collection, in *nāḍi-dal*, the collection (i.e. totality) of the tubes in the body that convey the vital airs, 80. See *nāḍi*.
dil, the heart, K. Pr. 56, 57; *dil dyun*ᵘ, to give heart, encourage, K. Pr. 46 (the corresponding L. V. 100 has *dam*, breath); sg. gen. *diluk*ᵘ, K. Pr. 57, (m. sg. dat.) *dilakis*, K. Pr. 56.
*dol*ᵘ, m. the front skirt of a garment; pl. nom. *dȧl*ⁱ *trŏv*ⁱ*mas*, I spread out my skirts before him, i.e. I knelt before him and meditated on him, 49.
dam, 1, m. vital air, breath of life, breath; suppression of the breath as a religious exercise; the time occupied in taking a breath, a very short time, a moment; *dam karun*, to practise suppression of the breath, 4; *dam dyun*ᵘ, to give breath (to a bellows; the corresponding K. Pr. 46 has *dil*, heart), 100; to suppress breath, and also to give forth breath, to shout, threaten, 101 (a double meaning); *damāh*, a single breath, hence, as adv. for a moment, for a short time; gradually, 4 (both meanings are applicable); *dȧmiy* . . . *dȧmiy*, at (or for) one moment . . . at (or for) another moment, 96, 97; K. Pr. 47.
dam, 2, m. self-restraint, in the phrase *shĕm ta dam*, quietude and self-restraint, 29; sg. abl. *shĕma dama*, 63.
dima, see *dyun*ᵘ.
damun, m. a pair of bellows; sg. dat. *damanas*, K. Pr. 46; *daman-basta*, f. the leathern bag that forms the body of

a bellows, sg. dat. *-basti* 100 = K. Pr. 46; *daman-hāl*, f. the pipe of a bellows, hence (4) used metaphorically for the windpipe; sg. dat. *-hālē* (for *hāli*), 4; *daman-khār*, a blacksmith (who uses bellows), 100 = K. Pr. 46.

dumaṭh, m. a vaulted building, a dome; a boundary-pillar (usually made of brick and whitewashed), 66; sg. dat. *dumaṭas*, 66.

dān, 1, m. a gift, a present; esp. a gift given in charity or for pious purposes, 62.

dān, 2, f. a stream (of water or the like); sg. ag. *dŏñi* (m. c. for *dŏñ^ü*), 39, 40.

dāna, m. corn, grain, 77.

dĕn, m. a day, K. Pr. 102; the day-time, as opposed to night, 22, 42; sg. dat. *dĕnas*, K. Pr. 102; *dŏh-dĕn*, see *dŏh*; *dĕn-kār*, the day's work, all one's duties, 108; *dĕn-rāth*, day and night, 91; as adv. by day and by night, continually, perpetually, without cessation, 55; *dĕn-rāth barȧnⁱ*, to pass day and night, to pass all one's time, 91; *dĕn kyōh rāth*, day and night, 3; met. joy and sorrow, 5; as adv. day and night, perpetually, 65; *lūstum dĕn kyōh rāth*, day and night set for me, vanished for me, passed for me, 3; *dĕn kyāwu rāth*, i. q. *dĕn kyōh rāth*; as adv. perpetually, 19.

dhēn, f. a milch cow; sg. abl. *dhēni*, 38.

dūn^u, m. a man who cards cotton, a cotton-carder; sg. ag. *dūnⁱ*, 102.

ḍingun, to be wrapped in sleep; fut. sg. 3, *ḍingi*, 78 (used as present).

doñ^u, adj. fortunate, happy, rich, opulent; m. pl. nom., with emph. *y*, *dȧñiy*, 27.

dŏñi, see *dān*, 2.

dīph, m. a lamp, 4; esp. the small lamp used in worship, 45.

dapun, to say; fut. sg. 3, with suff. 2nd pers. sg. dat. *dapiy*, he will (may) say to thee, 20; impve. pres. pl. 3, with suff. 1st pers. sg. dat. *dȧpⁱnĕm*, let them say to me, 21 (modern Ksh. would be *dȧpⁱnam*); p. p. m. sg. with suff. 3rd pers. sg. ag. and 1st pers. sg. dat. *dop^unam*, he said to me, 94; pl. *dȧpⁱ*, (Lal) said (verses, m.), 76.

dār, f. a stream, a current; *sȯd^ari-dār*, the current (or tide) of the ocean, 74; sg. dat. *dārĕ* (for *dāri*), 74; *chōra-dār*, see *chōr*.

dōrⁱ, adj. holding, supporting; *nāsika-pawana-dōrⁱ*, holding (i. e. borne upon) the vital airs that issue through the nose (sc. from the heart) (of the syllable *ōṁ*), 33; see *anāhath*.

dōr^ü, f. a side-door, a small door, a window; pl. nom. *dārĕ*, 101.

dūr^u, adj. far, distant, 27; adv. afar, 30; *dūrē*, adv. afar, at

a distance, 36; *dūrᵘ karun*, to make distant, to put far off, to put away, K. Pr. 56 (f. *dūrü*).
drŏgᵘ, adj. dear, high-priced; hence, rare, hard to obtain, 30.
durlab, adj. hard to obtain, rare, 29.
drām, see *nĕrun*.
dramun, m. a kind of grass, the *dūb*-grass of India, *cynodon dactylon*; hence, metaphorically, the luxuriant weeds of worldly pursuits, 36.
darun, to be firm, steadfast; fut. sg. 3, *darē* (for *dari*), 34 (in sense of pres. subj.).
dārun, to put, to place; to lay, or offer, (an animal in sacrifice), 63; *nām dārun*, to bear a name, to be called (so and so), 8; *thar dārüñü*, to offer the back, to place the back at one's disposal (of a riding animal), 88.

Fut. sg. 3, with suff. 2nd pers. sg. dat. *dāriy*, 88; p. p. m. pl. with suff. 3rd pers. sg. ag. *dörin*, 8; f. sg. *dörü*, 63.
darshĕn, m. seeing, esp. seeing, visiting, (a holy place or a god); abl. *darshĕna-myūlᵘ*, union (brought about) by visiting; *swa-darshĕna-myūlᵘ*, union with the Self (i.e. God) brought about by visiting a holy place, 36, but see art. *swa*.
druwᵘ, adj. firm, steady, immovable, 71.
drāyĕs, see *nĕrun*.
dās, m. a servant, 43.
dashĕ, card. ten, in *dashĕ-nāḍi-wāv*, the air (which passes along) the ten (chief) *nāḍis*, 69; see *nāḍi*. This word is borrowed from the Sanskrit *daśa-*. The regular Kāshmīrī word is *dah*.
dēsh, m. a country, a tract of country, 52, 53.
dish, f. a point of the compass, quarter, direction; sg. abl. *kami dishi*, from what direction? whence?, 41.
dēshun or *ḍēshun*, to see; fut. sg. 2, *dēshĕkh*, 36: p. p. m. sg. with emph. *y*, *ḍyūṭhuy*, 5; with suff. 1st pers. sg. ag. *ḍyūṭhum*, 31, 93, 96 (bis), 97 = K. Pr. 47; with suff. 2nd pers. nom. *ḍyūkhukh*, 44; with suff. 3rd pers. pl. ag. *ḍyūṭhukh*, 59; f. sg. with suff. 1st pers. sg. ag. *ḍīṭhüm*, 96 (bis) = K. Pr. 47, 97 (ter) = K. Pr. 47; m. pl. with suff. 1st pers. sg. ag. and 3rd pers. sg. dat. *ḍīṭhimas*, I saw (bolts) on His (doors), 48.
dōshĕway, card. the two, both, 56.
ditⁱ, *ditō*, *dith*, see *dyunᵘ*.
ḍīṭhüm, *ḍīṭhimas*, see *dēshun*.
ditith, *ditⁱtham*, see *dyunᵘ*.
dēv, m. a god, 14, 15, 33 (bis); the image of a god, an idol, 17; sg. dat. *dēwas* (in sense of gen. = Prakrit *dēvassa*), 33.
dĕwa, adv. perhaps, K. Pr. 56.
dwādashānth, m. N. of a certain ventricle in the brain (? the fourth, see *Śivasūtra-vimarśinī*, iii. 16; trans. p. 48).

The commentary to L. V. 33 describes it as the centre of the brain, or, alternatively, as the tip of the nose; *dwādashānta-maṇḍal*, m. the locality of the *dwādashānth*, i.e. the *Brahma-randhra* (see Note on Yōga, 5, 27), 33.

dwār, m. a door, a gate, 29; *dwār bazun*, to resort to a door to approach, or wait at, a door, 51.

*diwor*ᵘ, m. a lofty, stone-built, shrine for receiving the image of a god, a masonry temple, 17.

day, m. God, the Supreme Being, 106; sg. dat. *dayĕs*, K. Pr. 201; gen. *dayĕ-sond*ᵘ, 105.

dāy, m. advice, counsel; esp. instruction as to God, right teaching as to the nature of the Supreme, 41.

diyĕ, diyi, see *dyun*ᵘ.

döy, interj. in *bŏ-döy*, I, good Sir! 67.

ḍyūkhukh, old form for *ḍyūṭhukh*, see *dēshun*.

*ḍyol*ᵘ, adj. loose, slack; (of a parcel) untied, 108.

dhyān, m. contemplation, profound religious meditation, 59.

*dyun*ᵘ, to give, 12, 44, 54, 63, 71, 98; K. Pr. 18, 102 (ter); *cākh dyun*ᵘ, to cut to pieces, 104; *dil dyun*ᵘ, to give heart (to), to encourage, K. Pr. 46; *dam dyun*ᵘ (see *dam* 1), 100, 101; *goḍ*ᵘ *dyun*ᵘ, to asperge (an idol, as an act of worship), 39, 40; *ganḍāh dit*ⁱ, put knots (on a net), 6; *phālav dyun*ᵘ, to close the door and shutters of a shop, to shut up shop, K. Pr. 102; *pàn*ⁱ *din*ⁱ, to thrust in pegs, 66; *tār dyun*ᵘ, to cross (a person) over, to ferry across, 106.

Conj. part. *dith*, K. Pr. 102; *dith karith* (modern *dith kĕth*), 12.

Fut. sg. 1, *dima*, 98, K. Pr. 18; 3, *diyi*, 106; *diyē* (at end of line), 54.

Impve. sg. 2, with suff. 3rd pers. sg. dat. *dikh*, give to them, 71; pol. sg. 2, *ditō*, 100, K. Pr. 46; fut. with suff. 3rd pers. sg. dat. *dizĕs*, thou shouldst give to him or to it, 39, 40, 63.

Past part. m. sg. with suff. 1st pers. sg. ag. *dyutum*, I gave, 44; and also with suff. 3rd pers. sg. dat. *dyut*ᵘ*mas*, I gave to him or to it, 101, 104; with suff. 2nd pers. sg. ag. and 1st pers. sg. dat. (a *dativus commodi*), *dyut*ᵘ*tham*, thou gavest for me (i.e. in my presence), K. Pr. 102 (bis); pl. *dit*ⁱ, 6; with suff. 2nd pers. sg. ag. *ditith*, thou gavest (them), 66; and also with suff. 1st pers. sg. dat. (a *dativus commodi*), *dit*ⁱ*tham*, thou gavest (them) for me (i.e. in my presence), K. Pr. 102.

ḍyūṭhukh, ḍyūṭhum, ḍyūṭhuy, see *dēshun*.

*dyutum, dyut*ᵘ*mas, dyut*ᵘ*tham*, see *dyun*ᵘ.

dhyēy. m. the object of *dhyān*, q.v., the object of religious meditation, that which is meditated upon, 59.

dizĕs, see *dyunᵘ*.

dazawunᵘ, n. ag. that which burns, burning, blazing; f. *dazawüñüy*, 97 (with emph. *y*).

goḍᵘ, m. aspersion, ceremonial sprinkling (of an idol or the like) with water. *goḍᵘ dyunᵘ*, to asperge, 39, 40.

göfil, see *göphil*.

gagan, m. the sky, firmament (in contrast to the earth), 22, 42. Used as an equivalent to the Śaiva technical term *ākāśa* or the wide expanse of empty space; hence, ethereality or the principle of vacuity (in 1 used as synonymous with *shūñ*), one of the five physical factors, or *bhūtas*, viz. the principles of the experience of (1) solidity, (2) liquidity, (3) formativity, (4) aeriality, (5) ethereality or vacuity (see *Kashmir Śaivism*, 48, 131, 133, 140, 141, 145). It is also conceived as sound as such, i.e. sound conceived, not as a sensation within the brain, but as an objective entity. It is supposed to fill the inside of the body, its centre being the heart (cf. Note on Yōga, § 23). But by the word 'heart' is not meant the physiological organ, but the centre of the body, imagined as a hollow, and filled with this *akāśa* (translation of *Śivasūtra-vimarśinī*, p. 29). *Gagan* is used in this sense of the principle of vacuity in 1 and 26.

Sg. dat. *gaganas-kun*, (the earth spreads out) to the sky, 22; *gaganas*, in the vacuity, 1; old sg. loc. *gagànⁱ*, 26.

gēh, m. a house, house and home, a house and all that it connotes, 55. *gēh bazun*, to serve a house, to be occupied in household affairs, to be a householder as distinct from an ascetic, 32, cf. *gih*.

gih, m. i.q. *gēh*, a house, household affairs, life as a householder as opposed to an ascetic life, 64.

güjü, f. the opening of a native cooking-range through which the fuel is fed; hence, a cooking-hearth (as a part for the whole), 97.

gal, f. the throat, neck; sg. voc. *shyāma-galā*, O thou with the blue throat, i.e. Śiva, whose throat was dyed blue by drinking the deadly *kāla-kūṭa* poison, 13.

gāl, f. abuse, foul language, contumelious language; *gāl ganḍüñü*, to bind abuse (to a person), to abuse, 21.

golᵘ, 1, m. the inner corner of the mouth; *golᵘ hyonᵘ*, to take the mouth, hence, to conceal one's mouth; the mouth, or orifice, of the upper receptacle, through which grain is gradually delivered to the stones of a mill to be ground. When the stones cease to revolve, this orifice becomes blocked up; so *gràṭan hyotᵘ goluy* (emph. *y*), (when the mill stopped revolving, then) the mill concealed its orifice;

i.e. the orifice was hidden by the accumulating grain that should have issued from it, and became blocked up (86).

gol^{u}, 2, see *galun*.

gul, m. a rose-flower, a flower generally, 96 = K. Pr. 47.

gŏlāla, m. the red poppy; pl. nom. *gŏlāla*, K. Pr. 102.

galun, to melt away, disappear, be destroyed; in 64 (*kalan tsĕ gol*^{u}), *gol*^{u}, in the past, is used impersonally, and *kalan* is in the dative plural, the whole being an instance of the *bhāvĕ prayōga*, with regard to, or as to, thy longings disappearance was done for thee, i.e. thy longings disappeared.

Fut. sg. 3, *gali*, 11, 28; past m. sg. 3, *gol*^{u}, 1, 9, 11, 64.

gaman, m. the act of going; *wūrdhwa-gaman*, the act of going upwards, ascending into the sky, 38.

gaṇḍ, m. a knot; *gaṇḍāh dyun*^{u} (with suff. of indef. art.), to make a knot, to add a knot to something already knotted; in *gaṇḍāh shĕth shĕt*^{i} *dit*^{i} (6), *gaṇḍāh* is pl. although with the indef. art., he added knots (one by one) by hundreds; *aṭa-gaṇḍ*, a shoulder-knot, a knot by which the rope supporting a burden on the shoulders is tightened, 108.

goṇḍ^{u}, m. a rhinoceros; pl. nom. *gȧṇḍ*^{i}, 47.

gaṇḍun, to knot, tie up; to bind, fasten, tie up, 24, 101; to tie on, or put on, clothes, to dress oneself, 27 (bis); *gāl gaṇḍüñ*^{u}, to bind abuse (on a person), to abuse, 21; inf. sg. abl. *gaṇḍana-nishĕ*, from (i.e. by) dressing oneself, 27; conj. part. *gaṇḍith*, 27; fut. sg. 3, (in meaning of pres. subj.), *gaṇḍē*, 24; impve. pl. 3, with suff. 1st pers. sg. dat. *gȧṇḍ*^{i}*nĕm* (modern Kāshmīrī would be *gȧṇḍ*^{i}*nam*), 21; p. p. m. sg. with suff. 1st pers. sg. ag. *goṇḍum*, 101.

gang, f. the Ganges; sg. dat. *gangi-hyuh*^{u}, like the Ganges, K. Pr. 201.

ganun, to become established, firmly fixed; II past, f. sg. 3, *ganēyĕ*, 48.

gaṇz^{a}*run*, to count; hence, to think about, meditate upon, 55; conj. part. *gaṇz*^{a}*rith*, 55.

gȫphil, adj. negligent, heedless, unmindful; sg. voc. *gȫphilō*, 99; *gȫfilō*, K. Pr. 46.

gara, m. a house, 3, K. Pr. 57; a home, 106; *gara gatshun*, to go home, 106; *sōma-gara*, the home of the moon, 34, see *sōm*; sg. abl. *garē*, in the house, 34; *panani garē*, (I saw a learned man) in my own house, 3; (expelled) from my own house, K. Pr. 57. Note the old loc. pl. *garu*, in *lūka-garu*, 53, (enters) people's houses.

garē, see *gara* and *garun*.

gŏr, m. a spiritual teacher, a guru; sg. voc. *yē gŏrā*, 56; ag. *gŏran*, 94; *gŏra-kath*, the word, or teaching, of a guru, 45, 62; *gŏra-sond*^{u} *wanun*, id. 108. Cf. *guru*.

gōr, m. molasses, 66. It is given to a cow to increase her milk.

*gur*ᵘ, m. a horse, 14.

guru, m. a spiritual teacher or preceptor, i.q. *gŏr*, q.v.; *sura-guru*, usually means 'the preceptor of the gods', i.e. Bṛhaspati. He is a deity who is the chief offerer of prayers and sacrifices, and who is also the *purōhita* of the gods, with whom he intercedes for men. He is the god of wisdom and eloquence. In 5 and 65, *sura-guru-nāth* would therefore be expected to mean 'the lord of Bṛhaspati'. It is, however, not so interpreted, but *sura-guru* is said to be equivalent to the Sanskrit *dēva-dēva*, the chief of the gods, and *sura-guru-nāth* is said to mean 'Lord of the chiefest of the gods', i.e. Śiva. Cf. *Mahābhārata*, i. 1628.

*gūr*ü, f. a *ghaṛī* or space of time of about 24 minutes, hence, indefinitely, any short space of time; abl. sg. *gari gari*, at every *ghaṛī*, frequently, again and again, K. Pr. 150.

garb, m. the womb; hence, a foetus; with suff. of indef. art. *garbā*, a foetus, (even whilst thou wast) yet in thy mother's womb, 87.

garun, to frame, to build; fut. sg. 3 (with meaning of present), *garē*, 34. Cf. *gaṭun*.

gārun, to search eagerly for, 30, 43, 109 (bis); to remember affectionately, long for, and hence, to cherish affectionately, 7; pres. part. *gārān*, 109 (bis); impve. sg. 2, with suff. of 3rd pers. sg. acc. *gārun*, search thou for it, 30; past part. m. sg. with suff. 1st pers. sg. ag. *gōrum*, I cherished, 7; with suff. 3rd pers. sg. ag. *gōrun*, he sought for, 43. Cf. *gwārun*.

grāsun, to swallow down, to devour in one mouthful; past part. m. sg. *grōs*ᵘ, 22.

graṭa, m. a corn-mill, 86; sg. dat. *graṭas*, 52; ag, *graṭan*, 86; *graṭa-wōl*ᵘ, m. a miller, 86.

gösil, f. the condition of being littered with dirty straw, grass, weeds, &c., K. Pr. 56.

gaṭa, f. darkness, sg. dat. *gaṭi*, in the darkness, 4.

*got*ᵘ, in *wata-got*ᵘ, m. one who goes along a road, a wayfarer, 57.

gath, 1, f. going, gait, progress, movement, course; way, conduct, works; *hamsa-gath*, the way, or course, of the *haṁsa mantra*, 65. Like the syllable *ōṁ*, the course of this mantra is said to be unobstructed (*anāhata* or *avyāhata*). It is one of the mystic sounds heard by the Yōgī (Note on Yōga, § 23). See *hams* and *anāhath*. *parama-gath*, the way of the Supreme, final beatitude, 103. sg. dat. *gūś*ü; *cyāně gūś*ü *namaskār*, reverence to Thy (mighty) works! K. Pr. 102.

gath, 2, in *sarwa-gath*, adj. going everywhere, omnipresent, universally immanent (of the Deity), 64.

guthᵃr, m. family, race, lineage, 15.

gaṭakh, f. darkness, spiritual darkness; with suff. of indef. art. *gaṭakāh*, 104.

gāṭulᵘ, adj. wise, skilful, learned; with suff. of indef. art. *gāṭulwāh*, a learned man, a scholar, 83.

gaṭun, to put together, make, manufacture, compound (e. g. an elixir); cf. *garun*, of which it is an older form.

Conj. part. *gaṭith*; *zānun gaṭith*, to know how to compound, 80.

güȼü, see *gath*, 1.

gaȼhun, 1, to be wanted, to be required, to be necessary. This verb uses the future in the sense of the present, 29, 45; *gaȼhun gaȼhē*, going (*gaȼhun*, 2) is necessary, one must go, one has to go, 19; so *pakun gaȼhē*, one has to progress, 19.

Fut. sg. 3, *gaȼhi*, 29; *gaȼhē*, 19, 45.

gaȼhun, 2, to go, 19 (see *gaȼhun*, 1), 36 (to = dat.), 41, 61, 98 (= K. Pr. 18), K. Pr. 20; (*gara gaȼhun*, to go home, 106); to go away, depart, 95, K. Pr. 102; to go away, to disappear, be annihilated, 9; to become, 16, 59, 66, 86, 94, 108; *gaȼhiy hösil*, there will become a product for thee, it will be turned into (dat.) for thee, 100 (= K. Pr. 46); *kyāh gōm*, what became to me? what happened to me? 84, 85; *gayĕm*, it (fem.) happened to me, 102; *gauv mĕ kyāh*, what happened to me? i. e. what benefit was it to me? 81.

With the conjunctive participle of another verb, *gaȼhun* forms intensive compounds, as in *khàsⁱtⁱ* (for *khasith*) *gaȼhun*, to ascend, 27; *mīlith gaȼhun*, to become united (in), absorbed in (dat.), 11, 29, 30, 69; *mashith gaȼhun*, to become forgetful, to become ignorant, to become full of ignorance, 59; *ȼaṭith gaȼhun*, (?) to become cut, 84.

Fut. pass. part. m. sg. *gaȼhun*, 19; pres. part. used in sense of 3rd pl. pres. *gaȼhān*, 36.

Fut. sg. 1, *gaȼha*, 41, 61; 3, *gaȼhi*, 29; with suff. 2nd pers. sg. dat. *gaȼhiy*, 100 = K. Pr. 46.

Past. Cond. sg. 1, *gaȼhahö*, 106.

Past. m. sg. 3, *gauv*, 11, 30, 59, 69, 81, 86, 94; with suff. 1st pers. sg. dat. *gōm*, 84, 85, 108 (ter); pl. 3, *gay*, 9, 16, 27, 59, K. Pr. 102; *gaiy*, 95; *gàyⁱ*, 66; f. sg. 1, *gayĕs*, 98 = K. Pr. 18; 3, *gayĕ*, K. Pr. 20; with suff. 1st pers. sg. dat. *gayĕm*, 102.

gāv, f. a cow, 95.

gwāh, m. illumination, becoming illumined, 22. In modern Kāshmīrī this word is usually *gāsh*. For the insertion of *w*, cf. *gārun* and *gwārun*.

gwārun, to search eagerly for, i. q. *gārun*, q. v.; pres. part. *gwāran*, 48; inf. dat. (= inf. of purpose), *gwārani*, 36.

gyān, m. i.q. *jñān*, q.v., knowledge, esp. knowledge of the divine, ultimate wisdom; sg. dat. *gyānas*, 60.

ha, interj.; *ha māli*, O father (i.e. Sir!), 107. This may als be read as one word, *hamāli*; see *hamāl*.
hā, interj.; *hā manashĕ*, O man! 107.
hē, interj.; *hē nārān*, O Nārāyaṇa (the god)! 109 (ter).
huda-huda, a word of unknown meaning. In modern Kāshmīrī *hud* means a 'tunnel' or 'mine'. sg. gen. (f. sg. dat. or pl. nom.) with emph. *y*, *huda-hudañĕy*, 84.
hŏdun to become dry, withered; 1 p. p. f. sg. with suff. 1st pers. sg. gen. *hŏzüm*, 25.
hiḍis, see *hyuḍu*.
hah, m. cold breath, as it issues from the mouth,—said to take its rise from the *Brahma-randhra*, 56, 57.
hāh, m. warm breath, as it issues from the mouth—said to take its rise from the navel, 56, 57.
hihi, *hihĕn*, see *hyuhu*.
haka, adv. speedily, quickly, with energy, 99, K. Pr. 46.
hākh, m. a vegetable; *hāka-wörü*, f. a vegetable-garden, 63.
hĕkun, to carry out successfully some difficult task, 108; with the conj. part. of another verb, to be able, to can, *phirith hĕkun*, to be able to reverse, 107.

Fut. sg. 1, *hĕka*, 108 (bis); 3, with suff. of pron. of 2nd pers. sg. dat. *hĕkiy*, he will be able (to reverse) for thee, 107.

hal, m. striving, straining, making great efforts;—*karun*, to strive, strain oneself, 48.
hāl, f. in *daman-hāl*, the main pipe of a blacksmith's bellows; sg. dat. *-hālē* (for *-hāli*), 4.
holu, crooked, awry, 108 (metaphorically, of labour).
hlād, m. rejoicing, joy, happiness, 73.
hamāl, m. a burden-bearer, a porter; voc. *hamāli*, 107, also capable of being read as *ha māli*, O father!
himun, to become snow, to be turned into snow; fut. sg. 3, *himi*, 16 (in sense of pres.).
hams, 1, m. in *rāza-hams*, a swan, q.v., 86.
hams, 2, a reverse representation in Kāshmīrī of *sō 'ham*, or *ahaṁ saḥ*, 'that is I', or 'I am that', i.e. 'the Supreme is one with me', or 'I am one with the Supreme'. It is used as the title of a *mantra*, or mystic formula, and is an *anāhath shĕbd* (see *anāhath*), or unobstructed sound; *hamsa-gath*, the unobstructed course of this sound uttered by the deity dwelling within the body, as explained under *anāhath*, 65. The mantra '*sō 'ham*' leads to union with Śiva, and *hams* leads to union with manifested universes. See *Śivasūtra-vimarśinī*,

ii. 1 (trans. p. 25). For further particulars, see notes to verses 40 and 65.

han, f. a small piece, a fragment; sg. dat. *hani hani*, in small pieces, in fragments, 103.

hond^{u} (f. *hünz*^{ü}), suffix of the genitive (*a*) of all plural nouns, and (*b*) of all feminine singular nouns.

(*a*) *pāṇḍawan-hünz*^{ü} *mōj*^{ü}, the mother of the Pāṇḍavas, 97, K. Pr. 47.

(*b*) *wumri-hünz*^{ü} *hösil*, the results of life, K. Pr. 56.

The word *lūkh*, a person other than oneself, is masculine, but it takes *hond*^{u} in the genitive singular (being treated as if it were plural), as in *lūka-hünz*^{ü} *kŏng-wör*^{ü}, the saffron-plot of some one else, 88; *lūka-hanzay larĕ*, houses of other people, K. Pr. 57. Cf. *sond*^{u}.

honḍ^{u}, m. a large fat ram; pl. nom. *hanḍī* (m. c. for *hànḍ*^{i}), 77.

hūñ^{ü}, f. a female dog, a bitch, K. Pr. 102.

har, m. N. of the god Śiva in his capacity of destroyer (of sin, sorrow, misfortune, and stumbling-blocks against salvation); sg. dat. *haras*, 78, 79; *har-nāv*, the name of Śiva, 98.

hār, f. a cowry, 98 = K. Pr. 18.

hrĕd, f. the heart; sg. dat. in sense of loc. *hrĕdi*, 76.

hrĕday, m. the heart; sg. gen. (f. sg. dat.) *hrĕdayĕcĕ kūṭh*^{a}*rĕ-andar*, in the closet of my heart, 101.

haramŏkh, m. N. of a celebrated mountain in Kashmīr; sg. abl. *haramŏkha*, 50.

h^{a}*run*, to increase, grow greater; fut. sg. 3, with suff. 2nd pers. sg. dat. *h*^{a}*riy*, 87.

harun, to fall (as leaves from a tree), 83; to waste away, disappear, be destroyed, 72; pres. part. *harān*, 83; fut. sg. 3, *hari*, 72.

hishiy, see *hyuh*^{u}.

hushyār, adj. mindful, cautious, alert, on one's guard:—*rōzun*, to be on the alert, K. Pr. 46.

hösil, f. product, produce, outcome, K. Pr. 56; *shĕst*^{a}*ras sŏn gatshiy hösil*, for iron, gold will become a product for thee, i.e. thine iron will be turned into gold, 100 = K. Pr. 46.

host^{u}, m. an elephant, 24; K. Pr. 150; *zala-host*^{u}, a sea-elephant (a fabulous monster), 47; sg. nom. with emph. *y*, *hostuy*, K. Pr. 150; sg. ag. *hàst*^{i}, K. Pr. 150; pl. nom. with emph. *y*, *hàstiy*, 47.

hĕta, see *hĕth*, 1, and *hyon*^{u}.

hōṭā, interj. indicating respect, 17.

hot^{u}, adj. smitten; frequent °—, as in *nĕndri-hot*^{u}, smitten by sleep, sunk in sleep; m. pl. nom. with emph. *y*, *nĕndri-hàtiy*, 32.

hĕth, 1, adj. pleasant, agreeable. This adj. is immutable, and its m. pl. nom. is also *hĕth*, but in 28, with *ā* added m. c., it takes the form *hĕtā*, which here may also be translated as equivalent to *hĕta*, pol. impve. of *hyonᵘ*, q.v. Cf. *hyotᵘ*, 1.

hĕth, 2, see *hyonᵘ*.

hetⁱnam, see *hyonᵘ*.

hutawah, m. that which conveys oblations (to heaven); hence, a furiously burning fire, 38.

hüṭsᵘ, f. murder, in *brahma-hüṭsᵘ*, murder of a Brāhmaṇ, with emph. *y*, *-hüṭsᵘy*, K. Pr. 102.

hāy, interj. alas, 67.

hĕyē, see *hyonᵘ*.

hyuḍᵘ, m. the gullet, esp. the top of the gullet near Adam's apple, which is properly *hiḍⁱ-gōgulᵘ*, the lump in the gullet; sg. dat. *hiḍis*, 57. In modern language this word is usually *hyurᵘ*.

hyuhᵘ, adj. like, alike, 10, 77; *hihĕn hihⁱ*, like (are united) to like, 109; (governing dat.) like, as in *sirĕs hyuhᵘ*, like the sun, and so on for other similitudes, K. Pr. 201.

M. sg. nom. *hyuhᵘ*, K. Pr. 201 (twelve times); pl. nom. *hihⁱ*, 109; dat. *hihĕn*, 109; f. sg. nom., with emph. *y*, *hishiy* (for *hishᵘy*), 10, 77. Cf. *hyuvᵘ*.

hyonᵘ, to take, 12, 45; to buy, 89; with inf. of another verb, to begin; *wuchun hyotᵘmas*, I began to look at it, 48; *hyotum naṭsun*, I began to dance, 94.

ambar hyonᵘ, to take clothes, to wear clothes, to dress oneself, 28; *athi* (or m. c. *athē*) *hyonᵘ*, to carry in the hand, 10; *golᵘ hyonᵘ*, 86, see *golᵘ*; *tal hyonᵘ*, to take below (oneself); to put beneath one's feet, (of an elephant) to crush beneath the feet, K. Pr. 150; *zuv hyonᵘ*, to take (a person's) life, to kill, 54.

hĕth raṭun, to take and hold, to keep hold of, 69; *hĕth ṭsalun*, to take and flee, to run away with (as a thief), 86 (bis).

Conj. part. *hĕth*, 10, 69, 86; *hĕth karith* (modern *hĕth kĕth*), 12; fut. sg. 3, *hĕyē* (m. c. for *hĕyi*), 45, 54; impve. pl. 2, *hĕyiv*, 89; pol. impve. sg. 2, *hĕtā* (m. c. for *hĕta*), 28 (in this passage, the word may also be translated as equivalent to *hĕth*, 1, q. v.).

Past. part. m. sg. *hyotᵘ*, 86; with suff. 1st pers. sg. ag., *hyotum*, 94; and also with suff. 3rd pers. sg. dat., *hyotᵘmas*, 48; pl. with suff. 3rd pers. sg. ag. and also suff. 1st pers. sg. dat. (a *dativus commodi*), *hĕtⁱnam*, K. Pr. 150.

hyotᵘ, 1, adj. beneficial, advantageous, salutary, 61; i. q. *hĕth*, 1, q. v.

hyotᵘ, 2, *hyotum*, *hyotᵘmas*, see *hyonᵘ*.

*hyuv*ᵘ, i.q. *hyuh*ᵘ, q.v., like, alike, 5.
hĕyiv, see *hyon*ᵘ.
*hŏz*ᵘ*m*, see *hŏdun*.

jŏhil, adj. ignorant, illiterate; as subst., an ignorant fool, K. Pr. 46.

jān, adj. good, excellent, first-rate; *jān gatshun*, to turn out well, to have a happy result, 85; *jān kyāh*, how well! how excellently! 89.

jñān, m. knowledge; esp. the true knowledge (of the Śaiva religion), 12; *jñāna-mārg*, the path of knowledge, the way to the knowledge of the Supreme, 63; *jñāna-prakāsh*, the light of knowledge, illumination consisting in the true knowledge, 6; sg. gen. (in m. pl. nom.) *jñānak*ⁱ *ambar pairith*, having put on the garments of knowledge, 76. Cf. *gyān* and *zān*.

jāy, f. the position, or place, of anything; *arshĕs jāy*, a position in the sky (the whole world, being flooded, is represented as merely a waste of waters bounded by the sky), 50.

jyōti, f. brilliance, illumination, bright light; *tsĕth-jyōti*, the illumination of the intelligence, the pure light of Intelligence, pure Intelligence, i.e. the Supreme, or *Śiva-tattva*, the first stage in the process of the universal manifestation of the Supreme Śiva, looked upon as pure light, without anything to shine upon, or as the pure 'I', without even the thought or feeling of 'I am', i.e. of being. See *Kashmir Shaivism*, fasc. i., p. 63. Sg. dat. *tsĕth-jyōti*, (absorbed) in this Śiva-tattva, 76.

kō, in *kō-zana*, see *kō-zana*.

kŏch, f. the lap, the lower part of the bosom; dat. (for acc.) *kŏchĕ*, 70.

*kŏḍ*ᵘ, m. one who extracts seeds from raw cotton, a cotton-cleaner; sg. ag. *kŏḍ*ⁱ, 102.

kŏ-dēh, m. an evil body, a vile body, (this) vile body (of mine), 7.

kadam, m. the foot;—*tulun*, to raise the foot, to walk quickly or vigorously, to step out, 99; K. Pr. 46.

kaḍun, to extract; conj. part. *kaḍith nyun*ᵘ, to carry out, bring forth (from a house), carry forth, K. Pr. 57.

*kădur*ᵘ, m. a baker; sg. dat. *kădris*, K. Pr. 20.

kha, m. the sky, firmament; the ether, the principle of vacuity (i.q. *shūñ*, q.v.); *kha-swarūph*, he who consists of absolute vacuity, the impersonal Supreme Deity, 15.

kāh, card. eleven; pl. dat. (for gen.) *kāhan*, 95; *kāhan gāv*, the cow of eleven owners, i.e. a cow owned by eleven different persons (each of whom pulls her in a different direction), 95. The 'cow' is the body. Its eleven owners are the five *jñānêndriyas* or faculties of perception [i.e. the senses of (1) smell (*ghrāṇa*), (2) taste (*rasanā*), (3) sight (*darśana*), (4) touch (*sparśa*), and (5) hearing (*śravaṇa*)], plus the five *karmêndriyas* or organs of action [i.e. the organs of (1) voice (*vāc*), (2) handling (*hasta*), (3) locomotion (*pāda*), (4) excretion (*pāyu*), and (5) generation (*upastha*)], plus the mind (*manaḥ*), which is the regulating organ of the other ten.

kẽh, indef. pron. Subst. sg. nom. an. m. *kũh*, 35, 60; *kãh*, 107; *kũṭsh*, 60; inan. com. gend. *kũh*, 2; *kẽh*, 9, 11, 19, 23, 31, 90; dat. (for gen.) an. m. *kaĩsi*, 35; pl. nom. an. m. *kẽh*, 32; *kẽh*, K. Pr. 102; dat. *kẽtsan*, 32; *kĕntsan*, K. Pr. 102 (many times); ag. *kĕntsav*, K. Pr. 102.

Adj. sg. nom. inan. m. *kãh*, K. Pr. 201; *kãtsh*, 41; *kẽtsh*, 59; inan. f. *kõh* (in *kõh-ti*), 77.

Subst. any one, 35, 60; anything, 2, 31.

Adj. any, K. Pr. 201.

kẽh . . . *kẽh*, some . . . others, 32; K. Pr. 102 (*kẽh* . . . *kẽh*).

na kãh, no one, 107; *na kũh*, no one, 35; *nā kẽh*, nothing, 23; *kẽtsh nā*, no (adj.), 59; *na kũtsh*, no one, 60; *kẽh na-ta kyāh*, nothing at all, 19; *kẽh-ti nā*, nothing at all, 9, 11; *kẽh-ti nō*, nothing at all, 90; *kõh-ti na khĕth*, no harm at all, 77; *kãtsh-ti nō sath*, no substance at all, 41.

kĕhō, conj. or, K. Pr. 102.

khēd, m. distress, pain, feeling of trouble, 18.

khĕn, m. food, 71.

khũñ[u], f. a kind of warm woollen blanket worn as a cloak in cold weather; sg. dat. *khañi*, K. Pr. 201.

khar, m. an ass, 88.

khār, 1, m. a blacksmith; *daman-khār*, a blacksmith who uses bellows, 100 = K. Pr. 46.

khār, 2, m. a thorn, 96 = K. Pr. 47.

khŏr, see *khọsh*[u].

khura-khura, m. longing for something difficult to obtain or unobtainable, K. Pr. 57 (translated in original 'proudness of heart').

khārun, to raise, lift; to lift off (spun thread from a spinning-wheel), 102; *khārĕnam*, she raised fem. things of me, 102.

khọsh[u], left-handed; *khŏsh*[i]*-khŏr*, f. acting in a left-handed way, acting contrary to custom, 10, 77.

khasun, to ascend, go up, 27, 75; impve. sg. 2, *khas*, 75; conj. part. irreg. *khăs*[i]*t*[i] for *khasith*, 27.

khĕth, 1, f. loss, harm, injury, 10, 77.

khĕth, 2, see *khyon*[u].

khaṭun, to conceal; to cause to disappear, overwhelm, get the mastery over, 16; I. p. p. m. sg. *khoṭu*, 16.
kahyū, interrog. adv. how? by what means? 108.
khyolu, m. a flock, a herd, 108.
khyonu, to eat, 27, 63, 77, 81, 88; to bite, K. Pr. 102; esp. to eat the good things of this life, to enjoy oneself, 27, 90 (with double meaning, also simply 'to eat').

Inf. sg. abl. *khĕna-nishĕ*, (abstain) from enjoyment, 27; *khĕna khĕna*, by continued eating, 63; conj. part. *khĕth*, 27, 77; impve. fut. *nō khĕzē* (m. c. for *khĕzi*), thou shouldst not eat, 90; fut. sg. 3, *khĕyi*; *khĕyiy*, it will eat for thee, i.e. thy (ass) will eat, 88; *zang khĕyiwō* (m. c. for *khĕyiwa*), it will eat (bite) your leg, K. Pr. 102; 1 p. p. *khyauv*; m. pl. with suff. 1st pers. sg. sg. *khyēm*, I ate (masc. things), 81.
kal, 1, f. longing, yearning. —*ganüñü*, longing to increase, 48; pl. dat. *kalan*, 64.
kal, 2, an art, a skill; sg. abl. *yōga-kali*, by the art of *yōga*, by practising *yōga*, 14.
kal, 3, f. a digit of the moon; *shĕshi-kal*, id. 25, 69. Cf. *sōm*.
kāl, m. time, a time, period of time, age; the present, or iron, age, the *kali-kāl*, 91; *kāla-zōli*, by efflux of time, 64.
kŏl, m. race, tribe, family; as a Śaiva technical term (=Sanskrit *kula*), the sphere of cosmic action, as opposed to the *akŏl* (Skr. *akula*), the sphere of the Absolute or of Transcendental Being. It is supposed to be situate at the lower end of the Suṣumnā nāḍī (see Note on Yōga, §§ 12, 19). It is said to consist of the *jīva* (individual soul), *prakṛti* (primal matter), space, time, ether, earth, water, fire, and air. When the mind transcends these it is in a state of grace. Hence, *kŏl-akŏl*, the visible creation and that which transcends it, the totality of all creation, 2.
kolu, adj. dumb, 20; with emph. *y*, *koluy*, 86.
kŏlu, adj. of or belonging to (a certain) time, used —°; *path-kāli*, in former times, 91; *kŏli*, at the (destined) time, 74; *brōṭh-kŏli*, in the future, in future times, 92.
kalan, see *kal*, 1.
kalpan, f. imagination, vain imaginings, vain desires, desire, 30, 33.
klēsh, m. pain, torment, affliction, 80; — *karun*, to cause affliction (to), 51.
kam, see *kyāh*.
kām, m. sexual love, carnal appetite, 71. One of the six enemies, see *lūb*.
kami, see *kyāh*.
kumbu, m. a jar; hence, a particular religious exercise consist-

ing of profound meditation accompanied by 'bottling up' of inhaled breath (Skr. *kumbhaka*); cf. Note on Yōga, § 21. With emph. *y*, *kumbuy*, only the *kumbhaka* exercise, 34. See *nāḍi*.

kŏmbun, to practise the *kumbhaka* upon some impediment to religious welfare, to suppress by means of the *kumbhaka* meditation; conj. part. *kŏmbith*, 75.

kamalaza-nāth, m. the lord who was born in a lotus, N. of the god Brahmā, 8.

kan, m. the ear; *kan thāwun*, to offer the ear, to attend (to), give heed (to), 91.

kān, m. an arrow; *kān barun*, to aim an arrow, 71.

kun, postpos. governing dat., to, towards; *gaganas-kun vikāsē*, (the surface of the earth) will become extended to the sky, 22.

kunē, m. c. for *kuni*, adv. anywhere; *nā kunē*, nowhere, 9, 11; *na kunē*, id. K. Pr. 201.

kun^u, card. one, only one; with emph. *y*, *kunuy*, only one, 84, 94; (of several apparently different things) one and the same, 90.

kandā-purā, m. the 'city of the *kanda*', i.e. the *kanda* or 'bulb' which is supposed to be the root of the *nāḍis* (q. v.), or tubes, through which the *prāṇa*, or life-wind, circulates. It is said to be situated between the pudendum and the navel, 56. See Note on Yōga, § 5. Cf. *nāb*, *nāḍi*, and *prān*, 2.

kond^u, occurring only in the pl. ag. *kandĕv . . . kandĕv*, by several . . . by several, by some . . . by others, 55.

kŏng, m. saffron, the saffron crocus; *kŏng-wör^ü*, f. a saffron garden, 88.

koñ^u, adj. tawny-coloured; *koñ^u dād*, a tawny ox. In 66 the sg. dat. is *kàñ^i dādas*. In modern Kāshmīrī it would be *kañis dādas*.

küñ^ü, f. a stone; *dŏb^i-küñ^ü*, a washerman's stone, on which he washes clothes; sg. dat. *dŏb^i-kañĕ-pĕṭhay*, on a washerman's stone, 103.

kūph, m. anger, wrath; sg. abl. *kūpa*, 23.

kapas, f. the cotton-plant; *kapasi-pōsh*, the blossom of the cotton-plant, 102.

kapaṭh, m. deceit; *kapaṭa-ṭarith*, m. actions of deceit, jugglery, false and quack methods for obtaining salvation, 38.

kar, adv. when? *kar-bā*, when, Sir? 87.

kār, 1, m. in *ōm-kār*, the mystic syllable *ōṁ*, the *praṇava*, 34.

kār, 2, m. work, business; *dĕn-kār*, the day's work, all that one does each day, 108.

kŏr^u (= *kŏn^u*), one-eyed, 20.

kūr^ü, f. a daughter; pl. nom. *mājĕ-kōrĕ*, mother and daughter, 92.

krūd, m. anger, 71. One of the six enemies. See *lūb*.

krözjü, f. a potter's wife; *kröjⁱ-mās*, the aunt of a potter's wife, with emph. *y*, *kröjiy-mās*, 97 = K. Pr. 47. (The Pāṇḍavas and their mother Kuntī, during Draupadī's *svayaṁvara* had their home in a potter's house. See *Mahābhārata*, i. 6950, but there does not here appear to be any mention of the potter's children calling Kuntī their mother's aunt.)

karm, 1, m. an action, act, 58, 61; pl. nom. *karm*, 75. Actions are of two kinds, good or evil (75).

karm, 2, m. Fate; sg. gen. f. *karmüñü rᵃkh*, the line of Fate written on the forehead by Nārāyaṇa; *karmañĕ rᵃkhi*, (what Nārāyaṇa wrote) on the line of Fate, 107.

kāran, m. a cause; a means; sg. ag. *kāranⁱ pranawākⁱ*, by means of the *praṇava*, 76. In Śaiva philosophy, there are three causes of the material world, viz. the impurities (*mala*) that affect the soul. These are (1) *āṇava-mala*, or the impurity due to the soul, which in reality is identical with Śiva, deeming itself to be finite; (2) *māyīya-mala*, or impurity due to cognition of the differentiation of things, i.e. that one thing is different from another; and (3) *kārma-mala*, or the impurity due to action, resulting in pleasure or pain, 75.

karun, to do, 34, 37, 58, 61, 68, 74, 91, 95; to make, 17, 65, 81, 82, 85, 87, 89, 99 = K. Pr. 46; K. Pr. 102; *lālⁱ lālⁱ karān*, making the sound '*Lālⁱ Lālⁱ*', i.e. crying out, 'It is I, Lal; it is I, Lal', 105; *shiwa shiwa karān*, uttering (or calling to mind) the words 'Śiva, Śiva', 65.

klēsh karun, to give trouble, to cause pangs, 51; *nād karun*, to utter a cry, 72; *vishēsh karun*, to do a speciality, to act in a special character, 54; *ċĕtas karun*, to impress upon the mind, 34.

karith gaċhun, to make completely, 95; in *hĕth karith* and *dith karith*, both in 12, *karith*, like the modern *kĕth*, and like the Hindī *kar*, has little more than the force of a suffix of the conjunctive participle.

This verb makes many nominal compounds. Thus, *athawās karith*, holding each other's hand, = encouraging each other, 92; *cyōñü ċinth karān*, he takes thought for thee, 72; *dam karun*, to suppress the breath (as an ascetic exercise), 4; *dūrᵘ karun*, to drive away, K. Pr. 56; *hal karun*, to exert oneself, strive hard, 48; *lath karüñü*, to kick, 102; *lay karüñü*, to devote oneself ardently to any object, 60, 68; *lay karun*, to cause to be absorbed, 76; *pūz karüñü*, to worship (dat. of obj.), 17, 21; *snān karun*, to bathe oneself, 32, 46; *thaph karüñü*, to grasp (dat. of obj.), 4.

The following forms occur; inf. *karun*, 37; conj. part.

karith, 12, 32, 51, 65, 85, 92, 95; pres. part. *karān*, 65, 72, 105;

impve. sg. 2, *kar*, 17, 72, 99 = K. Pr. 46; K. Pr. 56; pl. 3, with suff. 1st pers. sg. dat. *kårⁱnĕm* (mod. *kårⁱnam*), 21;

fut. and pres. subj. sg. 1, *kara*, 61, 95; 2, *karakh*, 17; 3, *kari*, 46, 54, 68; *karē*, 34 (bis); pl. 1, *karav*, K. Pr. 102; 2, *kariv*, 91; 3, with suff. 2nd pers. sg. dat. *karinĕy* (mod. *karinay*), 74;

1 past part. m. sg. *korᵘ*, 76; with suff. 1st pers. sg. ag., *korum*, 58, 82, 89; with the same, and also with suff. 3rd pers. sg. dat. *korᵘmas*, 4, 48;

f. sg., with suff. 1st pers. sg. ag. *kürᵘ̈m*, 68; with the same, and also with suff. 3rd pers. sg. dat. *kürᵘ̈mas*, 4, 60; with suff. 3rd pers. sg. ag. and also with suff. 1st pers. sg. dat. *kürᵘ̈nam*, 102;

f. pl., with suff. 1st pers. sg. ag. *kiyĕm* (mod. *karĕm*), 81;

2 past part. m. sg., with suff. 2nd pers. sg. ag., *karyōth*, 87.

kēran, m. pl. the various natures of men and women (kindly, crooked, good, evil, tender, cruel, and so on), 92.

krünḍᵘ̈, f. a kind of large open basket; sg. dat. *kranjĕ*, 24.

krūrᵘ, adj. terrible, fierce, pitiless, 27.

krūṭhᵘ, adj. hard, severe, difficult to conquer (of a disease); hence, to be obtained with great difficulty, hard to find, 51–54, 80.

kartal, f. a sword, 62, 88.

kriy, 1, adj. doing, maker, used —°, as in *sarwa-kriy*, the maker of all things, the Creator, 59.

kriy, 2, f. an action, 63; esp. a good work, an act of devotion, act of worship, a holy action, in *kriyĕ-pūñᵘ̈*, a hedge of good works, 63.

kas, *kus*, *kusᵘ*, see *kyāh*.

kush, m. *kuśa*-grass, *Poa cynosuroides*, the sacred grass used at various religious ceremonies, 45.

kshŏd, f. hunger, 28, 72 (mod. *chŏd*).

kēshĕv, m. N. of Viṣṇu, Kēśava, 8, 14.

kusūm, m. a flower; pl. nom. *kusum*, 39, 40; abl. *kusumav*, 21.

kāsun, to remove, put away, dispel; pol. impve. sg. 2, with suff. 1st pers. sg. dat., *kāstam*, K. Pr. 57; 3, with same suff., *kösⁱtam*, 8; fut. sg. 3, with suff. 2nd pers. sg. dat., *kāsiy*, 73, 74; past part. f. sg., with suff. 3rd pers. sg. ag. *kösᵘ̈n*, 76.

kaũsar, m. N. of a sacred lake in Kashmīr, the ancient *Kramasaraḥ*, and the *Kōnsᵃr* of Sir Aurel Stein's translation of the *Rāja-taraṅgiṇī*, II, 393. The name is also given to the peak at the foot of which it lies, 50. This peak forms a part of the Pīr Pantsāl Range. Sg. abl. *kaũsara*, 50.

kọssa, see *kyāh*.

kati, adv. whence?, where?; in 106 employed, like the Hindī *kyā*, merely to indicate that the sentence is interrogative.

*k°t*ᵘ, adj. damp, moist, full of juice, juicy, 51; m. pl. nom. *kᵃtiy* (with emph. *y*), 51.

*kot*ᵘ, adv. to what direction?, whither?, 9.

*kūt*ᵘ, pron. adj. how much?; pl. how many?; m. pl. nom. *kaitⁱ*, 81; f. pl. nom. *kaiša*, 81.

*kūṭ*ᵘ, m. a beam (of wood); sg. abl. *kōṭi*, 23.

kath, f. a word, a statement, 91; *gŏra-kath*, the word of a *guru*, the spiritual teaching of a *guru*, 45, 62; pl. dat. *kathan*, 91.

kāṭh, m. wood; *kāṭha-dhēn*, a cow made of wood, a wooden cow, 38.

kĕth, termination of the conj. part., as in *vĕsarzith kĕth*, having taken leave, having departed, 9. Cf. *karith*, s. v. *karun*.

kĕtha, adv. how?, 10; *kĕthō*, id., 91 (used in addressing a person at some distance).

*kŏṭh*ᵘ, m. a knee; pl. dat. *kŏṭhĕn hyuh*ᵘ, like the knees, K. Pr. 201.

kuṭhun, to be in distress, to become hard up, to have one's income diminished; *hence*, to become more and more contracted, (of times) to become harder and harder, 91; pres. part. *kuṭhān*, 91.

kūṭhᵘrᵘ, f. a small dark room, a closet, a cupboard; sg. dat. *kūṭhᵃrĕ-andar*, 101.

kuṭun, to pound, crush, reduce to powder; conj. part. *kuṭith*, 80.

kōtur, m. a pigeon; *kōtar-mor*ᵘ, a pigeon-house, a dove-cote, K. Pr. 57.

kaiša, see *kūt*ᵘ.

kōšᵘ, f. a pair of scissors for cutting cloth or the like; with emph. *y*, *kōšᵘy*, 103.

kāv, m. a crow; pl. dat. *wan-kāwan*, for the forest-crows, 28.

kawa, see *kyāh*, 1.

kēwal, adv. only, nothing but, 72.

kyāh, 1, pron. interrog. who?, which?, what?

animate singular. Nom. m. subst. *kus*, who?, 7, 78; *kus-tām*, some one or other, 86; *kus-bā*, who, Sir?, 88; adj. *kus*ᵘ *push*ᵘ, what florist?, 39; *kus dēv*, what god?, 14; f. subst. *bŏh kŏssa*, who am I?, 7; adj. *kŏssa pūshŏñī*, what florist (f.)?, 39; dat. c. g. *kas*, to whom?, 17, 21, 33.

inanimate singular. Nom. subst. *kus*, in third line of 78, what? This is really an adjective with the substantive understood, what (thing)?; *kyāh*, what? 21, 34, 42, 68, 71, 73, 81, 84, 85, 91 (bis), 95, 98 = K. Pr. 18; K. Pr. 102; *kyāh-tām*, something or other, 86; *kēh na ta kyāh*, there is nothing, so what (is there?), = all is vanity, 19; *jān kyāh*, what a good thing!, how well!, 89; adj. *kus sar*, what lake?, 78; *kus parama-pad*, what supreme state?, 78.

Abl. subst. *kawa*, by what?, used adverbially to mean 'how?', 41, 'why?', 56 (bis); adj. *kami dishi*, from what direction?, by what direction?, 41 (bis); *kami watē*, by what road?, 41; *kami shātha*, on what bank?, 84, 85; *kawa dōñī*, with what stream?, 39; *kawa-sana mantra*, with what kind of *mantra*?, 39.

Plural nom. adj. *kam kusum*, what flowers?, 39; *kam vihi*, what sports?, 109.

kyāh, 2, adv. interrog. why?, 67, 74. Used as a mere interrogative particle, indicating a question, 18, 66.

kyōh, conj. as well as, and, in the adverbial phrase *dĕn kyōh rāth*, day and night, i.e. continually, always, 3, 5, 65. A variant form is *dĕn kyāwu rāth*, 19.

kiyĕm, see *karun*.

kyutu, postpos. of dat.; *biyis kyutu*, for some one else, 61.

kyuthu, pron. adj. interrog. what sort of?, of what kind?, 84, 85; with another adj., *kyuthu druwu*, how firm?, 71.

kyāwu, see *kyōh*.

kyāzi, adv. why?, 95, 107.

kō-zana, adv. or interj. who knows?; used in anxiety or the like, as in *kō-zana kyāh bani tas*, who knows what will happen to him, i.e. some calamity will probably occur to him. But Lal seems to use it as a mere adv. meaning 'by what means', quasi 'who knows what means (will effect so and so)', 73, 74. In 72, she has *kō-zanañi*, i.e. in the ablative feminine of the genitive, and uses it as a relative adverb meaning 'how', 'by what means' (God takes thought as to the means by which hunger will depart from thee).

lūb, desire, greed, cupidity, the chief of the six 'enemies', or sins which impede union with the Supreme. The six are *kāma*, sexual desire; *krōdha*, wrath; *lōbha*, desire; *mada*, arrogance; *mōha*, delusion of mind; and *matsara*, jealousy. In Monier Williams's *Sanskrit Dictionary*, s.v. *ṣaḍ-varga*, *harṣa*, joy, and *māna*, pride, are substituted for *mōha* and *matsara*; but the above is the list given in *Kirātārjunīya*, i. 9, viz.:—

kāmaḥ krōdhas tathā lōbhō mada-mōhau ca matsaraḥ.

In L. V. 12 and 30, *lōbha*, or Ksh. *lūb*, is mentioned alone, to indicate all six. In 43, three,—*lōbha*, *manmatha* (= *kāma*), and *mada*,—and in 71, *kāma*, *krōdha* (Ksh. *krūd*), and *lōbha*, are in each case mentioned to indicate all six. Cf. 13.

lūba-vĕnā, without desire, free from desire, 12.

labun, to get, obtain, acquire, find; fut. sg. 2, *labakh*, 75; 3, *labi*, 90, with emph. *y*, *labiy*, K. Pr. 46; past part. m. sg. with suff. 1st pers. sg. ag. *lobum*, 35, 90; f. sg. with same suff. *lüb*ᵘ*m*, 31.

lach, card. a hundred thousand; *yōzana-lach*, a hundred thousand leagues, 26; sg. abl. *lachĕ* (for *lacha*)-*manza*, (but one) out of a hundred thousand, K. Pr. 150.

lācār, adj. helpless, without resource; as subst., a helpless person, f. sg. ag. *lācāri*, 89.

ladun, to build (a house or the like); pres. part. *ladān*, K. Pr. 57.

lāg, f. aim, object, that which is aimed at, the result for which a person works; sg. abl. *lāgi-rost*ᵘ, one who is devoid of aim, one who works without considering the resultant reward, disinterested, 61, 65.

lagun, to be joined (to), connected (with); to come to anchor, to run aground, 84, 85; to come into close contact or connexion (with), to be absorbed (in), to be incorporated (in), to become one (with), 58; to become joined (to a condition), to experience, 70; to happen, befall, be met with, be obtained, 41; *achĕ lagañĕ tālav*, the eyes to be attached to the ceiling, i.e. to be turned upwards, K. Pr. 102.

Fut. sg. 1, *laga*, 84, 85; 3, *lagi*, 70; with suff. 1st pers. sg. dat. and emph. *y*, *lagimay* (for *lagĕmay*), 41; past. m. sg. 3, with suff. 1st pers. sg. dat. and interj. *ō*, *log*ᵘ*mō*, 58; f. pl. 3, *lajĕ*, K. Pr. 102.

lāgun, to join, unite, apply (*pānas lögith mĕtsĕ*, having applied earth to the body, 44, see below); to employ (an article for a certain use), to apply (something to a certain purpose), esp. to employ (a thing in worship), to make an offering (of something), 39, 40, 42, 78, 79; to act the part of (so and so), to perform the office (of so and so), to act in (such and such) a capacity, 43; in 44 (see above) *pānas lögith* also (by a pun) means 'having become hidden in thyself', i.e. of God, 'having become indiscrete'.

Conj. part. *lögith*, 44; fut. sg. 3, *lāgi*, 78, 79; impve. fut., with suff. 2nd pers. sg. dat. *lög*ⁱ*ziy*, 42; with suff. 3rd pers. sg. dat., *lög*ⁱ*zĕs*, 39, 40; past part. m. sg. with suff. 3rd pers. sg. ag., *lǒgun*, 43.

lah, adv. lightly, gently; *wāwa lah*, (leaves fall) gently with the wind, i.e. in a gentle wind, 83.

lŏh-langar, m. an iron anchor, an anchor; met. that which ties one down to this world, the things of this world (as opposed to spiritual things), worldly possessions and business, 67; sg. gen. (f. sg. nom.) *lŏh-langarüc*ᵘ, 67.

lĕjü, f. a cooking-pot; sg. dat. *lĕjĕ*, 95.

lĕkh, f. abusive language (usually indecent); *lĕkā-lĕkh*, mutual abuse, 23.

lūkh, m. people, persons, K. Pr. 57; people in general, 53; a stranger, one who is not related by blood, marriage or other connexion, other people than oneself, 88; K. Pr. 57. Note that the genitive of this word is twice *lūka-hondu*, 88; K. Pr. 57.

lūka-garu, into other people's houses (see *gara*), 53; *lūka-sāsā*, a thousand people, K. Pr. 57; *lūka-hanzay larĕ*, houses of other people, K. Pr. 57; see *hondu*.

lēkhun, to write; past part. m. sg. with suff. 2nd pers. sg. dat. *lyūkhuy*, (what) was written for thee (by Nārāyaṇa), i.e. what Nārāyaṇa wrote (on) thy (forehead),—an allusion to the lines of Fate written on the forehead of a person's skull on the sixth night after birth, 107.

lal, f. N. P., N. of Lal Dĕd, known in Sanskrit as Lallā, the authoress of the poems edited in this volume, 3, 48, 49, 68, 81, 82, 83, 93, 102; with emph. *i*, *làli*, even Lal; *làli làli karān*, making (the cry) (i.e. crying out) '(it is) even (I) Lal, (it is) even (I) Lal,' 105; sg. dat. *lali*, 84, 94; ag. *lali*, 76, 93, 103, 104; (m. c.) *lalē*, 76.

lāla, m. a darling, a beloved one, 105 (alluding to a specially loved god).

lōl, m. passionate love, eager and loving longing; sg. abl. *lōla*, 3; sg. gen. (m. sg. abl.) *lōlaki nāra*, (parched) with the fire of love, 25.

līlàmi, f. pl. actings, taking parts in a theatrical performance, 81. The word has not been noted elsewhere, and its form, as a feminine plural, is unexpected. It is a question whether we should not read *līla mĕ*, *līla* being the f. nom. pl. of *līl* or *līla* (Skr. *līlā*), and *mĕ* being the agent case of *bŏh*, I.

lalanāwun, to dandle a child to quiet it; hence, to fondle, to soothe (a pain); past part. f. sg. with suff. 1st pers. sg. ag. *lalanövüm*, 105.

lalith, adv. artlessly, gently, 67 (bis).

lāmā, f. one of the divine mothers or personified energies (*śakti*) of the principal deities, in Sanskrit *mātṛkā*, variously reckoned as 7, 8, 9, or 16 in number. They are closely connected with the worship of Śiva; *lāmā-tsakar*, the circle or assemblage of these mothers (Skr. *mātṛkā-maṇḍala*); *lāmā-tsakra-poshu*, a beast devoted for sacrifice in the joint worship of all these mothers,—used met. to signify anything devoted, or destined, to destruction, 63.

lamun, to pull (*razi*, a rope), 95; to tow (*nāvi*, a boat), 106; pres. f. sg. 1, *chĕs lamān*, 106; cond. past, pl. 3, *lamahŏn*, 95.

lar, f. the side or flank of the body; *dachiñi lari*, (lying) on the right side, K. Pr. 57.

lārᵘ, f. a house; sg. dat. *larĕ*, 101; pl. nom. *larĕ*, K. Pr. 57.

lūrun, to pull down or destroy (a house, wall, or the like); conj. part. *lūrith*, 74.

lasun, to live long, to live in good health and prosperously, 27, 35; to live, to be a survivor amongst a number of mortals, K. Pr. 150; fut. sg. 1, *lasa*, 35; past m. sg. 3, with emph. *y*, *lūstuy*, K. Pr. 150; pl. 3 (really conj. part., see App. II, p. 140) *làsⁱtⁱ*, 27.

lōsun, to become weary, 48, 60, K. Pr., 57; (of the day), to fail, to become evening, (or of the night) to fade away, to become morning, 3, 44, 98; K. Pr. 18. The past part. of this verb is *lūsᵘ* or *lūstᵘ*; fem. sg. *lūsᵘ* or *lūćhᵘ*, pl. *lōsa*.

Past m. sg. 3, with suff. 1st pers. sg. dat., *lūstum*, (the day) passed away for me, 3, 44, 98; K. Pr. 18; f. sg. 1 *lūćhᵘs*, 48, 60; f. pl. 3, with suff. 1st pers. sg. gen. *narĕ lōsam*, my arms grew weary, K. Pr. 57.

lūst, see *lasun* and *lōsun*.

lath, f. a kick, 102 (bis).

lūćhᵘs, see *lōsun*.

lawan, m. salt; *lawan-zàn*, like salt, 29.

lawar, ? gend., a rope; *sĕki-lawar*, a rope of sand, 107. The word does not occur in vocabularies of modern Kāshmīrī, but cf. mod. Ksh. *lar*, f. the strand of a rope.

lay, 1, m. absorption; (with dat.) *lay karun*, to make absorption (in anything), to become absorbed in, 76. This word is generally feminine. See *lay*, 2.

lay, 2, f. absorption; ardent affection or desire, K. Pr. 201; destruction; *lay karüñᵘ*, (with dat.) to practise (anything) steadfastly and with ardent devotion, to devote oneself (to any particular practice), 60, 68; *layĕ anun*, to bring (anything) to absorption, to bring (anything) under one's own power by concentration of mind, 82; *layĕ wŏthun*, to rise to destruction, to become dissolved into nothingness, 1. Cf. *lay*, 1. Sg. dat. 1, 82; *layi-hyuhᵘ*, like ardent love, K. Pr. 201.

lyūkhuy, see *lĕkhun*.

layun, to become absorbed (in the Supreme), to reach final beatitude; to become dissolved into nothingness; past m. pl. 3 *làyⁱ* (in both meanings), 59.

ma, prohibitive particle, used with the imperative. With the interj. *bā*, *ma-bā trāwun*, do not, Sir, let it go, 88. With the pol. impve. *mata*, q. v., is used. Other forms of *ma* are *mau* and *mō*, see *mō*.

mā, the interrogative form of *ma*. Used with the imperative it gives practically the force of a negative interrogative future, as in *hĕyiv mā*, will ye not buy? i.e. why do ye not buy?, 89.

mau, see *mō*.

mĕ, see *bŏh*.

mō or *mau*, i.q. *ma*, q.v. *mō gārun*, do not seek it, 30; *mau ās*, be not, 36; *bhayĕ mō bar*, to not feel fear, 72.

mŏchĕ, see *mŏṭhᵘ*.

mad, m. intoxication; hence, arrogance (one of the six 'enemies', see *lūb*), 43; intoxicating liquor, wine, 81.

mūḍ, m. a fool, a lout, an ignorant person, 20, 66; sg. dat. *mūḍas*, 66.

maidān, m. a field; sg. dat. *manz maidānas*, in a field, K. Pr. 57.

mūḍun, see *mūrun*.

mudra, f. name of particular positions or intertwinings of the fingers, commonly practised in religious worship. They have an occult meaning, and are believed to have magical efficacy; sg. ag. *mudri*, 2.

muh, m. illusion (in a religious sense); sg. abl. *muha*, by means of, under the influence of, illusion, 74; sg. gen. f. *muhücᵘ māy*, the desire of (i.e. begotten by) illusion, 67.

muhun, to suffer illusion, to be deceived; past f. sg. 1, *mushᵘs*, I was deceived, 13.

mŏjᵘ, f. a mother, K. Pr. 47; sg. nom. *mŏjī* (m. c.), 97; pl. nom. *mājĕ-kōrĕ*, mothers and daughters, 92.

mọkhᵒtᵘ, adj. released; esp, released from transmigration, saved (in a religious sense), finally emancipated, united with the Supreme; m. pl. nom. *zīwántⁱ mọkhᵃtⁱ*, released, or saved, while yet alive, 6.

mŏkᵃtⁱ, f. release from transmigration, final emancipation; sg. abl. *mŏkti-dwār*, the gate (or door) of final emancipation, 29.

makur or *makorᵘ*, m. a mirror; sg. dat. *makaris*, 18; *makuras*, 31.

mal, m. dirt, foulness, 18, 31, 49; *mal pyonᵘ*, dirt to fall (on anything, dat.), 18.

mŏlᵘ, m. a father; voc. *māli*, O father, used as a title of respect, equivalent to 'Good Sir!' or 'Sir!', 91, 107; K. Pr. 57; *ha māli*, id. 107, also capable of being read as *hamāli*, O burden-bearer!

mall, m. a hero, a strong man; sg. ag. *mállⁱ*, 24.

mēlun, to be united (with), to become one with, to be absorbed (in, dat.), 1, 68, 105; to be joined (to a person), to be got (by, dat.), to be attained to (by, dat.), 78, 79; *mīlith gaṭshun*, having become united to go; to go away together, or in a body, 9; (as intensive compound) to become united (to), mingled (with, dat.), absorbed (in, dat.), 11, 29, 30, 69.

Conj. part. *mīlith*, 1, 9, 11, 29, 30, 68, 69, 105; fut. sg. 3, with suff. 2nd pers. sg. dat. *mēliy*, 78, 79; past m. sg. 3, *myūl^u*, 1 (cf. also *myul^u* and *myūl^u*, 2, s. vv.).

milawun, caus. of *mēlun*, to join, unite; conj. part. *milavith*, 69.

māms, m. flesh; sg. gen. (m. pl. nom.) *māmsăk^i*, 81.

man, m. the mind, the thinking faculty (Skr. *manas*), 5, 12, 17, 18, 45, 65, 93; K. Pr. 57. This is roughly the meaning of the word, and will suit for the translation of the above passages, but, as a term of Śaiva philosophy, it is not sufficiently accurate. According to Deussen (*Allgemeine Geschichte der Philosophie*, I, 3, p. 490; cf. ib., pp. 58 ff., 352, 374, 604 ff., 648), the functions of the *manas* are that 'on the one hand, it forms the impressions delivered by the organ of cognition (*buddhi*) into conceptions, which are then preserved as finished products of cognition in the *buddhi*. On the other hand, it executes the decisions derived from the *buddhi* by influencing the organs of action'. This technical meaning of *manas* (Ksh. *man*) can be traced in its use in 23, 27, 31, 40, 79, 80, 105.

In L. V. 71, the meaning of *man* is further extended to indicate the exercise of the thinking faculty, careful thought. *Man raṭun*, to seize the mind, to bring it under subjection, 55; *swa-man*, one's own mind, 68, 98. In 68, there is a play upon words, *swaman* being also used as equivalent to *sŏman* or *suman*, the jasmine.

Sg. dat. *manas*, 17, 31; with emph. *y*, *manasay*, 23; loc. *mani*, 18, 45; abl. *mana*, 80, 98; with emph. *y*, *manay*, 71; gen. (m. sg. abl.) *manaki*, K. Pr. 57.

mān, m. the possession of a good reputation, respectability, 24.

maṇḍal, m. a circular disk, 75 (cf. *sūrya*); a district, locality, 33 (cf. *dwādashānth*).

mangun, to ask for, demand; fut. pl. 3, with suff. 2nd pers. sg. dat., *manganay*, they will demand from thee, K. Pr. 56; past part. m. sg., *mong^u*, with suff. 3rd pers. sg. ag. and 1st pers. sg. dat., *mong^unam*, he demanded from me, K. Pr. 150.

manmath, m. carnal desire, sexual appetite, 43; i. q. *kām*, see *lūb*.

mānun, to heed, to look upon as, consider (a thing to be so and so); conj. part. *mŏnith*, 73; impve. sg. 2, *mān*, 23; past part. (used as past tense), m. sg. *mŏn^u*, 5 (bis).

mānas, m. i.q. *man*, q.v., the mind, the thinking faculty, 2; the faculty of imagination (see *man*), 27.

manush, m. a man, a human being; voc. *hā manushĕ*, O man!, 107; *manushĕ-māms*, human flesh, 81.

manth^{a}*r*, m. a religious mystic formula (Skr. *mantra*), 11, 34 (bis), 39, 40, 58. A *mantra* is an aggregation of apparently unmeaning sounds. It has no efficacy unless the utterer is aware of the mystic meaning of each sound, which has to be taught by a *guru*, or spiritual preceptor. By meditating on a *mantra*, with full knowledge, unity with the Supreme is attained.

Sg. abl. *mantra*, 39, 40; pl. nom. *manth*^{a}*r*, 34.

manz, postpos. governing dat., in; *pānas-manz*, in myself, 44. In 98, it means 'having reached the middle', and exceptionally governs the abl. (*swamana-sŏthi manz*, having reached the middle of the embankment of (the illusions of) my own mind, or *suman-sŏthi manz*, having reached the middle of an embankment (furnished) with small bridges). In K. Pr. 57, *manz* precedes the word it governs,—*manz maidānas*, in a field.

manza, postpos. governing abl., from among, out of (so many); *laçhĕ-manza sāsa-manza*, out of a hundred thousand (or) out of a thousand (only one is saved), K. Pr. 150.

mār, m. killing, slaughter; *māra-būth* (pl. nom.), m. murderous demons, 71.

mor^{u}, m. a cote (for pigeons or the like); sg. abl. *marē* (m. c. for *mari*), K. Pr. 57.

mrag, m. a deer; pl. nom. *mrag*, 47.

mārg, m. a way, a path; *jñāna-mārg*, the path of knowledge, the way to the knowledge of the Supreme, 63; *sath-mārg*, the good way, the path of Wisdom, or (alternatively) the seventh road, 82,

marun, to die; inf. sg. abl. *marana brŏṭhay*, even before dying, even before thy death, 87; gen. (f. sg. nom.) *maranüñ*^{ü} *shŏkh*, the fear of death, 73–76; conj. part. *marith*, having died, i.e. after death, 87; K. Pr. 56; pres. part. *marān*, dying, 83; impve. sg. 2, *mar bā*, die, Sir!, 87; fut. sg. 1, *mara*, 35; with suff. 3rd pers. sg. dat., *maras*, I shall die in it, 68; 3, *mari*, 12; with suff. 1st pers. sg. gen., *marĕm na kūh*, no one belonging to me will die, 35.

mārun, to kill, destroy; met. to reduce to absolute quietism, 49; to beat, smite, 83; conj. part. *mörith*, 43, 77; pres. part. *mārān*, 83; impve. sg. 2, with suff. 3rd pers. sg. acc. *mārun*, destroy it, 30; with suff. 3rd pers. pl. acc. *mārukh*, destroy them, 71; fut. pl. 3, with suff. 2nd pers. sg. gen. *mārinĕy* (for modern *māranay*) *pān*, they will kill thy Self, 71; past part. m. sg., with suff. 1st pers. sg. ag., *mŏrum*, I pacified, 49; with suff. 3rd pers. sg. ag., *mŏrun*, he killed, 43.

mūrun or *mūḍun*, to husk grain by trituration in the hand; hence, met. *kŏchĕ mūrun*, to husk the bosom by rubbing, (of a suckling child) to snuggle or nestle in the bosom, to be at rest in the bosom; fut. sg. 3, *mūrē* or *mūḍē* (m. c. for *mūri*, *mūḍi*), 70.

martaba, ? m. honour, dignity, 87.

mas, m. wine, 104; K. Pr. 102.

mās, f. an aunt (mother's sister), 97 = K. Pr. 47.

mashun, to be forgetful, to forget (in this sense, the verb in the past participial tenses takes the subject in the dative case), 67; to be forgetful, to be deluded, to become subject to delusion; *mashith gatshun*, to become subject to delusion, as ab., 59.

Conj. part. *mashith*, 59; past part. m. sg. with suff. 2nd pers. sg. dat. *moṭhuy*, it was forgotten for thee, thou forgottest, 67.

mushᵘs, see *muhun*.

mast, m. the hair of the head; *mast-wāl*, a single hair, 24.

mata, prohibitive particle, used only with the polite imperative, do not, 53 (bis), where it has practically the force of a negative interrogative, 'does it not?'

maut, m. death, K. Pr. 56.

mŏtū, see *mŏtsun*.

motᵘ, m. a madman, 105.

mŏṭhᵘ, f. the closed fist; sg. dat. (in sense of loc.) *mŏchĕ*, 24.

mathun, to rub, knead, work, squeeze; past part. f. sg., with suff. 3rd pers. sg. ag., and 1st pers. sg. dat., *mütshᵘnam*, he rubbed (a fem. object) into me, 103.

moṭhuy, see *mashun*.

mātru-rūpⁱ, f. (a woman) in the character of a mother, performing the duty of a mother, 54.

mọtuy, *mọtᵘyĕy*, see *mŏtsun*.

mĕtsᵘ, f. earth, clay; met. earthly things, non-spiritual things, 44; sg. dat. *mĕtsĕ*, 44, where the word is repeatedly used in a double sense, viz. in the above meaning, and also in the sense of *mĕ tsĕ*, me (and) thee, or *mĕ tsᵃh*, me (and) thou.

mŏtsē, see *mŏtsun*.

mütshᵘnam, see *mathun*.

mŏtsun, to remain over and above, to be left remaining; fut. sg. 3, *mŏtsi*, with emph. *y*, *mŏtsiy*, 63; m. c. *mŏtsĕ*, 11, or *mōtsĕ*, 21; past m. sg. 3, with emph. *y*, *mọtuy*, 9, 11, and also with conditional suffix *ay*, *mọtᵘyĕy*, 2; also *mŏtū* for *mọtᵘ* (m. c.), past m. sg. 3, in 1.

māwās, ? f. the day of the new moon; old loc. *māwạsē*, 22.

may = Skr. *maya*, in *Shiva-may*, consisting only of Śiva, 16.

māy, f. love, affection, love for earthly things, delusion, *māyā*, 67; the love of God, K, Pr. 201; *māyi-hyuh*[u], like the love of God, K. Pr. 201.

māyĕ-rūp[i], f. (a woman) acting in the character of a deceiver, a Delilah, 54.

myul[u], m. union, identity with; hence, the knowledge of the fact of such identity, 7. Cf. *myūl*[u], 2.

myūl[u], 1, m. see *mēlun.*

myūl[u], 2, i. q. *myul*[u], union, identity; esp. union, or identity, with God, 36; see art. *swa.*

myōn[u], *myānuv*, see *bŏh.*

na, negative, not, 26, 35 (bis), 37, 60 (bis), 77, 90, 98 (bis, and in v. l.), 104, 107 (bis); K. Pr. 18, 102, 201 (many times). *na . . . na*, neither . . . nor, K. Pr. 46; *na ta*, and not, nor, 96 (bis), 97; K. Pr. 47 (bis), 102; *na . . . na . . . ta*, not . . . nor . . . nor, 15; *na-ta*, otherwise, or else, 19 (ter), 71; K. Pr. 150; *nay* (*na* + *ay*), if not, see s. v. Cf. *nā*, 1, and *nō*. The negative used with the present impve. is *ma*, and with the pol.-impve. *mata*, qq. v. With the fut. impve. *na* is generally used, but cf. *nō*.

nā, 1, negative, i. q. *na*, 2 (ter), 9, 11, 12 (ter), 18, 23, 27 (bis), 45 (bis), 47, 55, 59 (quater); *nā . . . nā*, neither . . . nor, 7; *zĕn nā zĕn*, they are being born (and) they are not being born, i. e. when they are hardly born, immediately on being born, 47.

nā, 2, verbal suffix indicating a negative interrogative; *ṭshĕnĕm-nā*, will it not be cut for me?, 83.

nō, negative, i. q. *na* and *nā*, 1; 29 (bis), 31, 41, 67, 70 (bis), 90 (bis); K. Pr. 46. In 70 and 90, *nō* is used with the future impve. Cf. *na.*

nāb, f, the navel; a focus, or central point, hence the focus of the body, the *kanda*, or bulb, between the pudendum and the navel, which is the root of the *nāḍis*, or tubes, through which the *prāṇa*, or life-wind, circulates. See Note on Yōga, § 5. Sg. abl. *nābi*, 34; *nābi-sthāna*, of the region of the *kanda*, 57. Regarding the heat in the navel, see *prān*, 2.

nābad, m. sugar-candy; *nābăd*[i]*-bār*, a load of sugar-candy, 108.

nĕbar, adv. outside, abroad, 4; K. Pr. 102 (bis); *nĕb*[a]*ra*, from outside, 94.

nĕch, adj. good, 35 (bis); as adv. well, successfully, fortunately, 37. The more usual form of this word is *nēkh*, cf. Prs. *nēk.*

nĕchatur, m. a lunar asterism; the season during which the sun, or the moon, is passing through a lunar asterism; hence, a time or moment fixed by astrology, 3.

nad, f. a river, 57, 96; K. Pr. 47; sg. dat. *sūti nadi*, (contact) with the river, 57.

nād, m. a cry, call, loud sound, 72. For *nāda-bindu* (15), see *bindu*.

nāḍi, f. a tube, artery, vein; esp. the tubes through which the *vāyu*, or life-winds, circulate. See Note on Yōga, §§ 5, 6, 21. There are fourteen of these,—rising from the *kanda*, or region between the pudendum and the navel (cf. *nāb*). Of these fourteen, ten (named *iḍā*, *piṅgalā*, *suṣumnā*, *gāndhārī*, *hastijihvā*, *pūṣā*, *yaśasvinī*, *alambuṣā*, *kuhū*, and *śaṅkhinī*) are the principal (hence the *dashĕ-nāḍi-wāv* of L. V. 69). The principal vital airs are five in number, viz. *prāṇa*, or upward flowing air, which has its seat in the lungs; *apāna*, or downward flowing air; *udāna*, which rises in the throat, and enters the head; *samāna*, which has its seat in the cavity of the navel, and is essential to digestion; and *vyāna*, that which is diffused through the whole body. These course through the various *nāḍis*, and the object of the Śaiva ascetic is to restrain them by *prāṇāyāma*. For this exercise, see Note on Yōga, § 21. By it, the *prāṇa* and *apāna* are united to the *udāna*. The fire of *udāna* then rises in the central *nāḍi*, which causes the dissolution of *prāṇa* and *apāna*, thus leading to *samādhi*, or consciousness independent of objects (see Translation of *Śivasūtra-vimarśinī*, pp. x and 41). Hence, L. V. 69 mentions the uniting of the winds of the ten *nāḍis*. In L. V. 80, *nāḍi-dal* is 'the collection of *nāḍis*', 'the whole group of *nāḍis*'. The authoress wishes that she had been able to bring the ten *nāḍis* under her mental control (by *prāṇāyāma*, &c.), and thus been able to obtain *samādhi*.

nadoru, 1, m. the stalk of the lotus, which is eaten when cooked with oil and condiments, 89, with play on the meaning of *nadoru*, 2.

nadoru, 2, adj. not firm; hence, worthless, of no value, 89, with play on the meaning of *nadoru*, 1.

nĕhāl, adj. prosperous, favoured, successful, 24.

nāl, m. the collar, or neckpiece, of a garment; *nāla raṭun*, to seize by the neck of the coat, hence, to seize forcibly and retain, K. Pr. 102; *nöli tshunun*, to cast on the neck (e.g. a garland, or a heavy chain), K. Pr. 102.

nolu, m. an unbroken cowry-shell; hence, a small piece of anything, 81; pl. nom. *nalī*, m. c. for *nāli*, 81.

nām, m. a name; pl. nom. *nām*, 8. Cf. *nāv*, 1.

nimēsh, m. the twinkling of the eye; sg. abl. *nimēshĕ aki*, in a single twinkling of the eye, 26.

namaskār, m. reverence, adoration, K. Pr. 102.

nonu, adj. naked; as subst. a naked ascetic, 46; the naked, or bare, body, 88; m. sg. nom. with emph. *y*, *nonuy*, 46; dat. *nanis*, 88. Cf. *nanga*.

nĕ̄ndᵃr, f. sleep; *nĕ̄ndri-hotᵘ*, smitten by sleep, sunk in sleep, 32.

nanga, adj. naked; f. sg. nom. with emph. *y*, *nangay*, 94. Cf. *nonᵘ*.

nĕnga, m. a time, an occasion; sg. abl. *aki nĕngi*, on one occasion, once, 50; *trayi nĕngi*, three times, 50; *sati nĕngi*, seven times, 50.

nanun, to become naked; hence, to become manifest, 4; past f. sg. 3, with suff. 1st pers. sg. dat., *nanyēyĕm*, became manifest to me, 4.

naphs, m. the breath; hence, the soul, K. Pr. 150, with emph. *y*, *naphsᵘ̈y*.

nār, m. fire, 97; sg. abl. *lōlaki nāra*, by the fire of love, 25; sg. gen. (f. sg. nom.), *nārücᵘ̈*, 23.

nürᵘ̈, f. the arm; pl. nom. *narĕ lōsam*, my arms grew weary, K. Pr. 57; acc. *narĕ ālawañĕ*, to wave the arms (in grief), K. Pr. 57.

nārān, m. Nārāyaṇa, God, the Supreme Being; sg. ag. *nārönⁱ*, 107; voc. *hē nārān*, 109 (ter).

nērun, to go forth, to go out (of the house), 3, 92, 102; K. Pr. 57, 102 (bis); to issue (as a result), 23; *lal nāv drām*, the name 'Lal' issued for me, i.e. I became known as Lal, 49.

impve. pl. 1, *nērav*, K. Pr. 102 (bis); fut. sg. 3, *nēri*, K. Pr. 57; with suff. 3rd pers. sg. dat., *nērĕs*, will issue from it, 23; pl. 3, *nēran*, 92.

past m. sg. 3, *drāv*, with suff. 1st pers. sg. dat., *drām*, 49; f. sg. 1, *drāyĕs*, 3, 102.

nāruťsᵘ, m. a barbed fishing-spear; *nārăťsⁱ-chŏkh*, the (very painful) wound caused by such a spear, 23.

nishĕ, 1, adv. near, close by, 30, 46.

nishĕ, 2, postpos. governing dat., near; *nishĕ pānas*, near myself, 31.

nishĕ, 3, postpos. governing abl., from; *gaṇḍana-nishĕ*, from (i.e. by means of) dressing oneself, 27; *rasa-nishĕ ti*, (efforts) even from (i.e. beyond) my strength, 48.

nōshᵘ, m. a destroyer, in *wata-nōshᵘ*, a way-destroyer, a highway robber; pl. nom. *-nöshⁱ*, 43.

nĕ̄shᵉbŏ̄dᵘ, m. one who has no wits, a fool, 83.

nishpath, adj. without trust, unbelieving, 36.

nāsikh, f. the nose; *nāsika-pawana-dörⁱ*, holding (i.e. borne upon) the vital air that issues through the nose (sc. from the heart) (of the syllable *ōṁ*), 33. See *anāhath*.

nĕsar, f. deep sleep, 32.

nāth, m. a lord, a chief; sg. voc. *nātha*, O Lord!, 7; *kamalaza-nāth*, the lord who was born in a lotus, i.e. Brahmā, 8;

sura-guru-nāth, the lord of the chief of the gods, i.e. the Supreme Śiva, 5, 65 (cf. *guru*).

nĕth, adv. perpetually, continually, 65; with emph. *y*, *nĕthąy*, 46. Cf. *nityĕ*.

nāṭy, m. dancing; *nāṭĕ-ras*, the pleasure of watching dances, 73.

nityĕ, adv. i.q. *nĕth*, q.v., 45.

naċun, to dance; inf. *hyotum naċun*, I began to dance, 94.

nāv, 1, m. a name, 15, 49; *har-nāv*, the name of Hara, 98. Cf. *nām*.

nāv, 2, f. a boat, a ship, 107; sg. dat. *nāvi lamun*, to tow a boat, 106; *nāwa-tār*, the act of ferrying a person in a boat, 98 = K. Pr. 18.

now[u], adj. new; with emph. *y*, continually new, ever new and new, 93 (bis); so *nawam-nowuy* (fem. *nawam-nüw*[ü]*y*), ever new and new, 93 (m. and f.).

nāwun, to scrub, scour, clean; past part. m. sg. with emph. *y*, *nŏwuy*, 93.

nay, a compound of *na*, not, and *ay*, if; if not, K. Pr. 46.

nyūl[u], adj. dark blue: (also) green; hence, (of vegetation) green and luxuriant, 36.

niyĕm, m. a fixed rule or law. — *karun*, to make a vow as to a future rule of conduct, 87.

nyun[u], to take; *kaḍith nyun*[u], to take out, to take forth, K. Pr. 57; fut. pl. 3, *nin*, with suff. 2nd pers. sg. dat. *ninanay* (apparently for *ninay*), they will carry thee (forth), K. Pr. 57.

niz, adj. own, one's own; *niza-swarūph*, the nature of what is one's own, the nature of Self, 67.

pad, 1, m. a position, site; *parama-pad*, or (77) *paramu pad*, the Supreme Śiva, 10, 77, 78, 79. See *param*.

pad, 2, m. a verse of poetry, such as Lallā's own verses; pl. nom. *pad*, 76; dat. (for loc.) *padan*, 84.

paida, adj. created, produced; — *karun*, to make (for oneself), 99 = K. Pr. 46.

paḍun or *parun*, to read; to study, 36; to recite, give forth (e.g. a stream of abuse), 18, 21.

Conj. part. *parith*, 36; impve. sg, 3, with suff. 1st pers. sg. dat., *pāḍ*[i]*nĕm* or *pār*[i]*nĕm* (modern Ksh. would be *-nam*), 18; pl. 3, with same suff., and with identical form, 21.

puh, m. the month Pauṣa (Dec.–Jan.). It is the month in which the leaves fall. Sg. gen. (m. sg. abl.) *puhani wāwa*, (leaves falling) with the wind of Pauṣa, 83.

phŏkh, m. expelling breath from the mouth with the lips contracted, blowing a long puff; sg. dat. *phŏkas*, 41.

phal, m. fruit, a crop or harvest of grain, 86 (see *phol*^{u}); *phal-hond*^{u}, a fruit-ram, a large ram fattened on fruit, 77.

phol^{u}, m. a single grain, or a small quantity of any kind of grain or seed; used —°. *sår*^{i}*-phol*^{u}, a single mustard-seed, 47; in *phal-phol*^{u}, 86, *phol*^{u} means simply 'grain', and defines *phal*. *Phal* means any fruit, and *phol*^{u} defines it as grain.

pahŏl^{u}, m. a shepherd; *pahāli-rost*^{u}, shepherdless, 108.

phalun, to bear fruit; cond. past sg. 3, with suff. 2nd pers. sing. dat., *phalihiy* (mod. Ksh. would be *-hīy*), 66.

phŏlun, to blossom, to bloom; fut. sg. 3, with suff. 2nd pers. sg. dat., *phŏliy*, K. Pr. 46.

phālav, m. the set of shutters used for shutting up a shop; *phālav dyun*^{u}, to shut up (shop, dat.), K. Pr. 102.

phŏlawun^{u}, n. ag. that which blossoms, flowering; f. sg. nom., with emph. *y*, *phŏlawüñ*^{ü}*y*, 96 = K. Pr. 47.

phērun, to return, come back (to a place, or to one's senses), 51, 89; to rest from work, take a holiday, 12. In 89, the 'returning' is in two senses, either 'coming back (to the market)', or 'coming (to my senses)'. Conj. part. *phīrith*, 51, 89; fut. sg. 3, *phēri*, 12.

phirun, to cause to revolve or to cause to come back; to turn over (of a washerman turning over clothes in the wash), 103; to reverse, cancel, 107; to ply (scissors), 103; conj. part. *phirith*, 107; past part. f. sg., with suff. 3rd pers. sg. ag. and 1st pers. sg. nom., *phir*^{ü}*nas*, 103; with suff. 3rd pers. sg. ag. and 1st pers. sg. dat., *phir*^{ü}*nam*, 103.

phuṭ^{a}*run*, to break (trans.); past part. m. pl., with suff. 3rd pers. sg. ag. and 3rd pers. sg. dat., *phuṭ*^{a}*r*^{i}*nas*, 26.

pöj^{i}, see *pālun*.

pŏkh, m. mud, a slough, 74.

pak^{a}*ch*, m. the wheel (of a vehicle), pl. nom. *pakh*^{a}*ch*, 26.

pakun, to move forward, progress; inf. *pakun gatshē*, one has to progress, 19; fut. sg. 3, with suff. 2nd pers. sg. dat. *pakiy*, 107.

pakawun^{u}, n. ag. one who progresses; (of a river) flowing on, K. Pr. 47; f. sg. nom., with emph. *y*, *pakawüñ*^{ü}*y*, K. Pr. 47.

pal, m. flesh, used in offering to a god, 10; *al-pal*, wine and flesh for a *Kaula* offering. In modern Ksh. the compound *al-pal* is used to mean 'wine, flesh, &c.', i.e. the five things commencing with *m* used in the *kaula* (not Lallā's sect) worship of Śiva. The five '*m*'s' are *madya*, wine; *māṁsa*, flesh; *matsya*, fish; *mudrā*, special attitudes; *maithuna*, sexual intercourse. Hence, in modern language, *al-pal* commonly means any vile or utterly impure food.

palān, m. a saddle (of a horse); sg. dat. *palānas*, 14.

pālun, to protect; hence, (of instruction or directions) to keep, to follow faithfully; past part. f. sg. *pöjⁱ* (mod. Ksh. *pöjü*), 62.

pan, 1, m. a leaf; pl. nom. *pan*, 83.

pan, 2, m. thread, sewing-thread; sg. abl. *pana*, 106.

pān, 1, the human body; voc. *pāna*, K. Pr. 57. In 44, the sg. dat. *pānas* is used with a double meaning, as the dat. of this word, and also as the dat. of *pāna*, self. See *pāna*.

pān, 2, m. i.q. *pāna*, the self, oneself, 5, 7, 71; *panunᵘ pān*, one's own self, one's own personality, 62, 82, 85.

pāna, self, oneself; myself, 31, 44 (bis), 60, 61; thyself, 44, 66; himself, he himself, 33, 59, 72; with emph. *y*, *pānay*, he himself, 33, 59; sg. dat. *pānas*, to myself, 61; for thyself, for thine own benefit, 66; *nishĕ pānas*, near myself, 31. In 44, *pānas* has three times a double meaning. It may here be the sg. dat. either of *pān*, the body, or of *pāna*, self. Thus, *pānas lögith*, having applied (earth) to my body, or having become absorbed in thyself; *pānas-manz*, (I saw earth) on my body, or (I saw thee) in myself; *pānas dyutum*, I gave to my body, or gave to myself.

pĕn, see *pyonᵘ*.

pönī, for *pönⁱ*, in *pönī-pānas*, for myself, 60.

ponᵘ, m. a wedge, a peg; pl. nom. *pånⁱ*, 66.

panca, card. five, in *panca-yindⁱ*, the five *indriyas*, or organs of sense, 79. The Skr. form of *pānẗs*, q.v.

pŏndun, to sneeze; fut. sg. 3 (in sense of pres.), *pŏndi*, 46.

paṇḍith, m. a learned man; esp. a *guru* or spiritual preceptor, 3.

pānḍav, m. pl. the Pāṇḍavas, the five heroes of the *Mahābhārata*. Their mother was Queen Kuntī. At one time, being reduced to great distress, she is said to have taken refuge in a potter's house, and to have passed as the maternal aunt of his children. Pl. gen. (f. sg. nom.) *pānḍawan-hünzü möjü* (or *möjī*, m. c.), the mother of the Pāṇḍavas, 97 = K. Pr. 47. See *kröjü*.

panunᵘ, pron. adj. one's own, 55, 62; my own, 3, 82, 85, 104; thy own, K. Pr. 57; his own, 45; with emph. *y*, *panunuy*, 62, 85, 104; m. sg. abl. *panani*, 3; K. Pr. 57; f. sg. dat. *panañĕ*, 45; *panunᵘ pān*, one's own self, one's own personality, 62, 82, 85.

pānẗs or *pönẗs*, card. five, 77 (*pönẗs*); pl. dat. *pönẗsan*, 95; *pānẗsan*, K. Pr. 47. There are five *bhūtas* (77, 95, see *būth*, 2); five *prāṇas*, or vital airs (95, see *prān*, 2); five *jñānĕndriyas*, or organs of sense, and five *karmĕndriyas*, or organs of action (95, see *yundᵘ*). Cf. *panca*.

pŏñ, m. a virtuous action (the opposite of *pāph*, sin), 62, 79; sg. abl. *pŏnĕ*, 62.

pŏñu, m. water, 24, 42, 47, 106; pl. nom. *pŏñi*, 42.

pūñu, f. a hedge (round a garden), 63.

pāph, m. a sin, a sinful act (opposite of *pŏñ*); sg. abl. *pāpa-pŏñĕ-bōji*, he who obtains the fruit of his sins and virtuous acts of a former life, 62. See *bōji*.

papun, to ripen, to become ripe; fut. pl. 3, *papan*, 92.

par, 1, adj. another than oneself, 5, 7.

par, 2, m. He Who is Supreme, the Supreme Deity, 59; *swa-para-vĕčār*, meditation on oneself and on the Supreme, or on the Supreme Self, 59, but see art. *swa*.

par, 3, a wing; pl. nom. *par*, 99 = K. Pr. 46.

pairiv, see *pūru*.

purā, see *kandā-purā*.

pūru, m. a foot; pl. abl. *pairiv*, on one's feet, 38.

probhu, m. a lord; hence, the Supreme Deity, 64.

parudu, m, a stranger, some one else, a person with whom one has no connexion; pl. dat. *paradĕn*, 92.

prah, f. adoring love, (to God) 105, (or for the world) 83; sg. dat. (in sense of instr.), *prahĕ* (m. c. for *prahi*), 105.

prakrĕth, f. *prakṛti*, i.e. (in Śaivism) primal matter (as opposed to spirit), primitive non-intelligent being, the root of all feeling, affection in the widest sense of the term, as experienced by the *puruṣa*, or individual soul (see *Kashmir Shaivism*, fasc. i., pp. 50, 89), 25; the nature of anything, 57. See Note on Yōga, § 1.

prakāsh, m. light, illumination, 4, 6, 9, 35, 82; K. Pr. 201 (ter); *bōdha-prakāsh* (35) or *jñāna-prakāsh* (6), the illumination of knowledge; *prakāshĕ-sthān*, the place of illumination, i.e. the stage of attainment of true wisdom, 82; sg. dat. *prakāshĕs*, 6.

paralōkh, m. the future world, the life after death; sg. dat. *paralōkas* (in sense of loc.), 75.

param or (77) *paramu*, adj. Supreme; *parama-gath*, the way of the Supreme, final beatitude, 103; *parama-pad* (10, 78, 79), the position of the Supreme, or *paramu pad* (77), the supreme position, hence, final beatitude; hence, also the Supreme Śiva (10, 77, 79); *parama-Shiv*, the supreme Śiva (gen. *-Shiwunu*), 58.

paramēshwar, m. the Supreme Lord, God; sg. voc. *paramēsh-warā*, 56.

prān, 1, m. an onion, 89, 90, in both cases with a double meaning, referring also to *prān*, 2. So, with similar double meaning, *prāna-čūr*, a thief of onions, or the thief of my vital breath, 101.

prān, 2, m. the vital breath (in 89, 90, 101, this word is used with a double meaning, in the sense of 'vital breath', and also in the sense of *prān*, 1, an onion); hence, life, the body as a living entity, 90 (ter).

According to Hindū scriptures there are five principal vital airs (*vāyu*) in the body, viz. *prāṇa*, *apāna*, *samāna*, *udāna*, and *vyāna*. See Note on Yōga, §§ 2, 16. Of these, two (*prāṇa* and *apāna*) are referred to by Lallā. There are also five secondary vital airs, or *upaprāṇa*, named *nāga*, *kūrma*, *kṛkala*, *dēvadatta*, and *dhanaṁjaya*, respectively.

According to the *Mahābhārata* (xii, 6844 ff.) *prāṇa* resides within the head, and, with the heat that is there, causes all kinds of exertion. The *prāṇa* is the living creature, the universal soul, the Eternal Being, the Mind, Intellect, and Consciousness of all living creatures, &c. Thus, the living being is, in every respect, caused by *prāṇa* to move about and exert himself.... The heat, residing between *apāna* and *prāṇa* in the region of the navel (cf. L. V. 57). operates, with the aid of these two breaths, in digesting all food that is taken by a living creature. There is a tube beginning from the mouth and ending in the anal canal. From this main tube numerous subsidiary tubes branch out in the bodies of all living creatures (see art. *nāḍi*). In consequence of the rush of the several breaths (the ten just mentioned,—see also below), these breaths mingle together. The heat that dwells in *prāṇa* causes digestion. . . . The *prāṇa*, bearing a current of heat, descends from the head downwards to the extremity of the anal canal, and thence is pushed upwards again. Coming back to its seat in the head, it once more sends back the heat that it bears. . . . The main tube leading from the mouth to the anus is the path by which *Yōgins* succeed in attaining to the Supreme by holding the soul within the brain (Sörensen's *Index to the Mahābhārata*, s. v. *prāṇa*).

The above is the account given in the *Mahābhārata*. Later accounts describe the five principal airs as follows:—*prāṇa* is the upward flowing air which has its seat in the lungs, and is exhaled through the mouth and nose (L. V. 57 accounts for its heat by stating that it rises from the region of the navel: see *nāb*); *apāna* is the downward flowing air, which is expelled from the anus; *udāna* is that which rises in the throat, and enters the head; *samāna* is that which has its seat in the cavity of the navel, and is essential to digestion; and *vyāna* that which is diffused through the whole body. These course through the various tubes, or *nāḍis*, and the object of the Śaiva ascetic is to restrain them, the process being called *prāṇāyāma*. For the methods by which this process is carried out, see Note on Yōga, § 21.

The main object is to bring *prāṇa* and *apāna* under complete control, as stated in L. V. 26. Cf. *pawan*, which Lallā uses as equivalent to *prān*. On the whole subject, see Deussen, *Allgemeine Geschichte der Philosophie*, I. 2, p. 248; 3, p. 70.

Reference has already been made to L. V. 26 and 57. In 89 (in one meaning) people are invited to take, or grasp, the vital breath (so as to bring it under control). In the other meaning, they are invited to buy onions (*prān*, 1). In 90, the word *prān* has, perhaps, the more general sense of the ordinary breath of life, or one's own body as a living being. In 101, *prāna-ṭsūr* may be translated 'a thief of onions', and also 'the thief of vital breath', i.e. the worldly temptations which prevent the proper control of the *prāṇa*. In 69, *wāv*, wind, is used, as a synonym of *prān*, for the vital airs.

prōnu, adj. old, of olden time; f. sg. nom. *prōñü*, 63.

pairun, to put on (clothes); conj. part. *pairith*, 76.

pūrun, to fill; hence, to inhale breath (37) in the process of *prāṇāyāma*; see *prān*, 2; conj. part. *pūrith*, 37.

In Sanskrit, the process of inhalation is called *pūraka*, while the retention, or 'bottling up' of the inhaled breath is called *kumbhaka*. See Note on Yōga, § 21, and *kumbu*.

pàrinĕm, see *paḍun*.

pranav, m. the name of the mystic syllable *ōṁ*, see *ōṁ* and *anāhath*; sg. gen. (m. sg. ag.) *pranawàki*, 76.

prārun, to wait for, await; pres. part. *prārān*, 83.

prasonu, adj. pleased, gratified; *tas prasonu*, pleased with him, 65.

parith, see *paḍun*.

pruthiwōnu, adj. of or belonging to the earth, 52.

prathuy, adv. implying distribution; *prathuy tīrthan*, (going) to every holy place, going from one holy place to another, 36.

parṭsun, m. recognition, 58.

pairiv, see *pūru*.

prawād, m. a proclamation, a crying out; — *karun*, to cry out, make proclamation, 89.

prāwun, to obtain; fut. sg. 2, *prāwakh*, 29; past part. sg. f., with suff. 1st pers. sg. ag., *prövüm*, I obtained (f. obj.), 103.

pravēsh, m. entering, entrance, 2.

parwāz, ? f. flying, flight; *parwāz tul*, take wings and fly, 99 = K. Pr. 46.

paryōkh, m. a bed; *tūla-paryōkh*, a bed (stuffed) with cotton, i.e. a luxurious bed, 73.

prazalun, to become lighted, to be set alight (of a lamp); 2 past, m. sg. 3, *prazalyōv*; with suff. 1st pers. sg. dat., *prazalyōm*, became lighted for me, 4.

parzānun, to recognize; pol. impve. sg. 2, with suff. 3rd pers. sg. acc., *parzāntan*, recognize him, 46; fut. sg. 3, with suff. 3rd pers. sg. dat. (for acc.), *parzānĕs*, he will recognize him, 14; past part. m. sg., with suff. 1st pers. sg. ag., *parzŏnum*, I recognized, 7.

pāsh, m. a net; sg. dat. *pāshĕs*, 6.

pōsh, m. a flower; sg. gen. (f. sg. abl.) *kapasi-pōshĕcĕ*, 102; pl. nom. *pōsh*, 42, 45.

*posh*ᵘ, m. a beast, an animal (as distinct from man), esp. a beast offered in sacrifice (see *lāmā*), 63.

*push*ᵘ, m. a florist, a professional garland maker, 39, 40. The fem. of this word is *pushöñ*ᵘ.

pashun, to see, 20, 59, in passive sense, to be seen, to be recognized (as so-and-so), 16; conj. part. *pashith*, 20, 59; fut. (or old present), sg. 3, *pashi*, or, with interjection *ā* added, *pashyā*, 16.

*pushöñ*ᵘ, f. a female florist, see *push*ᵘ; m. c. *pushöñī*, 39, 40.

pushĕrun, to make over (anything to anybody); inf. or verbal noun, *pushĕrun*, 61. In mod. Ksh. this verb is *push*ᵉ*run*.

pata, adv. afterwards, behind; *pata rōzun*, to remain behind, to survive, 67; *pata pata*, behind behind, i.e. continually behind; i.e. following after a person, dogging his footsteps, K. Pr. 56, 57.

pĕtā, see *pyon*ᵘ.

*pot*ᵘ, adj. of or belonging to the back, rear, back; although an adj., this word does not change for gender when in agreement with a fem. noun, as in the phrases *pot*ᵘ *kath* back-word, i.e. backbiting, *pot*ᵘ *kamöy*ⁱ, secret income, and so on. Similarly in L. V. 105 we have *pot*ᵘ *zūn* (f.), the end of the moonlight, i.e. the last hours of the night.

path, 1, ? m. a path, a way; sg. abl. *amara-pathi*, on the path (leading to) immortality, i.e. on the path of reflection on the Self or Ego, 70.

path, 2, adv. behind; in *path-kŏl*ᵘ, of or belonging to the time behind, i.e. of or belonging to former times; sg. abl. *path-kāli*, in former times, 91.

paṭh, m. a pavement, the floor of a flagged area; sg. dat. *paṭas*, 52.

pĕṭh, 1, adv. on the back, upon, 14, 15.

pĕṭh, 2, postpos. governing dat., on, upon; with emph. *y*, *dŏb*ⁱ-*kañĕ-pĕṭhay*, on a washerman's stone, 103. Sometimes, in frequently used phrases, *pĕṭh* does not govern the dat., but is simply compounded with the governed word, as in *bar-pĕṭh*, on (i.e. at) the door, K. Pr. 102.

pĕṭha, 1, adv. from above; *pĕṭha bŏna*, from above (and) from below, from top to bottom, 17.

pĕṭha, 2, postpos. governing abl., from above, from; *brahmānḍa-pĕṭha*, (down) from the *Brahma-randhra* (see *brahmānḍ*), 57; *yĕna-pĕṭha*, from which (time), i.e. since, 93.

pīṭhis, see *pyūṭhᵘ*.

pĕtarun, m. the burden, or responsibility, of carrying out any duty, 61.

paċun, to be trusting, to trust (a person, dat.), to show trust in, 104; esp. to show trust in a person by lending him money, to give a person credit, 27; past m. sg. 3, *poċᵘ*, 27; f. sg. 1, with suff. 3rd pers. sg. dat., *pūċᵘsas*, 104. Note that this verb is intransitive.

pawan, m. air, the vital breath (see *prān*, 2), 37, 42; sg. dat. *pawanas*, 17; abl. *nāsika-pawana-dörⁱ*, holding (i.e. borne upon) the vital air that (starting from the heart) issues through the nose, 33; *pawana-sötiy*, by means of the vital air (i.e. by means of suppressing the vital air), 25.

piwun, to drink; past part. m. sg., with suff. 1st pers. sg. ag., *pyuwum*, I drank, 81.

pay, m, milk, 54.

pĕyĕ, *pĕyē*, see *pyonᵘ*.

pyödil, m. the conduct, or behaviour, of a *pyāda* (lit. footman), or government messenger, who is looked upon as making his money by oppression, lying, and cheating; hence, wickedness generally, K. Pr. 46.

pyōm, see *pyonᵘ*.

pyonᵘ, to fall, 18, 32 (sleep fell), 47, 88 (the sword will fall); to fall (to, dat.), to apply oneself (to anything), to become engaged (in anything), 28, 45; to befall, happen, 67, 74, 84, 85, 87, 108.

pol. impve. sg. 2, *pĕtā* (m. c. for *pĕta*), 28; fut. impve. *pĕzē* (m. c. for *pĕzi*), 45;

fut. sg. 3, *pĕyē* (m. c. for *pĕyi*), 18; with suff. 2nd pers. sg. dat., *ċĕtas pĕyiy*, it will happen (i.e. come) to thy memory, 87; *pĕyiy*, (the sword) will fall (on) thy (body), 88; pl. 3 (old present), *pĕn*, they fall, 47;

past. m. sg. 3, with suff. 1st pers. sg. dat., *pyōm*, 84, 85, 108; f. sg. 3, *pĕyĕ*, 32; with suff. 2nd pers. sg. dat., *pĕyiy* (for *pĕyĕy*), happened to thee, 67, 74.

pāyirᵘ, f. a stirrup; pl. dat. *pāyirĕn*, 14.

pyūṭhᵘ, m. a pedestal, a throne; sg. dat. *pīṭhis*, 52.

pyuwum, see *piwun*.

pĕyiy, see *pyonᵘ*.

pĕzē, see *pyonᵘ*.

pūz, f. worship, ceremonial adoration; sg. dat. *pūzi*, 78, 79; *pūzē* (m. c.), 39, 40; *pūz karūñᵘ*, to offer worship (to, dat.), to worship, 17, 21.

pūzan, m. the performance of ceremonial worship, worship, 22.

rē, interj. O!, 3 (here pleonastic).
racyēyĕ, see *raṭun*.
rūdukh, see *rōzun*.
rāh, m. Rāhu, the demon of eclipse, 22.
ruhun, m. garlic, 89, 90, in both cases with a pun on the word *ruh*, soul or spirit (Ar. *rūḥ*).
rājy, m. a kingdom, the ruling of a kingdom; *rājy hyonᵘ*, to take ruling, to undertake the rule of a kingdom, 12; sg. dat. *rājĕs bōjⁱ*, one who gains a kingdom, 62.
rᵃkh, f. a line; met. a path or way as narrow as a line, 107; sg. dat. *karmañĕ rᵃkhi* (written) in the line of fate,—an allusion to the lines of fate supposed to be inscribed on a person's forehead on the 6th night after birth, 107.
rum, m. a hair of the down of the body; used met. to indicate a very small quantity or an instant of time; *pūšᵘsas na rumas* (sg. dat.), I did not trust in him by a single hair, or for a single instant, 104.
rainī or *rōnī*, f. a queen; hence, in voc. *rainyā*, (politely) O Lady!, 10.
rang, 1, m. the stage of a theatrical performance; hence, a theatrical performance; pl. dat. (in sense of gen.), *rangan*, 81.
rang, 2, m. mode, manner, fashion; *kyuthᵘ rang*, of what kind of fashion?, 84, 85.
rīnzⁱ, see *ryūnzᵘ*.
rūñᵘ, f. a wife, a man's wife (from the point of view of the husband); sg. dat. *rañĕ hyuhᵘ*, like a wife, K. Pr. 201; pl. nom. *rañĕ*, K. Pr. 102 (quater).
rūpⁱ, adj. used —°, possessing the appearance of, acting in the character of, in *bhāryĕ-rūpⁱ*, acting in the character of a wife, 54; *mātru-rūpⁱ*, in the character of a mother, 54; *māyĕ-rūpⁱ*, in the character of earthly love, 54; *zaḍa-rūpⁱ*, acting in the character of inanimate nature, stolid like an insentient block, 20.
rūph, m. shape, bodily form, 15.
ras, m. juice, sap, liquor, essence, distillate, 40; a person's essence, his power, energy, 48; charm, pleasure, delight; *nāṭĕ-ras*, the delights of (watching) dancing, 73.

Sg. abl. *shĕshi-rasa*, (water it) with the essence of the moon, i.e. with nectar, 40; *rasa-nishĕ-ti*, (I exerted myself) even beyond my natural power, 48.

rasan, f. the tongue; sg. abl. *rasani*, (uttered) by the tongue, 58.

rostu, adj. suff. signifying 'devoid of'; *lāgi-rostu*, one who is without (selfish) aim, disinterested, 61, 65; *pahāli-rostu*, shepherdless, 108.

rasāyĕn, m. an elixir, a magic potion, 80.

rotu, adj. good, beautiful, excellent; m. pl. nom. *rạti*, 51.

rāth, f. night, 42; *dĕn rāth* (55, 91), *dĕn kyōh rāth* (3, 5, 65), or *dĕn kyāwu rāth* (19), day and night, always, continually, without surcease.

rathu, m. a chariot, 73.

raṭun, to seize, grasp, take hold of, 3, 4, 24, 26, 101, 104, 107; K. Pr. 102; to seize, to bring into subjection, 55, 80; (of a road) to seize, to enter (a road) and follow (it) diligently, 82; *hĕth raṭun*, having taken to seize, i.e. to hold, 69.

Conj. part. *raṭith*, 55, 104; *raṭith zānun*, to know how to seize, &c., 26, 80.

Past part. 1, m. sg. *roṭu*, 24; with suff. 1st pers. sg. ag. *roṭum*, I seized, &c., 4, 69, 82, 101; also with suff. 3rd pers. sg. dat. *roṭumas*, I grasped it, 3: abl. *ami raṭi*, by this which had been grasped, i.e. by grasping this, 107.

Past part. 2, f. sg. *racyĕyĕ*, K. Pr. 102.

rōćun, to be preferred, to be liked; fut. (pres. subj.), sg. 3, *rōćē* (m. c. for *rōći*), 21.

rav, 1, m. a sound, an utterance, 33. See *anāhath*.

rav, 2, m. the sun, 16, 53.

rāwun, to be destroyed, be lost; inf. obl. *rāwan-tyolu*, lit. the blister caused by the destruction (of something desired), hence, an intolerable pain, 108; past, m. sg. 3, *rówu*, 66; past conditional, sg. 3, *rāvihē*, 95.

ryūnzu, a ball (the toy made of lac); pl. nom. *rīnzi*, 66.

raz, f. a rope; sg. dat. (for acc.) *razi*, 95.

ruz, ? f. a disease, 8. See *bhav*.

rāza-dŏñü, f. ? the work of a *rāz* (plasterer), ? plastering; sg. dat. *rāza-dāñĕ*, 85. The meaning of this word is now unknown, and that given here is a mere suggestion.

rāza-hams, m. a swan (said to have a beautiful voice), 86.

razan, ? f. the night, 22.

rōzun, to remain (in one place), abide, stay, 65; to remain, to remain concealed, to keep oneself hidden, 44; to remain over and above, to be left over, to survive, 2, 67; *hushyār rōzun*, to remain careful, to take care, K. Pr. 46.

Conj. part. *rūzith*, 65; impve. sg. 2, *rōz*, K. Pr. 46; fut. sg. 3, with suff. 2nd pers. sg. dat., *rōziy*, it will remain for thee (after death), 67; pl. 3, *rōzan*, 2 (old present); past. m. sg. 2, *rūdukh mĕ*, thou remainedst hidden from me, 44.

sab, adj. all (a Hindī word, the Kāshmīrī word being *sōr^u*, q.v.), 16.
sāban, f. soap, 103.
sād, m. eating with relish, tasting, enjoying, 90; hence, met., the true enjoyment, the pure happiness (begotten by the discrimination between that which is transient and that which is eternal), 45, 90 (with double meaning, i.e. both lit. and met.); sg. abl. *sāda*, 45.
sadā, adv. always, continually; with emph. *y*, *sadöy^i*, 7.
sĕda, adv. straightly; hence, with straight mind, attentively, heedfully, carefully, 91.
sadbhāv, m. pure devotional love, loving trust; sg. abl. *-bhāwa*, 45. Cf. *bāv*.
siddh, c. g. a holy person who has attained to one of the stages of beatitude; voc. *siddha-māli siddhō*, O respected Saint! (see *mōl^u*), 91.
sọd^ar, m. the sea, the ocean; sg. dat. *sọd^aras*, of (or to) the sea, K. Pr. 46; in the ocean, 106; abl. *bhawa-sọd^ari-dār*, the current (or tide) of the ocean of existence, 74.
sadöy^i, see *sadā*.
sagun, that which has properties, the material (as opposed to pure spirit), the material universe, 1.
shĕ, see *shĕh*.
soh^u, m. a money-lender, 27.
suh, see *tih*.
shūba-wōn^u, adj. possessing beauty, adorned; m. sg. dat. *-wönis*, 52.
shĕh (13) or *shĕ* (25), card. six; ag. sg. *shĕy^i*, by (a group of) six, 13; pl. dat. (for gen.) *shĕn*, (a lord) of six, 13.

The number six has various mystic meanings. Thus, there are six attributes of the Deity, viz. (1) *sarvajñatā*, omniscience, (2) *tṛpti*, contentment, (3) *anādibōdha*, having perception from eternity, (4) *svatantratā*, absolute independence, or absolute self-sufficiency, (5) *nityam-aluptaśakti*, having potency that is incapable of being diminished, and (6) *anantaśakti*, omnipotence. There are six enemies, or sins which impede union with the Supreme. For a list of these, see *lūb*. There are six *ūrmis*, or human infirmities, viz. (1) *śōka*, grief, (2) *mōha*, delusion, (3) *jarā*, old age, (4) *maraṇa*, death, (5) *kṣudh*, hunger, and (6) *pipāsā*, thirst. There are six *avasthās*, or periods of human life, (1) *śiśutva*, babyhood, (2) *bālya*, childhood, (3) *kaumāra*, youth, (4) *yauvana*, puberty, (5) *tāruṇya*, young manhood, and (6) *vārdhakya*, old age. Some omit numbers 1 and 5, and have only four periods, translating *yauvana* by 'manhood'. All these sextets are referred to in 13. There are, further, six *vikāras*, or changes of condition, in a man's life, indicated by the six verbs, *asti*, he exists; *jāyatē*, he is born; *vardhatē*, he grows up; *vipariṇamatē*, he is developed; *apakṣīyatē*, he declines; and *naśyati*, he is destroyed (82).

In 25 and 82, reference is made to the six *cakras*, or circles, regarding which, see Note on Yōga, §§ 9, 13 ff.

shĕholu, 1, m. coolness; *shĕholu karun*, to make coolness, to cool oneself, K. Pr. 102.

shĕholu, 2, adj. cool; f. sg. nom. *shĕhüjü*, K. Pr. 102.

shõkh, f. fear, apprehension, 73–6.

shēkun, to fear, to be afraid; impve. fut. *shīkizi*, 70.

shĕkath, f. the *śakti*, or energic power of a deity, conceived as the female consort of the latter; esp. in these poems, the Śakti of Śiva. She is the immanent aspect of Śiva, i.e. the aspect in which he pervades the universe. She is not in any way different from, or independent of, the Supreme Śiva, but is one and the same with him. She is immanent in every human being, and has herself an infinite number of aspects or modes. In order to obtain final emancipation, it is necessary to grasp the fact of her essential oneness with the Supreme, 68; *Shiwa-shĕkath*, Śiva and his Śakti, 2.

shēl, f. a large stone, a rock, 52 (ter).

shīl, m. good behaviour, right conduct, 24.

söhil, ? m. the seashore, K. Pr. 46.

shĕm, tranquillity, quietism, quietude, absence of passion, 71; *shĕm-dam*, quietude and self-restraint; sg. abl. *shĕma-dama-kriyĕ-pühü*, the hedge of holy acts joined to quietism and self-restraint, 63.

sō'ham (90), a Sanskrit formula meaning 'I am He', or 'I am That', and expressing the identity of the soul with the Supreme. With the letters reversed, it becomes *haṁsa*, which is used as a mantra, or mystic formula. See *hams*, 2.

shĕmbhu, Śambhu, a name of Śiva; sg. dat. *shĕmbhus*, 45.

shĕmun, to be quiet, to be at peace, 27; (of water) to be at rest (and gradually soak away), 106; pres. part. *shĕmān*, 106; fut. sg. 3, *shĕmi*, 27.

shĕṇkar, m. Śaṅkara, a name of Śiva, 25; *shĕnkar-swātma*, Śiva (recognized as) one with Self, 39, 40; *shĕnkara-boktu*, one who is full of devotional faith to Śiva, f. *-bhüküsü*, 18.

shūñ, m. the transcendental Void, emptiness (Skr. *śūnya*); in Śaiva philosophy, the imaginary body in which one feels oneself in dreams, a vague, indistinct, and undefined something which is practically 'Nothing', not unlike the 'nothing' of the experience of the really dreamless deep-sleep state in our waking life (see *Śiva-sūtra-vimarśinī*, trans. p. 18, and *Kashmir Shaivism*, pp. 77, 82). When a Universe comes into apparent existence, the Supreme Being, after a course of development through various phases (*K. Shaivism*, pp. 62 ff.), associates Himself with Māyā (illusion), and thereby becomes subjected to limited individual experience. In the first stage of this association, He, as the experiencer, loses the realization of Himself as the Self of the experience; and, as this happens, He becomes sleepy. In this sleep His perception of Himself as 'All This' becomes dim, as the vague, undefined, something, or *śūnya*, already mentioned. *Śūnya* may therefore be looked upon as the first stage in limited consciousness, and in the reverse order (of the soul becoming united with the Supreme) it is therefore the last stage of limited consciousness before the soul becomes conscious of universal experience as one with the Supreme in one of the five phases or conditions prior to this association with Māyā. In the microcosm of the body, Yōgīs locate this *śūnya* in the *sahasrāra*. See Note on Yōga, §§ 20, 24.

Hence Lallā, in 1, says that, when the *shūñ* (i.e. *śūnya*) became dissolved (in the course of union with the Deity) only pure (i.e. universal) consciousness remained.

Lallā is fond of the expression *shūñĕs shūñāh mīlith gauv* (11, 30, 69). Here *shūñĕs* is the dative singular, and *shūñāh* is the nominative singular with the suffix of the indefinite article, and the whole means literally 'a void became merged in the Void' that is to say, a thing which is really nothing, or mere emptiness, became merged in the Great *Śūnya* explained above. The thing which is really nothing is the apparent material existence,—the material world, or the consciousness of the material world. With the acquirement of true knowledge, its unreality is recognized, and the apparent reality disappears in the transcendental Void. Cf. the remarks on L. V. 69 in art. *sōm*.

Sg. nom. *shūñ*, 1; with suff. indef. art. *shūñāh*, 11, 30, 69; dat. *shūñĕs*, 11, 30, 69.

shūñākār, m. having the form of the Void, reduced to becoming nothing but the Great Void (see *shūñ*), 50.

shūñālay, m. he whose abode is the Great Void (see *shūñ*), i.e. the Supreme, 15.

shurᵘ, m. an infant; *dŏda-shurᵘ*, a milk-infant, a sucking child, 70.

shramāwun, to labour at; hence, *dŏd shramāwun*, to labour at milk, to milk, 38.

shrutawŏnᵘ, m. one who hears well, one who is the reverse of being deaf, 20.

shrōtsun, to become pure; 2 past, m. sg. 3, with suff. 1st pers. sg. gen. *shrōtsyōm*, 105.

shĕshi, m. the moon; *shĕshi-kal*, a digit of the moon, 25, 69; *shĕshi-ras*, moon-juice, the water of immortality, nectar, *amṛta*, sg. abl. *-rasa*, 40. For the mystic terminology in connexion with the moon in Śaiva theology, see art. *sōm*.

shās^{a}t^{a}r, m. a holy book, the general body of sacred writings; sg. abl. *shāstra*, 27.

shĕs^{a}t^{a}r, m. iron; sg. dat. *shĕst^{a}ras*, 100 = K. Pr. 46.

shāṭh, m. a sand-bank (hidden under water) in a stream, a shoal; sg. abl. with emph. *y*, *shāṭhay*, 84, 85.

shĕth, card. a hundred; *shĕth-shĕt^i*, hundreds, 6.

shiv, m. Śiva, the Supreme Deity, absorption in whom is final emancipation, 8, 14, 51–54, 80; sg. gen. *shiwun^u*, 58; dat. *shiwas*, 68; voc. *shiwa shiwa karān*, uttering the cry of 'Śiva! Śiva!', i.e. meditating on the fact that all that exists is one with Him, 65; *shiwa-may*, made up of Śiva, consisting of Śiva, 16; *shiwa-pūzan*, the worship of Śiva, 22; *shiwa-shĕk^{a}th*, Śiva and his *śakti*, or energic power, 2, cf. 68, and art. *shĕk^{a}th*; *parama-shiv*, the Supreme Śiva (gen. *-shiwun^u*), 58; *tsētana-shiv*, Śiva in his quality of Supreme Spirit, as opposed to his more material manifestations, 79.

shwās, m. a breathing, a complete breath, inspiration and expiration; sg. acc. *shwās*, 55.

sh^{ĕ}wot^u, m. the six-staged road, i.e. either the six *vikāras* or the six *cakras* (see art. *shĕh*), 82.

shyāma-gal, m. dark-blue-necked, a name of Śiva, whose neck was dyed a dark blue by drinking the *kālakūṭa* poison at the churning of the ocean; sg. voc. *shyāma-galā*, 13.

sahaz, adj. inborn, natural, innate; as subst. m. natural character, true nature, reality; hence, obl. sg. *sahaza*, as adv. naturally, innately, 18 (according to one interpretation), 45; as an epithet of the Supreme Śiva, *sahaz* means 'He who is real and true', 18 (according to another interpretation), 43; *sahaza-kusum*, a flower of the true nature, i.e. a flower born from one's inner soul, a flower which is a true offering of love; or (?) a flower of reality, a real flower, 21 (see note to the verse).

In Sanskrit, the compound *sahaja-vidyā* means 'the knowledge, or state of experience, in which the true relation of things is realized'. It is the consciousness of the identity of the Self with Śiva. Lallā frequently uses the word *sahaz*, by itself, with this meaning of 'the nature of Self'. Thus, in 29, she has *sahaza-vētsār*, discrimination as to the nature of Self, and in 30 she has *sahaz vĕċārun*, exercise this discrimination as to the nature of Self. From the idea of 'the nature of Self', it comes to mean 'knowledge of the nature of Self'. Thus, in 29, we are told that quietude and self-command are not necessary causes *sahazas*, i.e. of a knowledge of the nature of Self. Similarly, *sahaz* has the same meaning in 35 and 62.

Sg. nom. *sahaz*, 30, 35, 43; dat. *sahazas*, 29, 62; abl. and obl. *sahaza*, 18, 21, 29, 45.

sĕkh, f. sand; sg. obl. *sĕki-lawar*, a rope of sand, a rope made by twisting sand, an impossibility, 107.

sukh, m. happiness, ease, K. Pr. 201 (ter).

sakharun, to prepare for a journey, to set out; to set oneself to any task, busy oneself with, 10; impve. sg. 2, *sakhar*, 10.

sakol^u, adj. all, the whole, everything, 38; m. pl. nom. with emph. *y*, *sakaliy*, 1, all men, 47 (according to another interpretation, this is *sakaliy*, 2, below, q. v.).

sakaliy, 2, adv. without having eaten food, hungry and athirst, 47 (see the preceding).

sul, f. the early time, the time before any fixed time; hence, the propitious time (for doing anything), 99 (= K. Pr. 46), 100. The word often means 'early dawn', and perhaps also has this meaning in these passages.

salil, m. water, 16, 29; sg. dat. *salilas*, 29.

sōm, m. the moon. The moon plays a considerable part on the mystic side of Śaivism, and is frequently mentioned in this connexion in the *Lallā-vākyāni*. In these verses it appears under four different names, viz. *shĕshi* (25, 40, 69), *sōm* (34), *ċand^ar* (9, 22, 109), and *ċand^arama* (93), corresponding, respectively, to the Sanskrit *śaśin-*, *sōma-*, *candra-*, and *candramas-*. It will be convenient to bring together the various mentions of the moon, and to explain the mystic references thereto.

As explained in the Note on Yōga (§§ 9, 13 ff.), starting from the base of the abdomen,—the *mūlâdhāra*, or sacral plexus,—upwards along the spinal cord there are in the body six *cakras*, or circles. Over these is the seventh, the *sahasrâra*, or medulla oblongata (§§ 19, 27). In this sahasrâra, in mystic parlance, is the moon, and also the abode of the Parama Śiva, or Supreme Śiva,—the transcendental realm named Kailāsa or Akula (§ 19). By blocking up the breath in the *nāḍis*, while meditating upon this sahasrâra cakra, the Yōgī tries to enter into the highest *samādhi*, or mental absorption, in which the *citta*, or organ of thought, is absorbed, microcosmically, into sahasrâra, and, macrocosmically, into Parama Śiva (§ 21).

This is *mukti*, or final release,—what we should call salvation.

The above explains the reference in L. V. 25, in which the authoress says that by continual suppression of her vital breaths she had cut her way through the six forests (i.e. the *cakras*), so that the digit of the moon awoke and appeared to her.

Similarly, in 34, she refers to a Yōgī, in whose *kanda* or bulb (§ 5) the mystic syllable *ōṁ* is firmly fixed (§§ 23, 24), and whom the *kumbhaka* exercise (§ 21) leads to the home of the moon, or sahasrâra. He thus obtains *samādhi*.

In 69 she says, 'I held the steed of my *citta*, or thought, by the rein of absence of desire, after much practice having joined together the vital breaths of the ten *nāḍis*. Thereupon the digit of the moon (in the sahasrâra) melted and descended upon me, and the nothingness of the transient world became merged in the Nothing.' In the sahasrâra is the Void (§§ 20, 24), in which the empty world of matter becomes merged. The 'melting' of the moon means that the lunar nectar descends, as explained in the following remarks on No. 40.

In 40, the authoress advocates spiritual worship, in which the flowers offered to the object of worship (Śiva) are devotion, while over his (mental) image is to stream,—not material water, but—the juice of the digit of the moon (lunar nectar) abiding in the sahasrâra at the top of the vertebral column (§§ 8, 19 ff.). The nectar passes down through the *suṣumnā* and *iḍā nāḍis* (§ 8). The Yōgī who is becoming absorbed into sahasrâra drinks this nectar, and becomes master over himself and the *kula* (see *kŏl*) (§ 21). Thus the expression means that he is to devote himself to *samādhi* by absorption into sahasrâra.

The same ideas are found in No. 9. She states, 'when the sun disappeared, there came the moonlight; when the moon disappeared only *citta*, or thought, remained. When *citta* disappeared nothing was left anywhere'. Just as the moon is in the highest *cakra*, so the sun is in the lowest,—the *mūlādhāra*, near the perineum (§§ 5, 9). 'Disappeared' means 'ceased to be present in consciousness'. That is to say, the Yōgī raises his consciousness from the mūlâdhāra to the sahasrâra (§ 21), the sphere of absolute being. Here the sense of difference between his individual spirit and the Universal Being is sunk in the all-consuming consciousness of All-Being, All-Light.

In 93, there does not appear to be any reference to the moon of mysticism. It is stated that the *cit*, or pure spirit, is ever new and new, i.e. is ever full of new illusions, just as the natural moon is ever new and new, i.e. perpetually changes as it waxes and wanes.

Similarly, No. 109 presents no difficulty. Lallā states that after much searching she came from the inmost recesses of her soul into the moonlight, meaning either that she came into the light of true knowledge, or that her *citta*, or organ of thought, became absorbed into sahasrâra, as explained above.

There remains No. 22. This is dealt with in the note on the verse, and what is there said need not be repeated.

Sg. obl. *sōma-garē*, in the home of the moon, or the sahasrâra (see above), 34.

*som*ᵘ, adj. equal, alike, 5, 16. Sg. abl. *sami trața*, by equal, i.e. by thorough, union, 1; m. pl. nom. *samē* (m. c. for *sàm*ⁱ), 16.

sum, f. a bridge, 34, 50, 96 (= K. Pr. 47), 98; K. Pr. 46, 47. Pl. dat. *suman-sọth*ᵘ, an embankment with bridges, i.e. an embankment broken here and there, the gaps being covered each by a crazy foot-bridge of only two or three planks (v. l. *swamana-sọth*ᵘ), 98.

simhāsan, m. a throne, 73.

samun, to assemble, come together, unite for some purpose; cond. past, pl. 3, *samahŏn*, 95.

sŏman, m. jasmine; *sŏman-bāg*, a jasmine-garden, 68; see *swa*.

suman, see *sum*.

sĕmanz, K. Pr. 18 (= L. V. 98), *sĕmanz sŏthi* being translated 'in the middle of the way'. The correct reading is apparently *suman-sŏthi* or *swamana-sŏthi*, as in L. V. 98. See *sum* and *swa*.

samsār, m. the material universe, 35, 37; transmigration, the weary round of birth and rebirth, which must be endured by a soul till it obtains salvation, 6. Sg. gen. *samsārun*ᵘ, of which the m. sg. dat. is *samsāranis*, 6. In modern Ksh. this form of the genitive is reserved for masculine proper names; sg. dat. *samsāras*, 35, 37.

sana, a suffix added to interrogative words to indicate indefiniteness, as in *kyāh-sana*, sg. abl. *kawa-sana*, what kind of, 39.

sŏn, m. gold, 100 = K. Pr. 46.

*sond*ᵘ (f. *sünz*ᵘ), suffix of the genitive of all singular masculine animate nouns, except proper names. Cf. *hond*ᵘ. M. sg. nom. *gŏra-sond*ᵘ *wanun*, the word (i.e. instruction) of the teacher, 108; f. sg. dat. (in sense of instr.) *dayĕ-sanzĕ prahē*, with the love of God, 105.

sandēh, m. doubt, 7.

sandārun, to make steady, to put the brake on, to block (the wheels of a carriage), 26; to make (oneself) steady, to come to one's senses after a faint, to become cool and courageous after being subject to mental agitation, to take courage, 70; conj. part. *sandŏrith*, 26; impve. fut. *sandŏr*^{i}*zi*, 70.

sangāṭh, m. collection, bringing together into one place; *sangāṭh karun*, to bring together in this way (used especially of collecting appliances, materials, &c., before setting to at any work), 17.

snān, m. bathing, esp. bathing as a religious exercise (borrowed from Sanskrit); *snān karun*, to bathe as ab., 32, 46. The Ksh. form of this word is *shrān*.

sannyās, m. an ascetic, a wandering devotee, 36.

sapadun, conj. 2, to become; past m. sg. 2, *sapodukh*, thou becamest, i.e. thou hast become, 86.

sŏpanun, conj. 2, to become; past m. sg. 3, *sŏpon*^{u}, 5.

sparshun, to touch; fut. sg. 3, *sparshi*, 37.

sar, m. a lake, an ocean, 47 (bis), 50, 78, 79; *amrĕta-sar*, the lake of nectar, i.e. blissful union with the Supreme, 68; *bhawa-sar*, the ocean of existence, 23; with suff. of indef. art. *sarāh*, a certain lake, 50; sg. dat. *saras*, 23, 47, 68; sg. abl. *sari*, 47.

sȧr^{i}, adj. inundated, flooded, (of a lake) overflowing, 50.

sirĕ, m. the sun; sg. dat. *sirĕs*, K. Pr. 201.

sor^{u}, m. in *sȧr*^{i}*-phol*^{u}, a mustard-seed (as an example of minuteness), 47.

sŏr^{u}, adj. all. This word almost invariably takes emph. *y*, and becomes *sŏruy*; m. sg. nom. *sŏruy*, all that exists, everything, the totality of creation, 31, 42–3; m. pl. nom. *sŏriy*, all, every one, 95, K. Pr. 150; dat. *sārĕniy padan*, in all the verses, 84.

sur, m. a god; *sura-guru*, the chief of the gods (see art. *guru*); *sura-guru-nāth*, the lord of the chief of the gods, the Supreme Deity, 5, 65.

srugāl, m. a jackal; pl. nom. *srugāl*, 47.

sarun or *sŏrun*, to remember, 50, 91; to call to mind, to remember affectionately, meditate upon, 45, 65; conj. part. *sŏrith*, 65; pres. part. with force of pres. sg. 2, *sŏran*, dost thou remember?, 91; old pres. and fut. sg. 1, with suff. 3rd pers. sg. dat., *saras*, I remember it, 50 (quater); 3, *sŏri*, 45.

sȧr^{i}*-phol*^{u}, see *sor*^{u}.

saras, see *sar* and *sarun*.

sarwa, adj. all (borrowed from Sanskrit), in *sarwa-gath*, going to all places, hence, as an epithet of the Deity, All-pervading, Omnipresent, 64; *sarwa-kriy*, he who made all things, the All-Creator, 59. The Ksh. word is *sŏr*^{u}.

sūrya, the sun (borrowed from Sanskrit), in *sūrya-manḍal*, the orb, or disk, of the sun, used metaphorically to indicate the Supreme Deity, 75. The Ksh. word is *sirĕ*.

sās, 1, or *swās* (q. v.) m. ashes; sg. abl. *sāsa*, or (m. c.) *sāsā*, 18.

sās, 2, card. a thousand, 34; with suff. *ā* indicating the indef. art., *sāsā*, a thousand, i.e. any indefinite great number, 18, K. Pr. 57; sg. abl. *sāsa-manza*, out of a thousand, K. Pr. 150.

sūti, *sūty*, or (with emph. *y*) *sötiy*, postpos. governing dat., with, together with, 57, 92 (bis); governing abl., with, by means of, owing to, 25, 83; *sūti*, 57, 92 (bis); *sūty*, 83; *sötiy*, 25. In 57 it is a preposition, not a postposition.

sath, 1, m. substance, body; hence, ground for reliance, 41.

sath, 2, adj. good, 82; subst. m. a good man, a virtuous man; pl. nom. *sath*, 59, in both cases with alternative rendering of 'seven' (*sath*, 3).

sath, 3, card. seven; nom. *sath*, 59 (see *sath*, 2), 82; abl. *sati*, 50; *sati nĕngi*, seven times, on seven occasions, 50. The seven worlds (*lōka*) are the earth, sky, heaven, middle region, place of rebirths, mansion of the blest, and abode of truth. There are also seven lower regions, called, respectively, *Atala*, *Vitala*, *Sutala*, *Rasātala*, *Talātala*, *Mahātala*, and *Pātāla* (see 59). In 82, Lallā states that after going through six paths (i.e. the six *cakras*, or the six *vikāras*, see art. *shĕh*), she arrived at the *sath-mārg*, which means either 'the good road' or else 'the seventh *bhūmi*'. There are seven *jñāna-bhūmis*, or planes of knowledge; viz. *śubhēcchā*, or the plane of auspicious desire (for knowledge); *vicāraṇā*, or the plane of consideration; *tanu-mānasa*, or the plane of the subtile mind; *sattvāpatti*, the plane of acquirement of good sense; *saṁsakti*, the plane of intimate acquaintance; *padārtha-bhāvinī*, the plane of possession of the (true) meanings of words; and, seventhly, *turya-gā*, or that which conducts to the *turya* state, or condition leading to final emancipation.

sath, 4, f. hope; sg. dat., with emph. *y*, *sŭsuy*, 102. Cf. *satun*.

sāth, m. a particular moment of time, an instant, 25; an instant of time, a very short time, a moment, 104; a moment of time, (in astrology) a particular fortunate, or unfortunate, moment, 3; sg. dat. *sātas*, for a moment, for an instant, 104; sg. abl., with emph. *y*, *tamiy sötiy*, at that very moment, 25.

sŏthu, m. an embankment, e.g. along a river bank to confine the channel, and used as a road, 74, 98 = K, Pr. 18; sg. abl. *sŏthi manz* (for dat. *sŏthis manz*, see *manz*), 98, K. Pr. 18. Cf. *sum*.

sthān, m. a place, position, region, 57, 82; sg. abl. *sthāna*, 57.
sthir, adj. fixed, firm, permanent, 73.
satun, conj. 2, to hope; past f. sg. 1, with suff. 3rd pers. sg. dat. *süťüsas*, I hoped in it, 104. Cf. *sath*, 4.
sötiy, see *süťi* and *säth*.
süty, see *süťi*.
saťs, m. a tailor; sg. ag. *säťsi*, 103.
süťüsas, see *satun*.
süťüy, see *sath* 4.
swa, adj. and pron. own; self. This is a Sanskrit word, and occurs only in borrowed Sanskrit compounds. Owing to the fact that *wa* following a consonant, and *u* in borrowed words, are both, in Kāshmīrī, pronounced as *ŏ*, Lallā frequently makes use of this to effect double meaning. Thus: (28) *swa-para-vĕcār*, discrimination on the Self and on the Supreme, or on the Supreme, who is the Self. One of these two is here certainly the correct translation; but the words are also capable of being taken as *sŏ-para-vĕcār* (i.e. *su-para-vicāra*), discrimination on Him who is excellently Supreme; (36) *swa-darshĕna-myūlu*, union with the Self (i.e. God) (brought about by) visiting (holy places), or *sŏ-darshĕna-myūlu*, union brought about by the excellent visiting (of holy places); (68) *swa-man-bāg*, the garden of one's own heart, or,—taking *sŏman* as equivalent to the Persian *suman*,—*sŏman-bāg* means 'a jasmine-garden'; (98 = K. Pr. 18); *swa-mana-sọthu*, the embankment of (the illusions of) one's own mind, or *suman-sọthu*, an embankment with crazy bridges (see *sum*); (71, 79) *swa-vĕcār*, discrimination exercised as regards the Self, or *sŏ-vĕcār*, the good discrimination. *Swa-rūph*, m. own form, i.e. the nature of anything, identity with; thus, (15) *kha-swarūph*, He who is identical with, or consists of, absolute vacuity, the impersonal Supreme Deity; (67) *niza-swarūph*, the nature of what is one's own, the nature of Self.
sŏwu, adj. plenteous, abounding (of a crop), 66.
savikās, m. that which has wide expansion, the total expanse of creation, the visible creation, 1.
swömī, m. a lord, one who is master or owner; *shĕn swömī*, the owner of the six (attributes of the Deity), 13, see *shĕh*.
säwun, to cause to sleep, to put to sleep, to lay to sleep; conj. part. *sövith*, K. Pr. 57.
swar, m. heaven; *bhūr*, *bhuwaḥ*, *swar*, the earth, the atmosphere, and heaven,—i.e. the whole visible universe, 9.
swarg, m. heaven; sg. dat, *swargas böji*, a possessor of heaven, 62.
swarūph, see *swa*.

swās or *sās*, 1 (q.v.), m. ashes, 43.

swātma, m. one's own self; hence, the Self, recognized as identical with the Supreme; sg. dat. *swātmas*, to the Supreme Self, 61; *shĕnkar-swātma*, Śaṅkara (i.e. Śiva) recognized as one with Self, 39, 40.

swayam, oneself (borrowed from Sanskrit), 33.

sŏy, *suy*, see *tih*.

syund[u], m. the river Sindh, one of the three principal rivers of Kashmīr. Its waters are sacred. *syund*[u]*-zal*, pl. the waters of the Sindh, 81.

saz, f. fuller's earth, 103.

ta, 1, conj. and, 3, 4, 13, 17, 20, 22, 24, 29, 31, 35 (bis), 37, 39, 41, 44, 48, 52, 56–7, 78–9, 89, 90–1, 94–5, 101–2–3; K. Pr. 18 (bis), 102 (bis); *na ta*, and not, nor, 96–7; K. Pr. 47, 102; cf. *na ta* under *ta*, 2; *na* . . . *na* . . . *ta*, not . . . nor . . . nor, 15. A strengthened form of this word is *tŏy*, 1, q.v.

ta, 2, conj. then, and then, and next, thereupon (= Hindī *tō*) (in this sense often scarcely distinguishable from *ta*, 1), 1, 4, 19, 23, 43, 47, 68, 82, 104; then, and then, thereafter, but, 98; then, so, accordingly, therefore, 21, 30, 33, 42, 46, 51–2, 54, 70, 80–1, 89, 99 (bis), 100; K. Pr. 46 (quater); then, so that, 66; then, and yet, nevertheless, 60; then, used to indicate the apodosis of a conditional or quasi-conditional, sentence, 2, 27, 55, 87, or the antecedent clause of a relative clause, 61; often (like the Hindī *tō*) colouring a whole sentence, but itself hardly translatable, I wonder if, well then, verily, &c., according to the context, 9, 19, 92; *na ta* (= Hindī *nahī̃ tō*), otherwise, or else, 19, 71; K. Pr. 150; cf. *na ta* under *ta*, 1. A strengthened form of this word is *tŏy*, 2, q.v.

ti, conj. (= Hindī *bhī*) also, 48, 106; K. Pr. 18; even, 32, 48; *kĕh ti nā*, nothing at all, 9, 11; *kĕh ti nō*, nothing at all, 90; *kāńh ti nō sath*, no substance at all, 41; *kŏh ti na khĕth*, no harm at all, 77; *tō ti* (Hindī *tau bhī*), even then, 29.

tō, = *ta*, 2, in *tō ti* (Hindī *tau bhī*), even then, 29.

tōḍ[i], see *tŏr*[u].

taday, adv. then only, then and not till then, 77.

tagun, conj. 2, to be known how to be done, to be possible. This verb is used as a potential verb, the ability always being mental, not physical (cf. the Sanskrit *tajjñāna*-, by which paṇḍits translate this word); *tih yĕs tagi*, to whom that is possible, i.e. he who knows how to do that, 24; *tih yĕs karun tagi*, to whom the doing that is possible, he who knows how to do that, 37. If it is desired to indicate physical possibility the verb *hĕkun* (q.v.) must be used.

tih, pronoun of the third person, he, 5, 6, 8, 20, 24, 27, 31 (bis), 33–4, 37 (bis), 43 (bis), 65, 71–2, 76, 105; she; it, 70; K. Pr. 46 (bis); substantival demonstrative pronoun that, 20–1, 37, 57 (bis), 69, 75, 90, 94, 107; adjectival demonstrative pronoun, 3, 15, 25, 28 (bis), 34, 47, 52 (bis), 77, 81, 104; sometimes used substantively, but treated as an adjective (see below), 2, 12–13, 58 (bis), 94.

This pronoun is either animate or inanimate, and the animate forms may be either masculine or feminine. The inanimate forms are of common gender. Moreover, as seen above, there is a cross-division, according as it is used substantively or adjectivally. We shall consider the substantival forms first.

As an animate substantival pronoun, the following forms occur:—

masc. sg. nom. *suh*, he, 8, 24, 31, 33; with emph. *y*, *suy*, he only, he verily, 31, 34, 37.

dat. *tas*, to him, 20, 34, 37, 105; with emph. *ⁱ*, *tásⁱ*, to him only, 65.

gen. (m. sg. nom.) *tasondᵘ*; with emph. *y*, *tasonduy*, his only, 72.

ag. *tàmⁱ*, by him; with emph. *y*, *tàmiy*, by him alone, by him verily, 5, 43 (bis).

pl. nom. and acc. *tim*, they, 6; them, 76: with emph. *y*, *timay*, they alone, 27.

gen. (m. sg. nom.) *tihondᵘ*, their, 71.

There is no occurrence of the feminine pronoun used substantively in the songs.

As an inanimate substantival pronoun, we have the following:—

sg. nom. and acc. *tih*, it, that, 24, 37, 70, 107; with emph. *y*, *tiy*, 20, 21.

dat. *tath*, to it, K. Pr. 46 (bis).

abl. *tawa*, by that; used adverbially to mean 'for that reason', 'on that account', 'therefore', 57 (bis); with emph. *y*, *taway*, therefore, 69, 90, 94; by that means, 75.

pl. nom.; with emph. *y*, *timay*, those very, 13.

Used as an animate pronominal adjective, the following forms occur. They are the same as the corresponding substantival forms:—

m. sg. nom., with emph. *y*, *suy*, that very (god), 15.

pl. nom. *tim*, those (rams), 77.

f. sg. nom. *sŏh*; with emph. *y*, *sŏy*, (I am) only that (Lal), 81.

When used as an inanimate pronominal adjective, the substantival forms *tih* and *tiy* of the nominative are not used, the animate substantival forms (m. *suh*, *suy*; f. *sŏh*, *sŏy*) being used instead. On the other hand, the inanimate substantival form of the dative, *tath*, is also used as an adjective. Thus:—

m. sg. nom. *suh*, that (wine), 104; with emph. *y*, *suy*, that very (time) 3, (spell) 34.

dat. *tath*, in that (lake), 47.

abl, *tami*; with emph. *y*, *tamiy*, at that very (time), 25.

pl. acc. *tim*, those (foods), 28; those (garments), 28.

f. sg. nom. *sŏy*, that very (stone), 52 (bis).

As regards the use of the substantival forms of this pronoun, as semi-adjectives, this consists in the use of *suh*, *suy*, *sŏh*, or *sŏy*, instead of *tih* or *tiy*, when referring to something inanimate. This occurs:—

(1) When the substantival pronoun is the antecedent to an adjectival relative pronoun. The antecedent, although a substantive, is then treated also as an adjective. Thus:—*yih yih karm korum*, *suh arćun*, whatever act I performed, that was worshipping (God), 58. Here the relative *yih yih*, whatever, is an adjective, and therefore *suh* (the adjectival form of the antecedent) is used, and not *tih*, the substantival form. On the other hand, if the relative is inanimate and substantival, the inanimate substantival form, *tih*, is used for the antecedent. Thus, in the next line of the same verse, we have *yih wŏććorum*, *tiy manthar*, what I uttered, that verily was a mystic invocation.

(2) In a copulative sentence, when the subject is a pronoun, this, although substantival, is treated as an adjective in agreement with the complement. Thus, (2) *suy* (not *tiy*) *wŏpadēsh*, that alone is the instruction; (12) *suy* (not *tiy*) *chuy jñān*, that alone is (true) knowledge; (58) *suy yih tanthar*, that alone is this scripture; (94) *suy gauv wākh*, that became the (mystic) word.

thūjü, f. (this word is a feminine diminutive of *thal*), a small place; esp. a small sacred *cella* or small wooden temple, in which an image of a god and other appurtenances of worship are kept; sg. nom. (m. c.) *thaji*, 33.

thal, m. a place; sg. abl. *thali thali*, in every place, in every land, 53.

thamawun, to cause to stop, to stop, to prevent going on; inf. sg. nom. *thamawun*, 38.

thān, m. a place; *al-thān*, 60, see *al*; sg. dat. *-thānas*, 60.

tihondu, see *tih*.

thaph, f. the act of grasping or taking hold of; — *karūñū*, to grasp, 4.

thar, f. the back; — *dārūñū*, to offer the back, to place the back at one's disposal (of a riding animal), 88.

thūrū, f. a bush, a shrub, 96 = K. Pr. 47.

tahsīldār, m. a revenue collector, a tax-gatherer (looked upon as inevitable and merciless), K. Pr. 56.

thāwun, to put, to place, 70; *dūru thāwun*, to put far off, to put away, 27; *kan thāwun*, to place the ear, to give heed, attend, listen (to), 91; conj. part. *thövith*, 27; impve. sg. 2, *thāv*, 91; impve. fut. *thövizi*, 70.

ṭŏku, m. an earthen drinking vessel, an earthen goblet; pl. dat. *ṭākĕn*, 106.

tal, m. the lowest part or bottom of anything; *bhū-tal*, the surface of the earth, the whole earth as opposed to the sky, 22, 42; *hyonu tal*, to take below (oneself), to put beneath one's feet, (of an elephant) to crush beneath the feet, K. Pr. 150.

tĕl, m. sesame seed (used in offerings to a god), 45.

tĕli, adv. then, 49, 82 (in both cases the correlative of *yĕli*, when).

tul, m. weight, the weight of anything, 23; sg. abl. *tuli tōlun*, to weigh by weight, to weigh in the balance, 23.

tūl, m. cotton-wool; *tūla-paryōkh*, a bed (the pillows of which are stuffed) with cotton, a luxurious bed, 73.

tulā, in *tulā-kūṭu*, m. the beam or standard of a large weighing balance; hence, such a balance; sg. abl. *-kōṭi*, (weighing) in a scales, 23.

tēlun, (of water in a receptacle) to leak or ooze away; old pres., sg. 3, with emph. *y*, *tēliy*, 78–9.

tōlun, to weigh; past part. m. sg. *tūlu*, 23.

tulun, to raise, lift; *bam tulun*, to raise the skin, to raise weals (with a whip), 101; *kadam tulun*, to raise the step, to step out, walk alertly, 99 = K. Pr. 46; *parwāz tulun*, to raise flight, to take to oneself wings and fly, 99 = K. Pr. 46.

Impve. sg. 2, *tul*, 99 (bis) = K. Pr. 46 (bis); past part., with suff. 1st pers. sg. ag. and 3rd pers. sg. dat., *tulumas*, I raised his (skin), 101.

tālav, m. the ceiling of a room or house; *tālav-rāzadōñū*, ? the plastering of the ceiling of a room or house, 85; but the meaning of *rāzadōñū* (q. v.) is very doubtful. *achĕ lagañĕ tālav*, to attach the eyes to the ceiling, to turn up the eyes (in death), K. Pr. 102.

tam, m. darkness, spiritual darkness; sg. abl. *tama-pōkh*, the morass of spiritual darkness, 74.

tām, 1, suffix, converting an interrogative into an indefinite pronoun, as in *kus-tām*, some one or other, *kyāh-tām*, something or other, both in 86.

tām, 2, postpos. up to, as far as, governing dat.; *hiḍis-tām*, (from the navel) up to Adam's apple, 57.

tami, *tàmⁱ*, *tim*, *tamiy*, *tàmiy*, *timay*, see *tih*.

tan, f. the body, 93; sg. dat. *tanē* (m. c. for *tani*), 76.

tana, adv. since then, from that moment, 83, 93.

ṭang, m. a pear (the fruit); pl. nom. *ṭang*, 92.

tanthᵃr, m. the sacred books of the Śaiva religion, the *tantra*, 11, 58.

taph, m. austerities, esp. religious austerities, 62.

tāpun, to heat, cause to be hot, (of the sun) to shine upon; pol. impve. sg. 3, *tŏpⁱtan*, let him shine, i.e. does he not shine?, 53 (bis).

tapasy, m. asceticism; sg. abl., with emph. *y*, *tapasiy*, 35.

tār, m. a means for leading a person across (a river or the like), 96, 106; K. Pr. 46, 47: a fee paid to a ferryman, *nāwa-tār*, a ferry-fee, 98=K. Pr. 18; a name for the sacred syllable *ōṁ* (see *anāhath*), as that which crosses the soul over the sea of existence, 72; sg. dat. *tāras*, 98=K. Pr. 18; sg. gen. *tārukᵘ*, 72; *tār dyunᵘ*, to pass a person across (a river, &c.), 106.

tōr, adv. there; with emph. ⁱ, for *y*, *tūrⁱ*, there only, 19, 61.

tōrᵘ or *tōḍᵘ*, m. the bolt (of a door); pl. nom. *törⁱ* or *töḍⁱ*, 48.

tūrⁱ, see *tōr*,

tūrᵘ, f. cold, coldness, 16, 28; sg. ag. *tūri*, 16.

trāg, m. a pond, a lake, 84.

turogᵘ, m. a horse, 26, 69.

trᵃh, card. three, 16, 75; *trayi nĕngi*, adv. three times, 50. The modern form of this word is *trĕh* or *trih*. There are three impurities (*mala*) of the soul, which impede its final release (75). These are called *āṇava*, *māyīya*, and *kārma*. The first, *āṇava*, is the state or character of the soul deeming itself to be finite (the soul being looked upon as a very minute entity, *aṇu*), the second, *māyīya*, is that born of cosmic illusion, or the belief that one thing is different from another, and the third, *kārma*, is the impurity that results from action or 'works' (which may be good or bad). See Note on Yōga, § 24.

tᵃrunᵘ, adj. cool, cold, 56, 57.

tūrun, to become cold, (of water) to freeze; old pres. sg. 3, *tūrē* (for *tūri*), 16.

tᵃranāwun, to make cold, to extinguish (a fire); inf. *tᵃranāwun*, 38.

trŏpᵃrun, to shut (a door); past part. m. pl., with suff. 1st pers. sg. ag., *trŏpᵃrim*, I closed (the doors), 101.

trupti, f. contentment, satisfaction, 12.

trēsh, f. thirst, 37.

tīr^a^th, m. a sacred bathing-place, a place of pilgrimage, 36, 46; K. Pr. 201 (ter); pl. dat. *tīrthan*, 46; *prathuy tīrthan*, (going) to every holy place, going from one holy place to another, 36.

trāwun, to abandon, leave behind, K. Pr. 57; to abandon, discard, give up (sin, &c.), 27, 30; K. Pr. 46 (bis); to abandon, let loose, lose control of, 70, 88; (of a road) to leave (it, after passing along it), hence, to traverse completely, 82; *dȧlⁱ trāwȧnⁱ*, to throw out the skirt from the body, i.e. to sit with bended knees, 49.

Conj. part. *trövith*, 70, 82; K. Pr. 57; impve. sg. 2, *trāv*, 30; K. Pr. 46; with suff. 3rd pers. sg. acc., *trāwun*, 88; fut. sg. 2, *trāwakh*, K. Pr. 46; past part. m. pl., with suff. 1st pers. sg. ag. and 3rd pers. sg. dat., *trövⁱmas*, 49; f. sg. *trövᵘ*, 27.

trayi, see *trᵃh*.

tas, *tasonduy*, see *tih*.

tati, adv. there, 70, 88; m. c. *tatē*, there, in those circumstances, 41; with emph. *y*, *tatiy*, even there, there and then, 104; *tȧtⁱ*, even there, at that very place, 48, 49, 68; with emph. *y*, *tȧtiy*, at that very place, at the same place, 51.

totᵘ, 1, adj. hot, 56, 57.

totᵘ, 2, adv. there, K. Pr. 102 (bis); with emph. *y*, *totuy*, 47.

tath, see *tih*.

titha, adv. so, in that manner; with emph. *y*, *tithay . . . yitha*, so . . . as, 100.

tŏṭun, to be reduced to misery; past, f. sg. 1, *tŏṭᵘs*, 13.

tattwa, m. (in Śaiva philosophy) (in the plural) the fundamental and general factors of which the universe consists, see *Kashmir Shaivism*, p. 47; *tattwa-vyodᵘ*, one who knows and understands the *tattwas*, 20.

tawa, *taway*, see *tih*.

tᵃy, 1, a woman who spins a very fine kind of thread, a delicate spinner; sg. ag. *tᵃyĕ*, 102.

tᵃy, 2, f. very fine thread; pl. nom. *tᵃyĕ*, 102.

tiy, see *tih*.

töy, 1, conj. and, 5, 14, 40, 51, 62, 86. This is a strengthened form of *ta*, 1, q.v.

töy, 2, conj. then, and then, thereafter, thereupon, 9 (ter), 11 (ter), 16; then, therefore, accordingly, 24, 53; then, introducing the apodosis of a conditional sentence, 12. This is a strengthened form of *ta*, 2, q.v.

tyāgun, to let go, let loose; hence, (of a sword), to wield, to draw; past part. f. sg. *työjⁱ* (for *työjᵘ*), 62.

tyolᵘ, m. a blister, 108. See *rāwun*.

tyuthᵘ, pron. adj. and adv. of that kind, such, 66; with emph. *y*, *tyuthuy* (as correl. of *yuthuy*), such, 55 (adj.); so, 64 (adv.); m. pl. nom., with emph. *y*, *tithiy*, 92 (adj.).
tĕzun, to abandon; past part. m. pl. *tĕzⁱ*, 55.

ċidānand, m. pure spirit (*ċĕth*, 1, = Skr. *cit*) and joy (*ānand*); sg. dat. *ċidānandas*, 6.
ċᵃh, pron. of the second person, thou, 7 (ter), 13, 44 (bis), 59, 70, 91; with emph. *y*, *ċᵃy*, thou alone, 42 (quinquies), 109 (ter).

Sg. dat. *ċĕ*, 13 (to thee, belonging to thee), 44 (bis), 56, 72; *abēd ċĕ ta mĕ*, no distinction between thee and me, 13. Obsolete form of sg. dat. *tŏyĕ-vĕn*, distinct (different) from thee, 13.

sg. ag. *ċĕ golᵘ* (modern Ksh. would have *ċĕ goluth*), thou destroyedst, 64.

sg. gen. (f. sg. nom.) *cyŏñᵘ ċinth*, thought (care) for thee (objective genitive), 72; (f. sg. dat.) *cyāñĕ*, K. Pr. 102.

pl. nom. *tŏhⁱ*, ye, 91.
ċhāḍun or *ċhā̃ḍun*, to search, to wander about searching, 3, 48; to search for, seek, 44, 60, 99, 100; K. Pr. 46; pres. part. *ċhāḍān*, 3, 44, 60; *ċhāḍan*, 48; impve. sg. 2, with suff. 3rd pers. sg. acc. *ċhā̃ḍun*, 99, 100; K. Pr. 46.
ċhŏh, m. unrestrained conduct (in modern language used with reference to a person who, having obtained some post of authority, acts without self-restraint, and without fear of the consequences). In L. V. 44 it means the experiencing of unrestrained rapture; *ċhŏh dyutum*, I gave (to thee and to myself) the unrestrained rapture (of perfect union).
ċhanḍun, to pass over, traverse; fut. sg. 3, *ċhanḍi*, 26.
ċhĕnun, conj. 2, to become cut; hence, to be cut away from a person, to be torn away from; fut. sg. 3, with suff. 1st pers. sg. dat., and negative interrogative, *ċhĕnĕm-nā prah*, will not love (of the world) be cut away from me (i.e. be torn from my heart), 83.
ċhunun, to throw, but used in many idiomatic phrases. Thus, in K. Pr. 102, *nölⁱ ċhunun*, to throw (a halter) on to the neck. Past part. f. sg., with suff. 2nd pers. sg. ag. and 1st pers. sg. dat. *ċhuñᵘtham*, thou castedst for me (i.e. in my presence) (a feminine thing), K. Pr. 102.
ċhŏpa, f. silence, esp. silent meditation; sg. ag. (instr.) *ċhŏpi*, by silent meditation, 2; *ċhŏpi-mantra*, by the mystic formula of silence, i.e. the *azapā* (Skr. *ajapa*) mantra, which is not uttered, but which consists only in a number of exhalations and inhalations, 40. Cf. *prān*, 2.
ċhĕpith, adj. hidden, concealed, secret, 60.
ċhaṭun, to winnow (in a sieve); hence, met., to throw up into

the air, to cast abroad, to make public, 4; past part. m. sg., with suff. 1st pers. sg. ag., *ṭhoṭum*, 4.

ṭhāy, f. shade, K. Pr. 102; a shadow, the shadow cast by anything, 67.

ṭhĕzun, to become extinguished, (of daylight) to fade away, become extinct; fut. sg. 3, *ṭhĕzi*, 22.

ṭakh^{a}r, m. a circle; hence, a circle of individuals, a specific group of individuals, see *lāma*; sg. abl. (in composition), *ṭakra*, 63.

ṭala, in *ṭala-ṭitta*, O restless mind! 72.

ṭalun, conj. 2, to flee, to run away, to depart to a distance; *hĕth ṭalun*, having taken to run away, to run away with (as a thief), 86 (bis).

Fut. sg. 3, *ṭali*, 28; with suff. 3rd pers. sg. dat., *ṭaliy*, will flee from thee, 75; past m. sg. 3, with suff. 1st pers. sg. dat., *ṭolum*, fled from me, 31; with suff. 2nd pers. sg. dat., *ṭoluy hĕth*, ran away with from thee, 86 (bis); f. sg. 3, *ṭajī* (for *ṭüj^{ü}*), 33.

ṭĕlun, to force into, to cause forcibly to enter; hence, to train with much practice, to exercise thoroughly, to train with vigorous practice; conj. part. *ṭĕlith*, 69.

ṭŏmbun, to pierce, bore; conj. part. *ṭŏmbith*, 75.

ṭāmar, m. a fly-whisk, the tail of the *Bos grunniens*, one of the insignia of royalty, 73.

ṭanḍī, adj. voc. f. O hasty woman, 77.

ṭandan, m. sandal, 42.

ṭanḍ^{a}r, m. the moon, 9; sg. ag. *ṭanḍ^{a}r^{i}*, 22; loc., with emph. *y*, *ṭanḍ^{a}riy*, (I came) into the moonlight, 109. Regarding the mystic references to the moon in these poems, see art. *sōm*.

ṭanḍ^{a}rama, m. the moon, 93. See *sōm* for the meaning of this passage.

ṭēnun, to recognize; to recognize as such-and-such, to understand a thing to be (such-and-such), 28; hence, to accept when seen, to experience, gain the experience of anything, 6; to recognize as authoritative, to meditate upon (instruction given), 51–4, 80; impve. sg. 2 *ṭēn*, 51–4, 80; pol. impve. sg. 2, with suff. 3rd pers. sg. acc., *ṭēntan*, recognize it, 28; past part. m. sg. *ṭyūn^{u}*, 6.

ṭinth, f. care, anxiety; *cyōn^{ü} ṭinth karān*, he cares for thee, 72.

ṭēr, f. an apricot; pl. dat. *ṭēran-sūt^{i}*, together with apricots, 92.

ṭūr, m. a thief, 101; pl. nom. id., 43.

ṭarmun, m. that which is made of leather, the human skin; used met. for the human body, 66.

ṭarun, to go forward, progress, walk; conj. part. *ṭarith* (1), 38.

ṭraṭh, m. the noise caused by falling from a height on to the earth or into water, crash, flop; hence, compared to the fall itself, close union; sg. abl. *sami ćraṭā* (m. c. for *ćraṭa*), in intimate union, 1.

ćarith, 2, (for 1, see *ćarun*), m. a mode of action, conduct, 38.

ćarāćar, m. that which is movable and that which is immovable, the animate and the inanimate, i.e. the whole universe, 16.

ćĕth, 1, m. the pure spirit, the soul (the Skr. *cit*, to be carefully distinguished from *ćĕth*, 2, or *ćitt*, the organ of thought), 76, 93.

ćĕth, 2, m. i. q. *ćitt*, the organ of thought, the mind, intellect (the Skr. *citta*), 9, 11 (bis), 34, 70, 87; sg. dat. *ćĕtas karun*, to impress upon the mind, 34; *ćĕtas pĕyiy*, it will fall into thy mind, it will come to thy memory, 87.

ćūṭhᵘ, m. an apple; pl. nom. *ćūṭhⁱ*, 92.

ćaṭun, to cut, to tear, 66; to cut down, to cut one's way (through a forest), 25; to cut away, or tear away anything from anything, 80; *ćaṭith dyunᵘ*, to cut to pieces, to cut up, 104; *ćaṭith zānun*, to know how to cut, 80; in 84, *cang gōm ćaṭith* appears to mean 'my claw has become cut', but the passage is very obscure; conj. part. *ćaṭith*, 25, 66, 80, 84, 104.

ćētun, 1, m. remembering, calling to mind; esp., in a religious sense, calling to mind and realizing (the nature of the Supreme and the Self); sg. obl. (in composition) *ćētana-dāna-wakhur*, (feeding with) the grain and cates of this realization, 77; *ćētani wagi*, with the bridle of this realization, 26.

ćētun, 2, m., i. q. *ćaitany*, q. v.; sg. obl. (in composition) *ćētana-shiv*, Śiva in his quality of Supreme Spirit, as opposed to his more material manifestations, 79.

ćaitany, m. consciousness; (in Śaiva mysticism) the Supreme Consciousness, the Supreme Experiencing Principle, a name of the Supreme (see *Kashmir Shaivism*, p. 42); sg. obl. (in composition), *ćaitanyĕ-rav*, the sun of the Supreme Consciousness, 16.

ćitt, m. the organ of thought, mind, intellect, i. q. *ćĕth*, 2, q. v. To be carefully distinguished from *ćĕth*, 1, the pure spirit; sg. obl. *ćitta*, 22; *ćitta-turogᵘ*, the steed of the intellect, 26, 69; voc. *ćittā*, O mind!, 28, 36, 67; *ćala-ćitta*, O restless mind!, 72.

ćyūnᵘ, see *ćēnun*.

ćāyĕs, see *aćun*.

wā, conj. or, 64; *wā . . . wā*, either . . . or, whether . . . or, 8.

wuchun, to see, 3, 48, 68, 83 (bis); to see, look at, inspect, look into, search, 98; fut. pass. part. *wuchun hyotᵘmas*,

I began to look for him, 48; past part. m. sg., with suff. 1st pers. sg. ag., *wuchum*, I saw, &c., 3, 68, 83 (bis), 98 (= K. Pr. 18).

wudu, adj. awake, not asleep; m. pl. nom., with emph. *y*, *wudiy*, 32; pl. dat. *wudĕn*, 32.

wadal, interchange; *adal ta wadal*, confusion, K. Pr. 102.

wadun, to weep, lament; fut. sg. 1, with suff. 2nd pers. sg. dat. *waday*, I will weep for thee, 67.

wudun, conj. 2, to awake from sleep; met. to come forth from obscurity, to become actively manifest; past f. sg. 3, with suff. 1st pers. sg. dat., *wuzüm*, it (fem.) became manifest to me, 25. Cf. *wuzun*.

wŏdur, m. the womb; sg. dat. *wŏdaras*, 51.

vidis, see *vyodu*.

wag, f. a horse's bridle; sg. abl. *wagi anun*, to bring by the bridle or to the bridle, to bring under subjection, 37; *wagi hyonu*, to take (a horse) by the bridle, 69; *wagi raṭun*, to hold (a horse) by the bridle, 26.

vĕgalun, to melt, deliquesce; conj. part. *vĕgalith*, 69.

wāh, interj. of astonishment and admiration, 68.

vihi, see *vyuhu*.

wuhī, f. coal that has been set alight, burning coal, red-hot coal, 82.

wàhäri-waharas, adv. throughout the whole year, from year's end to year's end, 46.

wahawunu, nom. ag. (of a river) flowing, in full flood; f. sg. nom., with emph. *y*, *wahawüñüy*, 96; dat. *wahawañī* (m. c. for *-wañĕ*), 57.

wākh, m. voice, the power of expression by word, in Saiva philosophy one of the five *karmĕndriyas*, or faculties, or powers, of action, 2; a word, *wākh ta wakun*, a word and a sentence, esp. the mystic formula confided to a disciple by his preceptor, a guiding principle, 94; in 104, *wākh* is the equivalent of the Skr. *vākya*, i.e. Lallā's sayings (*Lallā-vākyāni*), or the verses composed and recited by her.

wakhun, m. a story, a tale, 84.

wakhur, m. a cake offered in sacrifice, a sacrificial cake, 10, 77.

wŏkh-shun, m. scraping out and emptying a pot with a ladle or spoon, taking out the food to the last scraps, 95.

vikās, m. expansion, wide extent; *sa-vikās*, that which has wide expanse, the total expanse of creation, the visible creation, 1.

vikāsun, to become widely expanded, to widen out and extend to some distant limit; fut. sg. 3, *vikāsē* (m. c. for *vikāsi*), 22.

wāl, m. a hair of the head; sg. abl. *mast-wāla*, (to bind) with a single hair of the head, 24.

wōlᵘ, m. a suffix forming nouns of agency or possession, as in *graṭa-wōlᵘ*, a miller, from *graṭa*, a mill, 86. Cf. *wōnᵘ*, 2.

wālun (causal of *wasun*, q.v.), to cause to descend, to bring down; past part. m. sg., with suff. 1st pers. sg. ag., *wōlum*, I brought down, 104.

wölinjü, f. the heart (as the seat of the affections), 25.

wŏlasun, to rejoice; hence, to rejoice in any business, to be zealously engaged in it; old pres. sg. 3, with suff. 3rd pers. sg. dat., *wŏlasĕs*, he is zealously engaged in it, 14.

wumr, f. age, a man's life; sg. gen. (f. sg. nom.) *wumri-hünzü*, K. Pr. 56.

vimarsh, m. consideration, reflection, examination, discussion; sg. abl. *vimarshĕ*, 15, or (m. c. *vimarshā*), 16.

wan, m. a forest; pl. nom. *wan*, 25; *wan-kāv*, a forest-crow, 28; *wan-wās*, abode in a forest, the life of a hermit, 55, 64.

wān, m. a shop; pl. dat. *wānan*, K. Pr. 102; *lōwᵃrⁱ-wān*, a weaver's workshop (sg. abl. *-wāna*), 102.

vĕn (13) or *vĕnā* (12), postpos. without, free from, 12; apart from, distinct from, 13.

wōnᵘ, 1, m. a shopkeeper; sg. dat. *wōnis*, K. Pr. 20.

wōnᵘ, 2, m. a suffix forming nouns of agency or possession, i.q. *wōlᵘ*, q.v.; as in *shruta-wōnᵘ*, a hearer, a person who can hear, i.e. who is not at all deaf, 20; *brama-wōnᵘ*, a wanderer, one who roams about, 26; *pruthi-wōnᵘ*, of or belonging to the earth, 52; sg. dat. *shūba-wōnis*, to (a mill) which possesses beauty, i.e. which is adorned, 52.

wŏnda, m. a man's inner feelings and thoughts, (as the seat of the feelings and thoughts) the heart or soul; sg. dat. *wŏndas*, 72; loc. *wŏndi*, 49.

vĕndun, to get; hence, to take to, have recourse to (some course of conduct or the like), 64; to look upon as, consider as, 43; impve. pl. 2, *vĕndiv*, 64 (bis); past part. m. sg., with suff. 3rd pers. sg. ag., *vyondun*, 43.

wanun, 1, to say, 89, 94; to say a thing is so-and-so, to call a thing by such-and-such a name, 15; past. part. m. sg. *wonᵘ*, 15; with suff. 1st pers. sg. ag., *wonum*, 89; with suff. 3rd pers. sg. ag. and 1st pers. sg. dat., *wonᵘnam*, he said to me, 94.

wanun, 2, m. a speech, a thing said, a saying, 108; (properly inf. or verbal noun of *wanun*, 1).

wuñĕ, adv. now, even now, at this very time, 99 (bis), (= K. Pr. 46).

wŏpadun, conj. 2, to come into being, be produced; pres. part. in sense of pres. pl. 3, *wŏpadān*, 56.

wŏpadēsh, m. instruction; esp. true instruction, right teaching, 1, 2, 51–4, 66, 80.

vĕphol^{u}, adj. fruitless, bearing no, or imperfect, fruit, 55.
wār, m. the right, or propitious, time (for anything); *dĕnas wār*, the propitious moment of the day (for giving a child); (Thou, i.e. God, didst not know) this moment (in respect to some people), i.e. hast given them no children, K. Pr. 102.
wör^{ü}, f. a garden; *hāka-wör*^{ü}, a vegetable-garden, 63; with emph. *y*, *wör*^{ü}*y*, only a garden, nothing but a garden, i.e. the bare ground with no produce on it, 63.
wūrdhwa-gaman, m. the act of going upwards, ascending into the sky, 38.
war^{a}*n*, m. colour, hue, 15.
warun, m. Name of the god of the waters, Varuṇa; hence, met., water generally, 53.
wās, m. an abode, 55; *wās hyon*^{u}, to take up an abode; with suff. of indef. art., *wāsā hyon*^{u}, 18; *wan-wās*, abode in a forest, the life of a hermit, 55, 64; *atha-wās*, hand-grasping, 92; see *atha*.
vishom^{u}, adj. uneven; hence, (of a net) tangled, complicated; m. sg. dat. *vishĕmis*, 6.
vishēsh, m. a special kind, a speciality; hence, *vishēsh karun*, to perform a speciality, to act perfectly in some particular character, 54.
vishĕy, m. the scene of action, ground of action, basis, 71.
wasun, conj. 2, to descend; past f. sg. 3, with suff. 1st pers. sg. dat., *wütsh*^{ü}*m*, it descended to me, 69. The causal of this verb is *wālun*, q. v.
vĕsarzun, to take one's leave, to depart; conj. part. *vĕsarzith kĕth*, having departed, 9.
wot^{u}, for *wath*, in *sh*^{ĕ}*wot*^{u}, q. v.
wath, f. a road, way, path, 41; sg. abl. *watē* (or *wati*), (going, &c.) by a road, 41, 98 (bis) (= K. Pr. 18); *wata-got*^{u}, adj. going along a road, going by way of, 57; *wata-nŏsh*^{u} (pl. nom. *-nŏsh*^{i}), a road-destroyer, a highway robber, 43.
waṭh, m. a round stone; with indef. art., *waṭā*, 17 (bis).
wāṭh, m. joining together, construction; hence, the material of which a thing is constructed, 17.
vĕth, f. the river Jihlam (in Skr. *Vitastā*), the principal river of Kashmīr, K. Pr. 102 (where it is used as a symbol of prosperity, owing to the fruitful crops produced by its waters).
wŏthun, conj. 2, to rise, arise; impve. sg. 2, *wŏth*, 10, 75; conj. part. *wŏthith*, 105; past m. sg. 3 *wŏthū* (m. c. for *wọth*^{u}), 1; *layĕ wŏthun*, to rise to absorption, to become dissolved into nothingness, 1.
wuṭhun, to twist (rope); pres. m. sg. 2, *chukh wuṭhān*, 107.
waṭun, to unite; *tsaṭun waṭun*, to cut and unite, to separate

and bind together; conj. part. *tatith waṭith zānun*, to know how to separate and to unite, 80.

wātun, conj. 2, to arrive, come (to); past m. sg. 3, with suff. 1st pers. sg. gen., *wŏtum*, arrived to my (understanding), 60; pl. 3, *wöt^i*, 51; f. sg. 1, *wöts^ü s*, 60, 82.

watari, adv. continually, without cessation, 78, 79.

wŏttom^u, adj. excellent, first-rate; *wŏttom^u wŏttom^u dēsh*, various lands, each of which is excellent, 53.

wütsh^ü m, see *wasun*.

watsun, m. a saying, a sentence of instruction, 94 (bis).

vĕtsun, conj. 2, to fit into; fut. sg. 3, with emph. *y*, *vĕtsiy*, 47.

vĕtsār, m. judging, meditating upon and deciding about anything, discriminating about anything, 28–9, 71, 79; sg. dat. *vĕtsāras*, 28; abl. *vĕtsāra*, 71, 79.

vĕtsārun, to meditate upon, discriminate concerning anything; impve. sg. 2, with suff. 3rd pers. sg. acc., *vĕtsārun*, meditate on it, 30.

wŏtstsarun, to utter, pronounce; past part. m. sg., with suff. 1st pers. sg. ag., *wŏtstsorum*, 58.

wāv, m. the wind, 24, 83; the vital airs circulating in the *nāḍis* (see *nāḍi*), a synonym of *prān*, 2, q. v., 69; sg. abl. *wāwa*, 83; pl. nom. *wāv*, 69.

vĕwahör^i, adj. occupied, busy, 65 (where it may mean either 'occupied in worldly pursuits', or else 'occupied in religious practices').

wawun, to sow; 2 past part. m. sg., with suff. 2nd pers. sg. ag., *wavyōth*, 66.

vyod^u, adj. known, 56; —°, one who knows, as in *tattwa-vyod^u*, one who knows and understands the *tattwas* (see *tattwa*), 20; m. sg. dat. *-vidis*, 20.

vyuh^u, m. sudden change from one condition to another; hence, the sudden 'sport' (*līlā*) of the Divinity, by which He manifests Himself in creation; pl. nom. *vih^i*, 109. In modern Ksh. this word is *vih*.

vyondun, see *vĕndun*.

wāz, m. a cook; sg. dat. *wāzas*, 83.

wuz^ü m, see *wudun*.

wuzun, conj. 2, i. q. *wudun*, q. v., to awake from sleep; to come forth from obscurity, to become actively manifest; fut. sg. 3, *wuzē* (m. c. for *wuzi*), 39, 40.

wuzanāwun, to awaken (another) from sleep; past part. m. sg., with suff. 1st pers. sg. ag., *wuzanŏwum*, 105.

yē, interj. O!, *yē gŏrā*, O teacher!, 56.

yid (18), *yud^u* (23, 24), *yod^u wanay* (10) or *yid^a way* (64), conj. if.

yōg, m. intense abstraction, religious ascetic abstraction and meditation; *yōga-kal*, the art, or practice, of such abstraction, 14.

yōgī, a yōgī, one who practises *yōg* (q. v.), 14.

yih, 1, proximate demonstrative pronoun, this, he; (as a pronoun) 20, 26, 54, 58 (bis), 84 (bis), 85 (bis), 109; (as a pronominal adjective) 7, 13, 28, 95; combined with *tih*, that, *suy yih*, that very, 58.

This pronoun is either animate or inanimate, and the animate forms may be either masculine or feminine. The inanimate forms are of common gender. Moreover, there is a cross-division, according as it is used as a pure pronoun, or as a pronominal adjective. We shall consider the purely pronominal forms first.

As an animate pronoun, the following forms occur:—

Masc. sg. nom. *yih*, 26.

Fem. sg. nom., with emph. *y*, *yihay*, she verily, this very woman, 54 (ter).

As an inanimate pronoun, we have:—

Sg. nom. *yih*, 84 (bis), 85 (bis); with emph. *y*, *yuhuy*, this very, this alone, 1, 20, 58; *suy yih*, that very, 58.

Pl. nom. *yim*, 109.

As a pronominal adjective, it occurs, in these poems, only as referring to inanimate things; viz.:—

M. sg. nom. *yih*, 7, 28; with emph. *y*, *yuhuy*, 13.

Dat. *yith*, 95.

yih, 2, relative pronoun, who, which, what. It is either animate or inanimate, and the animate forms may be either masculine or feminine, while the substantival inanimate forms are of common gender. There is also the cross-division into its forms as a pronominal substantive and into its forms as a pronominal adjective.

As an animate pronominal substantive, or pure pronoun, the following forms occur:—

m. sg. nom. *yus*ᵘ, 20, 24, 37, 45, 65.

m. sg. dat. *yĕs*, 15 (bis), 21, 33, 34, 37; *yĕmis*, or, with emph. *y*, *yĕmisay*, 5.

m. sg. ag. *yĕm*ⁱ, 5 (bis), 26, 43, 62 (bis).

m. pl. nom. *yim*, 95; ag. *yimav*, 6, 27.

As an inanimate pronominal substantive, we have:—

sg. nom. *yih*, 20, 21, 107.

sg. abl. *yĕwa*, by which; hence, in order that, so that 28 (bis), 75.

As a pronominal adjective, we have:—

m. sg. nom. (inan.) *yuh*ᵘ, 61; *yuh*, 8; *yih*, 58 (bis), 61.

f. sg. nom. (inan.), with emph. *y*, *yŏsay*, 52.

m. sg. dat. (inan.) *yĕth*; 47.
m. sg. ag. (an.) *yĕmi*, 24.
m. pl. nom. (inan.) *yim*, 76; with emph. *y*, *yimay*, 13.

This pronoun is often repeated in various idiomatic senses. Thus, *yusu yih dapiy*, who will say what to thee, i.e. whoever will say anything to thee, 20; *yĕs yih rōċĕ*, to whom what is pleasing, to whom anything is pleasing, i.e. whatever is pleasing to each, 21; *yih yih karm*, whatever work, 58; *yuhu yih karm*, whatever act, 61.

yēku, card. one; *yēkuy*, only one, nothing but, 7; *yēka-wāṭh*, of one construction, of the same material, 17 (see *wāṭh*). Cf. *oku* and *akh*.

yĕli, adv. at what time, when, 31, 44, 49, 82, 102, 103 (bis); K. Pr. 57.

yĕma, m. Yama, the god of death, and judge of souls after death; *yĕma-bayĕ*, the fear of Yama, the fear of death, 27; *yĕma-baṭh*, Yama's apparitors, who drag away the soul of a dying person to judgement, 74.

yęmbarzal, f. the narcissus, K. Pr. 56.

yĕna, adv. from what time, since; *yĕna-pĕṭha*, id. 93.

yunu, to come; fut. pl. 3, *yin*, which with suff. 2nd pers. sg. dat. appears in K. Pr. 57 as *yinanay*, they will come (i.e. return home) (after having abandoned) thee; past m. sg. 3, *āv*, 9, 91; pl. 3, *āy*, 19; f. sg. 1, *āyĕs*, 35, 41, 98, 109 (bis); K. Pr. 18; 3, *āyĕ*, K. Pr. 20.

yundu, m. an organ of sense or action, in Skr. *indriya*. There are five organs of sense (*buddhīndriya* or *jñānēndriya*), viz. the organ of smell (*ghrāṇēndriya*), of taste (*rasanēndriya*), of sight (*darśanēndriya*), of touch (*sparśēndriya*), and of hearing (*śravaṇēndriya*); there are also five organs of action (*karmēndriya*), viz. the organ of generation (*upasthēndriya*), of excretion (*pāyvindriya*), of locomotion (*pādēndriya*), of handling (*hastēndriya*), and of voice (*vāgindriya*). There are thus two pentads of sense and action, respectively. In 79, it is probably the latter pentad that is referred to. Pl. nom. *yindi*, 79.

yār, m. a friend, a beloved; the Beloved, i.e. God, 99 (bis), 100; K. Pr. 46 (ter).

yōr, relative adv. of place, where; with emph. *i*, for *y*, *yūri*, where even, in the exact place where, 61; *yōra*, whence, from where; with emph. *y*, *yōray*, from the very place whence, 19.

yīshwar, m. the Lord (Skr. *īśvara*), a title of the Supreme Śiva, connoting His power and lordliness, 43.

yaitu, rel. pron. adj. as much (mod. Ksh. *yūtu*), 81.

yĕti, rel. adv. of place, where, 88; from where, whence, 57.

yiti, adv. of place, here, in this place; hence, here, in this world, 73.

yutu (or *yitu*), adv. of place, here, in this place; hence, here, in this world, K. Pr. 102 (bis).

yūtu, see *yaitu*.

yitha, rel. pron. adv. of manner, as K. Pr. 46; *tithay . . . yitha*, so . . . as, exactly like, 100.

yuthu, rel. pron. adj. of manner, of what kind, as; with emph. *y*, *yuthuy*, 55; used adverbially, exactly as, 64.

yüťü, adj. many, much, 102; K. Pr. 102; as adv., very much, 103. In all these cases with emph. *y*, *yüťüy*.

yiťh, f. wish, desire, loving longing, 29, 40, 45; sg. abl. *yiťhi*, 29, or (m. c.) *yiťhē*, 45.

yōzan, m. a league; *yōzana-lach*, a hundred thousand leagues, 26.

zi, conj. that, so that (consecutive), 48.

zaḍ, adj. non-sentient, inert; *zaḍa-rūpi*, like an insentient thing, stolid, 20.

zūḍē, see *zūru*.

zadal, adj. pierced with holes (as in a sieve); *zadal ťhāy*, a shade full of holes, like that thrown by a broken thatch, K. Pr. 102.

zag, f. the world, 16.

zāgun, to watch a person (dat.), 48; to be watchful, to keep wide awake (in this sense used impersonally in the past tenses), 78, 79; fut. sg. 3, *zāgi*, 78, 79; past part. m. sg., with suff. 1st pers. sg. ag. and 3rd pers. sg. dat., *zōgumas*, I remained watching him, 48.

zigar, m. the liver (the seat of the affections and desires), 49.

zah, card. two, 75.

zal, m. water, 38–40, 45, 47, 81; sg. gen. *zaluku* (f. sg. ag. *zalaci dōñī*, with a stream of water, 39, 40); pl. dat. *zalan*, 81; *zala-hostu*, a water-elephant, a sea-elephant (a mythical animal), 47.

zōlu, m. the joint where a branch leaves the parent stem, or where two branches commence to fork; hence, met. *kāla-zōlu*, efflux, or passing, of time, 64; sg. ag. (or instr.) *zōli*, 64.

zalamay, m. that which is composed of water; hence, the waste of waters which is all that is left at the destruction of the universe, 93. Cf. *may*.

zālun, to burn (transitive), to burn up; past part. m. sg., with suff. 1st pers. sg. ag. *zōlum*, 49.

zalawunu, n. ag. burning, fiery hot, blazing; f. sg. nom. *zalawāñī* (m. c. for *zalawüñü*), 57.

zāmun, to yawn; fut. (in sense of pres.) sg. 3, *zāmi*, 46.

zan, 1, m. a man, a person; hence, the world of men, people 31; sg. dat. (in sense of loc.), *zanas*, 31.

zan, 2, adv. as it were, as though, like, 29, 31, 83, 106.

zān, f. knowledge; esp. the true knowledge of the Supreme; *lūb*^{ü}*m zanas zān*, I obtained (a reputation for) knowledge among people, 31.

zana, in *kō-zana* (73, 74) or *kō-zanañi* (72), see *kō-zana*.

zĕn, see *zyon*^{u}.

zin, m. a Jina, i.e. the Buddha, 8.

zūn, f. moonlight; sg. dat. *zūnē* (m. c. for *zūni*), in the moonlight, 9; *pot*^{u} *zūn*, the end of the moonlight, the last hours of the night; sg. dat. (for loc.) *pot*^{u} *zūni*, 105.

zinda, adj. alive; with emph. *y*, *zinday*, even while alive, 68.

zang, f. the leg, K. Pr. 102.

zānun, to know, 20, 30, 41, 64 (bis); K. Pr. 102; to get to know, to come to know, to accept as true, 7 (bis), 10, 71, 77, 85, 90; to know how; *raṭith zānun*, to know how to seize, 26, 80; *gaṭith zānun*, to know how to make, 80.

Conj. part. *zōnith*, 20, 64; impve. sg. 2, *zān*, 71; with suff. 3rd pers. sg. acc., *zānun*, know it, 30; fut. sg. 1, *zāna*, 41; 2, *zānakh*, 10 (pres. subj.), 77; *zānĕkh*, 64; 3, with suff. 1st pers. sg. gen., *zānĕm*, it, belonging to me, will know, 85; past. part. m. sg. *zŏn*^{u}, 26; with suff. 1st pers. sg. ag. *zŏnum*, 7 (bis), 90; with suff. 2nd pers. sg. ag. and 1st pers. sg. dat. (*dativus commodi*), *zŏn*^{u}*tham*, K. Pr. 102; cond. past sg. 1, *zānahö*, 80 (bis).

zanüñ^{ü}, f. a mother; sg. dat. *zanañĕ*, 51.

zūr^{u}, or *zūḍ*^{u}, m. a condition of bad conduct, bad habits; sg. dat. *zūrē* (or *zūḍē*) (m. c. for *zūrĕ* or *zūḍĕ*) *lagun*, to acquire bad habits, 70.

zösun (impersonal in the past tenses), to cough; fut. sg. 3 (in sense of pres.), *zŏsi*, 46.

zāth, f. nature, the true nature of anything, 4.

zīv, m. the life, soul; the soul in the sense of a living soul, a living being, a man, 12. Cf. *zuv*.

zuv, m. life, 54; the soul, 106; *zuv hyon*^{u}, to take life, to destroy life, 54. Cf. *zīv*.

zīwont^{u}, adj. living, alive, 6, 12; m. pl. nom. *zīwänt*^{i}, in *zīwänt*^{i}*-mọkh*^{ā}*t*^{i}, men who obtain final release while yet alive, 6.

zyon^{u}, to come into being, to be born; fut. sg. 3, *zĕyi*, 37; *zĕyē* (m. c.), 45; pl. 3 (old pres.), *zĕn nā zĕn*, they are being born, (and) they are not being born, i.e. when they are hardly born, immediately on being born, 47; 3 (remote) past, m. pl. 3, *zāyāy*, 51.

zöyyul^{u}, adj. (f. *zöyij*^{ü}), fine, ~~tenuous~~ (e.g. of a thread); f. pl. nom. *zöyijĕ*, 102.